Thomas Becket
murder and the
making of a saint

Lloyd de Beer
and Naomi Speakman

The British
Museum

This publication accompanies the exhibition *Thomas Becket: murder and the making of a saint* at the British Museum from 22 April to 22 August 2021

Supported by:
The Hintze Family Charitable Foundation
The Ruddock Foundation for the Arts
Jack Ryan and Zemen Paulos

This exhibition has been made possible as a result of the Government Indemnity Scheme. The British Museum would like to thank HM Government for providing Government Indemnity and the Department for Digital, Culture, Media and Sport and Arts Council England for arranging the indemnity.

First published in the United Kingdom in 2021
by The British Museum Press
A division of The British Museum Company Ltd

The British Museum
Great Russell Street
London WC1B 3DG
britishmuseum.org/publishing

Thomas Becket: murder and the making of a saint
© 2021 The Trustees of the British Museum

ISBN: 978 0 7141 2838 2

British Library Cataloguing-in-Publication Data
A catalogue record for this book is available from the British Library

Further information about the British Museum and its collection can be found at britishmuseum.org

Images © 2021 The Trustees of the British Museum, courtesy of the British Museum's Department of Photography and Imaging, unless otherwise stated on page 267

Designed by ADRIAN HUNT

Colour reproduction by ALTAIMAGE, LONDON

Printed in Belgium by GRAPHIUS

ON THE COVER
Front: Panel from an altarpiece showing Becket's martyrdom, *c.*1425–50. Alabaster. 38.5 × 28.4 cm. British Museum, London, 1890,0809.1
Back: Panel 45 from miracle window nIII, Canterbury Cathedral

FRONTISPIECE
Detail of reliquary casket showing the martyrdom and burial of Thomas Becket, *c.*1210. Wooden core, copper alloy, gilding and enamel. 13.6 × 13.7 × 6.5 cm. British Museum, London, 1854,0411.2

PAGES 244–5
Detail of panel 45 from miracle window nIII, Canterbury Cathedral

NOTE ON THE TEXT
Birth and death dates in this book follow the *Oxford Dictionary of National Biography*. Due to the global pandemic, it was not possible to source complete information on materials and dimensions for a select few objects before publication.

Contents

Director's foreword

Hartwig Fischer

The 850th anniversary of the murder of Thomas Becket was marked in 2020, a year that saw institutions across the UK delay their celebrations due to the global pandemic. The British Museum was no exception and it is thanks to the hard work of colleagues that this important exhibition has gone ahead.

Thomas Becket's remarkable life, his violent death and his legacy are the focus of the exhibition and this book. Born in London around 1120, he rose from ordinary beginnings to become chancellor and friend to King Henry II. When the position of Archbishop of Canterbury became vacant, Becket was a surprise appointment to the post. Soon their friendship soured and the two men famously clashed in a dispute regarding the division of power between the Crown and the Church. It culminated in Becket's murder on 29 December 1170 by four knights with close ties to Henry. For the archbishop to be killed in this way was profoundly shocking. News of the event spread across Europe like wildfire. Within just three years Thomas Becket was canonised and a widespread cult soon developed, with pilgrims visiting from across Latin Christendom. At first they sought his tomb and after 1220 their goal was his glittering shrine set at the heart of a purpose-built chapel, a journey famously evoked in Geoffrey Chaucer's *Canterbury Tales*. The impact of Becket's death cannot be overstated: his influence was strongly felt in religion, literature, art and culture from the twelfth century onwards. The conflict between Church and Crown that arose from Becket's dispute with Henry would also become an important touchstone in European politics. In the sixteenth century, during Henry VIII's reign, the destruction of Becket's shrine and almost total obliteration of his cult brought history full circle.

The story of Becket's enduring legacy is brought to life in this exhibition through an array of precious reliquaries, jewellery, pilgrims' badges and sculpture from the British Museum's collection. A number of spectacular and generous loans bring us close to the man himself, such as manuscripts from Trinity College and Corpus Christi College, Cambridge, which Becket commissioned or was gifted for his own use. A single surviving wax impression made from his own personal seal matrix, attached to a document in The National Archives, provides a tantalising glimpse of his personality. One of the earliest known representations of the murder, from a manuscript comprising Becket's collected letters and a biography by John of Salisbury, is lent from the British Library. Some loans to the exhibition have never left their country of origin before: a gilded reliquary casket from Hedalen Stave Church in Norway and a carved font from Lyngsjö Church in Sweden. They speak to the truly European dimension of Becket's cult. It is thanks to the Very Revd Robert Willis and staff at Canterbury Cathedral, a key partner in the organisation of the exhibition, that we are able to display one of the most extraordinary loans: a stunning window of stained glass from the Trinity Chapel, made within fifty years of the murder, which reveals the myriad miracles attributed to Becket.

List of lenders

We are grateful to our colleagues in institutions across the UK and Europe, who have contributed to this unique exhibition through their generous loans. My sincere thanks go to the British Library, the British Jesuit Province, Cambridge University Library, Canterbury Cathedral, Canterbury City Council, Canterbury Museums and Galleries, Hedalen Stave Church, Norway, Lyngsjö Church, Sweden, The National Archives, Nicholas and Jane Ferguson, the Parker Library, Corpus Christi College, Cambridge, the Queen's Most Excellent Majesty in Right of Her Duchy of Lancaster, the Society of Antiquaries of London, Eglwys Gadeiriol Tyddewi / St Davids Cathedral, Stonyhurst College, Trinity College Cambridge, the Victoria and Albert Museum, London, Westminster Cathedral, The Worshipful Company of Barbers, the Wyvern Collection and two private collections. This exhibition and book have drawn on the expertise of colleagues from museums and universities in the UK and around the world, to whom we are indebted.

Thomas Becket: murder and the making of a saint could not have taken place without the generosity and friendship of the Museum's long-term supporters The Hintze Family Charitable Foundation, The Ruddock Foundation for the Arts, and Jack Ryan and Zemen Paulos. We are enormously grateful to them. I would additionally like to thank Nicholas and Jane Ferguson for their continued support of the post of Curator of Medieval Europe, and the Paul Mellon Centre for Studies in British Art for supporting the post of Project Curator.

The British Library
British Jesuit Province
Cambridge University Library
Canterbury City Council
Canterbury Museums and Galleries
The Chapter, Canterbury Cathedral
Dean and Chapter of Eglwys Gadeiriol
 Tyddewi / St Davids Cathedral
Hedalen Stave Church
Lyngsjö Church
Nicholas and Jane Ferguson
The National Archives
Parker Library, Corpus Christi College,
 Cambridge
Private Collection
Private Collection
The Queen's Most Excellent Majesty in Right
 of Her Duchy of Lancaster
Society of Antiquaries of London
Stonyhurst College
Trinity College Cambridge
Victoria and Albert Museum, London
Westminster Cathedral
The Worshipful Company of Barbers
The Wyvern Collection

Introduction

On 29 December 1170, as the last light of the winter sun faded from view, Thomas Becket was murdered in Canterbury Cathedral. The spilling of blood in such a holy place was appalling, and all the more so because Becket was Archbishop of Canterbury and this his cathedral. Trained knights, for whom armed combat was a central part of life, entered the cathedral to arrest him. With a terrifying clatter of swords and armour, they were followed into the church by a motley entourage. Shouting, 'This way, king's men!', they let all those present know the true origin of their authority.[1] This was the knights' second attempt that day; the first had ended in a heated argument and it is clear they had no intention of leaving Canterbury without their man. Tempers were high and Becket refused to comply with their demands. After striking the fatal blow, and with the archbishop lying dead on the flagstones, the murderers fled.

Becket was once at the centre of power but times had changed. For many years he was the right hand to Henry II, King of England, having been appointed royal chancellor by him in 1154 and consecrated as archbishop in 1162. In the years leading up to his murder, however, he had found himself an outcast, after becoming embroiled in a six-year long dispute with his former friend the king. Canterbury Cathedral must have seemed like his last sanctuary, but it proved to be the stage for his violent demise. News of the event quickly made its way across Europe, reaching Church leaders and foreign princes alike. Their horrified reactions mirrored those who had witnessed it in person. Within days, miracles were attributed to Becket, whose death was interpreted as martyrdom by his supporters. They found in him a model of opposition to royal tyranny. In recognition of his miracle-working power, he was officially canonised as a saint in 1173.

By that time, his body lay encased in a marble tomb in the cathedral crypt and was visited by scores of pilgrims, many from far-flung destinations, all of whom sought the intervention of St Thomas of Canterbury. From Scotland to Sicily, images of his murder circulated widely. Jewel-like caskets covered in gilded-metal plaques, and enamelled in dazzling shades of blue, green and red, were made to hold his precious relics, probably pieces of cloth dipped in Becket's blood, or even small fragments of his body (fig. 0.1). Such objects tell the story of Becket's murder and sainthood, from the raised weapons of the knights to the moment of his death, and from Becket's entombment to his soul being triumphantly lifted into heaven by angels. What caused the knights to commit such a crime, and what impact the events had across Europe in the twelfth century and beyond, are the subject of *Thomas Becket: murder and the making of a saint*.

0.1
The Becket Casket, c.1180–90. Wooden core, copper
alloy, gilding and enamel. 29.5 × 34.4 × 12.4 cm.
Victoria and Albert Museum, London, M.66-1997. This
depiction of Becket's martyrdom is one of the earliest
known representations of the scene on a reliquary
casket. It has an English provenance dating back to
the early 1700s, when it was in the possession of a
Catholic family in St Neots, Cambridgeshire.

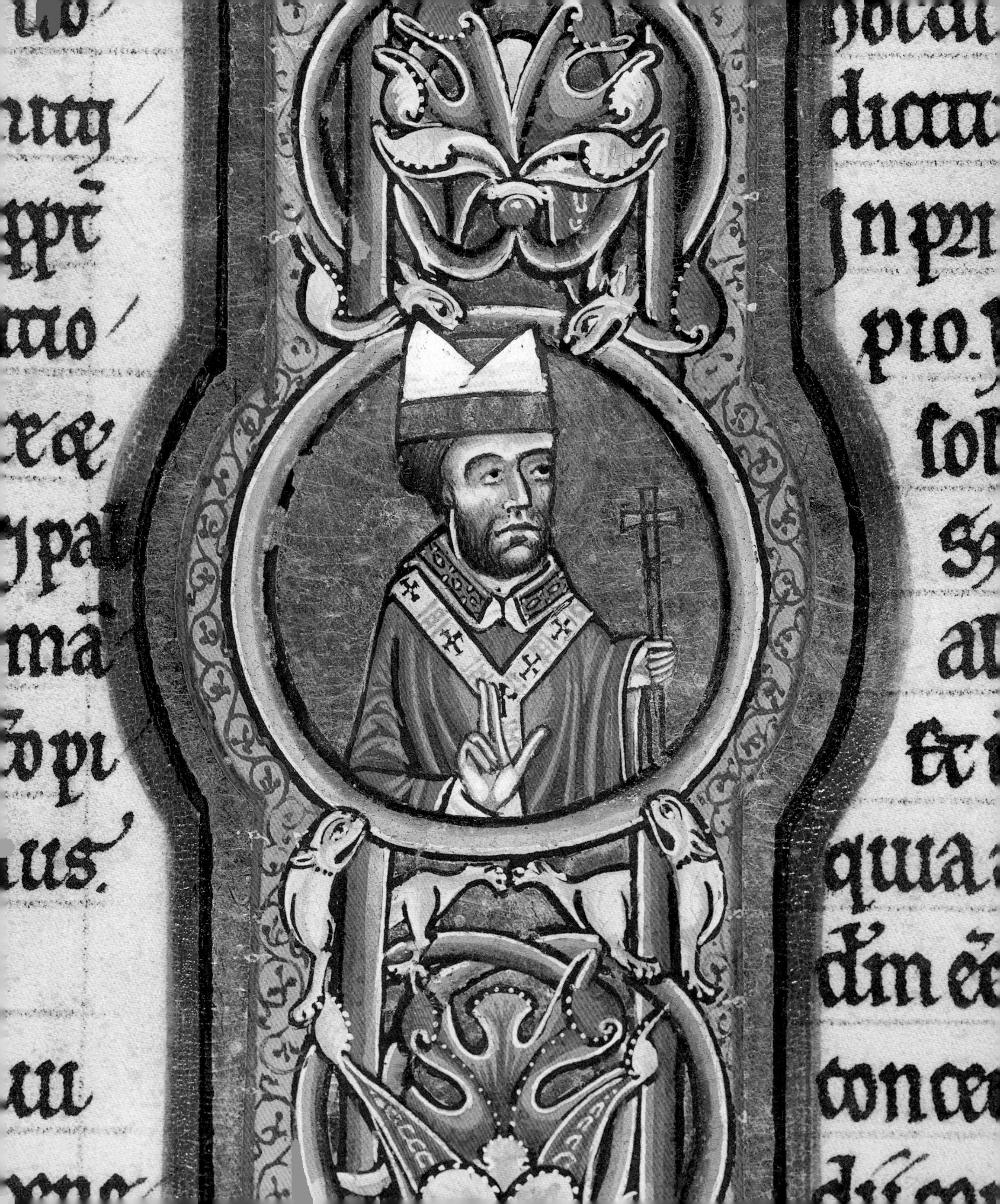

Rise: from Cheapside to the royal court

Thomas Becket was born in London around 1120 to Gilbert and Matilda, who had emigrated to England from Normandy (fig. 1.1).[2] In the decades that followed the Norman Conquest, London expanded considerably, although most of its citizens still lived within the area defined by the old Roman walls. As one of the country's major urban centres, London had long been a thriving focus of trade. Goods flowed in and out of the city from across Europe and much further afield. The 1100s were a lucrative time to do business in London, and its merchants, like Gilbert Becket, were becoming wealthier. In his day-to-day life Gilbert would have met with a broad cross section of people. Although he likely spoke French with his family at home, he would have heard a variety of languages throughout the city, including all sorts of French (from Normandy in the north to the dialects of the far south), Latin, English, Hebrew, Flemish, German and quite possibly Spanish and Italian. The chronicler William FitzStephen (d. *c*.1191), one of Becket's biographers, described the incredible array of luxury goods passing through the city:

Chosen before the foundation of the world in Christ, Saint Thomas in his propitious birth lit up the capital of the British Isles, London[1]

Edward Grim, *Life of St Thomas Becket*, 1171–2

Detail of fig. 1.17

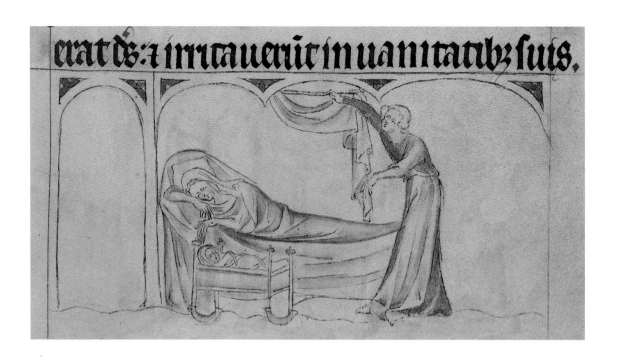

erat dei: 7 irritauerit in uanitatibz suis.

To this city, from every nation that is under heaven, merchants
rejoice to bring their trade in ships.
Gold from Arabia, from Sabaea spice
And incense; from the Scythians arms of steels
Well-tempered; oil from the rich groves of palm
That spring from the fat lands of Babylon;
Fine gems from Nile, from China crimson silks;
French wines; and sable, vair and miniver
From the far lands where Russ and Norsemen dwell.[3]

As London's prosperity grew, so did its population. Estimates suggest that
from 1100 to 1200 the number of inhabitants roughly doubled from possibly
around 20,000 to over 40,000, making it one of the largest cities in western
Europe.[4] With this influx came a demand for space, resulting in the building
of new roads and houses and pushing the limits of the city further north
(fig. 1.2). Growing up, Becket would have heard the sounds of construction
work across the city. London had a thriving and diverse religious community
too. By the 1170s there were thirteen monastic houses inside or adjacent
to the city and roughly one hundred parish churches within its walls.[5] The
growth of such churches went hand in hand with the rising population and

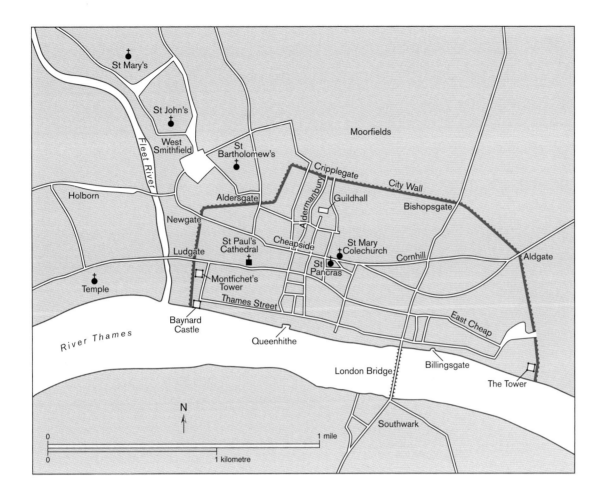

1.2

Simplified map of London, c.1200

its spiritual needs, and many were located along the densely packed streets leading down to the river.[6] London also had a sizeable Jewish population.[7] The Great Synagogue was situated in the Jewish quarter (now marked by a street named Old Jewry), which Becket must have passed frequently as it was close to his family home. Although the London that Becket knew as a boy has long since vanished, traces of it can still be seen in the fragments of material culture that have survived (fig. 1.3).

Compared with his adulthood, little is known about Becket's early life. According to his biographers, Matilda witnessed several incredible omens both while pregnant and when Thomas was a baby. In one vision, twelve stars fell from the sky into Matilda's lap, while in another she saw the Thames flowing inside her and heard a voice declaring that 'the one who is born to you … will rule over many people'.[8] After Thomas was born,

his mother had a dream in which she and her maid discovered that the purple cloth covering the infant was miraculous. On unravelling it, the cloth continuously expanded. Amazed by this, they heard a voice telling them it was large enough to cloak the whole of England.[9] These portents all served to underscore the same message: that the child was destined for future glory and his divinity was evident from the moment of his conception.

When exactly Becket was born is a matter of debate. His biographers do not specify a precise date of birth but it has been suggested that he was born on or just before 21 December 1120, the Feast of St Thomas the Apostle, and that he was named in honour of the saint.[10] A finely engraved copper-alloy dish, believed to have been discovered in the River Thames and made around the time of Becket's birth, depicts a popular aspect of the Apostle's legend (fig. 1.4). Made in England, or possibly in Germany and imported to London soon afterwards, the dish shows the story of Thomas the Apostle's mission to India.[11] Across several scenes, the saint performs conversions but is eventually beheaded on the orders of a king named in an inscription as 'Migdonius'. An association with Thomas the Apostle became a feature of Becket's saintly cult.[12]

Becket spent roughly the first twenty-five years of his life in and around London, except for a brief period when he left to study in Paris.[13] As a Londoner and a commoner, his experiences of a vibrant and cosmopolitan city fundamentally shaped the man he would become. These years were a stark contrast to the world of the royal court that he came to inhabit so effortlessly. When confronted with the task of reconciling Becket's saintly persona with his decidedly ordinary origins, his later biographers sometimes struggled. However, it is these modest beginnings that make his later achievements all the more extraordinary.

At home in London

Becket's family lived on Cheapside, London's commercial artery, which was then, as now, the main east to west thoroughfare through the city.[14] His childhood home would have been no modest affair.[15] London's twelfth-century expansion was marked by the increasing use of stone as a building material. Only the wealthiest could afford properties made entirely of stone, as castles and churches were, but archaeological evidence shows that more people were making use of stone foundations and basements to

support their timber-framed houses.[16] As a mercantile family on the rise, it is possible Becket's parents could have afforded such a luxury. Their home was probably furnished with locally made and imported wares, including glazed and decorated pottery. These were much finer than the coarse, unglazed ceramics that had been used widely before the 1100s.[17]

The Beckets' house was located in the parish of St Mary Colechurch, in the vicinity of the parish church where he was baptised. The church was small and located upstairs in a house adjacent to the Becket property.[18] St Mary Colechurch was destroyed by the Great Fire of London in 1666, but a surviving stone capital found nearby is suggestive of how the church may have been decorated (fig. 1.5). It was discovered on the site of Honey Lane Market, not far from Becket's home. Gilbert's business meant he would have

1.6
Ice skates, 12th–13th century.
Bone. Left: 25.2 × 5 × 3.7 cm.
Right: 23.7 × 5 × 2.9 cm.
British Museum, London,
1891,0420.51–2. Donated by Sir
Augustus Wollaston Franks

1.7
Two boys ice skating and
tobogganing, detail from a psalter,
c.1320–30. Parchment codex.
Bodleian Libraries, University of
Oxford, MS Douce 5, f. 1v

frequented the stalls in the market, which was a popular place for the trade in imported textiles, and probably knew its traders personally. Although it remains unknown which building the capital came from, a small chapel of All Hallows was located nearby and is a likely candidate.[19] It provides a momentary glimpse into the lost world of twelfth-century London, one that Becket encountered every day, and it no doubt adorned a structure that was decorated both inside and out.

London was a city of independently minded, entrepreneurial citizens. They did not elect their first mayor until the end of the century, but the city's wealth and size meant Londoners were able to negotiate a special relationship with the Crown.[20] Gilbert was an active member of London's civic community and in recognition of this he was elected as a sheriff (or portreeve) in the 1130s.[21] His appointment elevated his family's social standing, providing him with greater authority and a connection to the Crown: it was the sheriff's duty to collect the court fees and tolls levied on the market and harbour.[22] It is clear that Becket's family was well connected and in business they played host to other sheriffs and merchants.

In winter, when it was cold enough, many Londoners passed their time ice skating on the frozen marshes of Moorfields, north of the city walls. This activity is evocatively described by FitzStephen:

Others there are, more skilled to sport upon the ice, who fit to their feet the shin-bones of beasts, lashing them beneath their ankles, and with iron-shod poles in their hands they strike ever and anon against the ice and are borne along swift as a bird in flight or a bolt shot.[23]

Numerous bone skates have been uncovered in the city (fig. 1.6). They were tied to the wearer's shoes by winding a strap around the skate; this could be made more secure by using holes drilled into the bones or metal loops inserted into the back. Many surviving skate blades are worn smooth on the bottom from repeated use. Becket, like other boys his age, might well have enjoyed such traditional pursuits and skated on the frozen marshlands (fig. 1.7). His biographers tell us that as a young man he indulged in worldly activities, including hawking and hunting, but he also may have enjoyed the popular hobbies of twelfth-century Londoners, such as the game of tables or backgammon. Many bone, antler and horn gaming pieces have been found in the city. These are small discs, some decorated with concentric circles or ring-and-dot motifs (fig. 1.8). Wealthier members of society owned more elaborate pieces, carved with images of animals, creatures or mythical and biblical scenes, often made in costlier materials such as ivory.

1.8
Gaming pieces, 11th–13th century. Bone. Diam. 5 cm (largest piece). British Museum, London, 1896,0411.62–3 (donated by Sir Augustus Wollaston Franks), 1856,0701.1320, 1856,0701.1515, 1856,0701.1327

1.9

The Liberal Arts Casket, *c.*1190–1200.
Copper alloy, enamel, gilding.
6.9 × 10.4 × 6 cm. Victoria and Albert
Museum, London, 7955:2-1862. To the
right of Grammar, Rhetoric is shown
as a bearded man holding a set of
scales. Next to him is the female
figure of Music, who plays a stringed
instrument, called a psaltery, which
she holds in her lap.

From London to Paris

Becket's basic education would have been delivered at home by his mother.[24]
Around the age of ten, he left home for the first time. He was sent to Merton
Priory in Surrey, six miles south-west of the city, to continue his education,
returning a few years later to attend another school in London. After this,
he took up the chance of a lifetime: the opportunity to study in Paris. By
then, probably around 1138, he was in his late teens and remained in France
for about three years.[25] This was an exciting time to be a student in Paris.
It was one of the most desirable places in Europe for young men to study,
with the city playing host to some of the greatest thinkers and teachers of
the Middle Ages. It was the age of Peter Abelard (1079–1142), best known for

his scandalous love affair with Héloïse, and Paris was a hotbed of scholastic thinkers, artists and architects.[26] Abbot Suger's (1081–1151) Basilica of St-Denis was almost complete and Becket possibly saw it being built. There was no formal university at this time but instead a series of monastic and cathedral schools where students could learn from different masters.[27] In Paris the young Thomas was instructed by the Englishman Robert de Melun (c.1100–1167), who taught the art of reasoning and debate.[28]

As a student, Becket studied the liberal arts, a programme divided into seven parts comprising the trivium – grammar, rhetoric and dialectic – and the quadrivium – arithmetic, geometry, music and astronomy. This provided him with a good academic grounding for a future career in administration, where basic skills like reading and writing in Latin were essential but conquering more difficult skills, like dialectic, could prove something of a challenge. Allegorical representations of the seven disciplines were popular during the twelfth century, such as those on the facades of the cathedrals of Chartres (c.1140s), Laon (c.1190) and Sens (c.1200).[29] Similar images can be found in England too, as seen on the Liberal Arts Casket, a brightly enamelled box made in the late twelfth century (fig. 1.9).[30] The casket is decorated with personifications of six of the liberal arts, along with figures of Philosophy and Nature, who is suckling the child Knowledge. On the front, Grammar takes the form of a woman who, holding a rod, is seated next to a young boy carrying a scroll. Grammar was viewed widely as a starting point for scholarly study and was thus enforced with strict discipline.[31] Its importance was asserted by John of Salisbury (1115/20–1180), a brilliant scholar as well as Becket's biographer and friend, who stated that 'Grammar is accordingly first among the liberal arts.'[32] Such a depiction also suggests something of the student experience at the time Becket was in Paris. Hugh of St Victor (1096–1141), a highly celebrated and influential Parisian thinker, expected much of his pupils, arguing that, among other things, 'the good student, then, ought to be humble and docile, free alike from vain cares and from sensual indulgences, diligent and zealous to learn willingly from all, to presume never upon his own knowledge, to shun the authors of perverse doctrine as if they were poison'.[33] The reality was quite different and complaints were raised about the riotous behaviour of students, to which Becket may have been witness or in which he may even have participated.

Logic and dialectic, the great arts of reasoning, were the two core pillars of twelfth-century learning. They provided students with the capacity to construct effective arguments. In his discussion of logic, John of Salisbury wrote that 'while each study is fortified by its own particular principles, logic is their common servant. … Hence logic is most valuable … as a tool in argumentative reasoning and the various branches of learning that pertain to philosophy.'[34] Becket's intellectual curiosity was stimulated by the Parisian masters, who were known for valuing a healthy spirit of inquiry in their classrooms. The skills he acquired in Paris proved valuable and helped him as he moved on from his life as a student and into the working world.

Entering the household of Archbishop Theobald

After several years in Paris, Becket abandoned his studies and returned to England. There is some debate about why he did so. Was he in Paris only to cherry-pick aspects of the curriculum? Had his scholarly career been unsuccessful? Or had a misfortune affected his family?[35] Whatever the circumstances were, he arrived back in London around 1141. There he started working for a financier named Osbert Huitdeniers. Osbert's surname, translating as 'Eightpence', indicates his connections with the financial world and he may even have been a moneylender. At this time usury was forbidden but it took place nonetheless and served as an essential prop to both royal government and society more generally. A few years later Becket joined the household (or curia) of Theobald, Archbishop of Canterbury (c.1090–1161), a career move which set him on a path that changed his life. Theobald was primarily responsible for the spiritual guidance of the entire country, but his position also required that he be a savvy political manoeuvrer. Becket's training in the archbishop's household introduced him to the royal court and brought him into contact with the great and the good from all over England and the Continent. Theobald came to England from the Abbey of Bec in Normandy, a training ground for Canterbury archbishops from the time of Lanfranc (c.1010–1089). He had been consecrated as archbishop on 8 January 1139 and held the position until his death in 1161. Chroniclers record that Becket's employment came through two of Theobald's officials, who lodged with the Becket family when in London.[36] Joining the household was an excellent move for the young man, as he could now count on the backing of a powerful patron with impeccable connections. One of Becket's biographers provides an account of Theobald's character; he was 'a simple man, somewhat quick to temper, and not as wary of word, if his mind was now stirred, as the rule of meekness utmost demandeth'.[37]

The members of Theobald's household assisted with the archbishop's personal and professional concerns, including the management of episcopal estates and representation on official business.[38] Becket was one of several promising young Paris-educated clerks working for Theobald. It is proof of the rigorous training these clerks received, coupled with the archbishop's reportedly excellent judgement of character, that six went on to become bishops and four archbishops.[39] Working in the household required Becket to have a good grasp of law. As archbishop, Theobald issued over 300 surviving charters, covering a vast array of business from the confirmation of rents, tithes and other gifts to mediation in disputes.[40] The archbishop also strove to maintain a positive working relationship with the prior and community of monks who lived in the precincts of Canterbury Cathedral, which in the Middle Ages was known as 'the church of Christ', or simply 'Christ Church'. Over the course of the medieval period the relationship between the archbishop and the priory fluctuated.[41] Since the archbishop, in theory abbot or head of the monastic community, was so frequently absent on state affairs, a lesser monk known as the prior exercised day-to-day control at Canterbury, overseeing his fellow monks. Theobald appears to have maintained generally good relations with the prior and monks, enabling Christ Church to thrive. From 1152/3 to 1167 a man called Wibert (d. 1167) led the Canterbury monks as prior. He was a visionary who oversaw several ambitious projects, including a whole host of major building work in the cathedral precincts.[42] Wibert and Theobald cooperated with relatively little friction. Theobald's keen interest in the monastic community can be seen in a grant issued between 1155 and 1161, addressed to Wibert (fig. 1.10). Here, Theobald confirms new regulations governing monks who had fled from Canterbury or been expelled from the community. It states that, should they return, they will have the very lowliest status within the priory for the rest of their lives.[43] At the base of this document are two wax seals attached by means of parchment tags. To the left is Theobald's archiepiscopal seal. It conveys his status and position, showing him fully clad in vestments with a crozier in his left hand and his right hand held in blessing.[44] The reverse indicates something of his personality (fig. 1.11). Here the impression has been made by a smaller counterseal and has at its centre a bearded man in profile, surrounded by the Latin for 'secret seal'.[45] The matrix from which this impression was made is now sadly lost but it originally incorporated an ancient Roman gem: an engraved intaglio showing the head of a man. Reusing a classical gem in this way demonstrated Theobald's depth of

1.10
Grant to Prior Wibert of Christ Church Priory, showing the wax seals of Archbishop Theobald (left) and Christ Church Priory (right), 1155–61. 29 × 17.5 cm. Canterbury Cathedral Archives and Library, CCA-DCc/ChAnt/C/163

1.11
Archbishop Theobald's counterseal, attached to a grant to Prior Wibert of Christ Church Priory, 1155–61. Wax. Canterbury Cathedral Archives and Library, CCA-DCc/ChAnt/C/163

1.12
Thomas Becket's counterseal, attached to a confirmation of a grant to Walter, Bishop of Rochester, 1162–70. Wax. 9.3 × 6.3 cm. The National Archives, Kew, E40/4913. The inscription reads '+SIGILLUM TOME LUND' (the seal of Thomas of London).

learning and his familiarity with the classical world; he may well have acquired it while abroad in Italy.[46] To the right of Theobald's seal is that of Christ Church itself. At its centre is an image of the building with Christ resurrected in the main doorway, explicitly demonstrating his personal patronage of the institution. Surrounding the image is an inscription reading 'The Seal of Christ Church, Canterbury. Premier Seat of Britain.'[47] This statement declares the primacy of Canterbury among all English churches. Made between 1155 and 1158 to replace a much older seal that had probably been in use from before the Norman Conquest, this second seal was particularly innovative.[48] Its sheer size, being far larger than most comparable twelfth-century episcopal seals, invites the viewer to consider the cathedral's immense status at the time.

Becket's experiences in Theobald's household may have given him a taste for the luxury for which he was later well known.[49] It was perhaps during this phase that he had his own secret seal made (fig. 1.12). Only a single impression from it survives, attached to a charter now in The National Archives. Like Theobald, Becket was keen to stress his classical learning and scholarly credentials. When he had his own matrix made, he also opted for a reused Roman gem, possibly depicting Apollo, placing it at the centre of the seal.[50] The text declares that this is the 'seal of Thomas of London' and it must surely have been made before he was chancellor or archbishop, when he styled himself differently.[51] Becket's seal brings us close to the man himself and places him alongside the other learned clerks in Theobald's household, who also used seals with reused Roman gems, including John of Salisbury, William de Vere (d. 1198) and Roger de Pont l'Évêque (c.1115–1181).

Becket's time under Theobald was a profitable one. As a clerk in the household he was part of a select group of some of the brightest young minds in the country. Many of the friends, and in some cases enemies, he made here remained so throughout his life. One of these was John of Salisbury, who had studied in Paris around the same time as Becket. John, however, showed more commitment to his education. Prior to arriving in Canterbury, he had spent twelve years as a student in various monastic schools, eventually receiving the respected title of 'magister' (Master). Degrees in the modern sense did not exist at this time, but to become a Master was a public acknowledgement that the student had gained sufficient experience to teach. John worked in Theobald's household for twelve years, from 1147 to 1159, and, like Becket, his responsibilities involved travelling between European courts on diplomatic business, assisting with legal matters and compiling much of the archbishop's correspondence. John was frustrated by this work, complaining that it left him little time to study. Yet despite his protests he found time to write several books, the most famous of which, the *Policraticus*, was dedicated to Becket (see Chapter 2). Not everyone who worked with Becket in Theobald's household remained on such friendly terms with him. Roger de Pont l'Évêque and John of Canterbury (*c.*1120–*c.*1204) were two fellow clerks who went on to enjoy prestigious careers: Roger as Archdeacon of Canterbury and then as Archbishop of York, and John as Bishop of Poitiers and then Archbishop of Lyons. Early on, these two men formed a pact with Becket to help advance one another's careers.[52] It would seem that their deal was a success, but Roger later turned on him. Becket's medieval biographers tell us that Roger's skills drew particular praise from Theobald, who appreciated the young man's 'gentleness and wisdom' and his aptitude as an orator.[53] However, they also report that he was consumed by jealousy because of Theobald's favouritism towards Becket, to the extent that he 'grew resentful of him, and did his utmost, either by himself or by using others, to have him marginalized'.[54] The dispute became so serious that accusations of heinous crimes were levelled against Roger, including seducing a young man and fixing a trial so that this same individual was sentenced to death.[55] Years later, Roger would play a central role in Becket's argument with the king.

Theobald also sent Becket for further training, perhaps because, as one chronicler observed, he was not as well educated as his colleagues.[56] He travelled to the Continent, spending time in both Auxerre and Bologna, where he studied law, and making several visits to the papal curia in Rome.[57] Bologna was the most prestigious place to study law in Europe and it is thought Becket learnt both civil or Roman law, and ecclesiastical or canon law.[58] Such experiences no doubt shaped Becket personally and professionally. They allowed him to see the world beyond England and Paris, to learn practical legal and diplomatic skills, and to network with legal scholars and future church leaders. His work as a clerk also brought financial benefits. In 1154, when Roger moved into his new position as Archbishop of York, Becket was given his previous role as Archdeacon of Canterbury. According to John, the position was worth £100 a year, an enormous sum at the time.[59] For Becket this was beginning to be a lucrative career path. As archdeacon, he remained a member of the 'secular clergy', living in the world, albeit as a cleric, without many of the restrictions that were placed upon the 'regular clergy', who lived in retirement from the world according to a monastic rule.[60] Seculars, although they too were supposed to wear clerical dress and have their heads tonsured, could own property, made no vows of obedience and could carry arms.[61] Such freedoms enabled Becket to indulge in more worldly pursuits. The liberties enjoyed by clerks and the legal protection they were given by the Church were matters of heated debate that came to have major consequences for Becket.

Canterbury

During the twelve years that Becket worked under Theobald, Canterbury Cathedral was a powerhouse of artistic patronage and, although he was not permanently based in Canterbury, he would have witnessed at first hand the major works bringing splendour to the cathedral. He probably stayed

1.13
Quatrefoil showing the half figure of a king, *c.*1150–80. Caen limestone. 34.6 × 32.4 cm. Canterbury City Museum, CANCM 1984.32.1. This fragment was discovered in 1730 in a wall of the Aula Nova (High Hall) in Canterbury Cathedral's precincts.

1.14
Label stop showing an animal head, possibly a lion or a dog, holding the head of a man in its mouth, c.1150–80. Caen limestone. 10.5 × 10 cm. Canterbury Cathedral, 001196.5. This fragment was discovered in 1970 in Canterbury Cathedral's cloister.

in the Archbishop's Palace near to the hubbub of the stonemasons' yard, where blocks and sculptures were shaped before being hauled by labourers up wooden scaffolding and into position. A large group of broken limestone sculptures, the majority of which were discovered in the cathedral's cloister in the late 1960s and early 1970s, may date from this broad period of building work – that is to say, between 1150 and 1180 (figs 1.13–1.14).[62] The carvings include figurative pieces decorated with human forms, busts of kings and heads of queens, and even bearded men who probably represent masons, as well as animals and monstrous beasts.[63] It is unclear whether they were made for a screen that spanned the interior of the church, were intended for a structure in the monastic cloister or were from a partition screen produced around 1173 for the site of the martyrdom chapel, where Becket was killed.[64] In any case, they are indicative of the kind of lavish decoration Becket would have seen as part of the new building work going on in the cathedral.

Plans to rejuvenate the priory buildings in the mid-twelfth century included new gateways, ornate cloisters and a piped water system fed from a two-storied water tower.[65] The plan for this is shown in a unique survival,

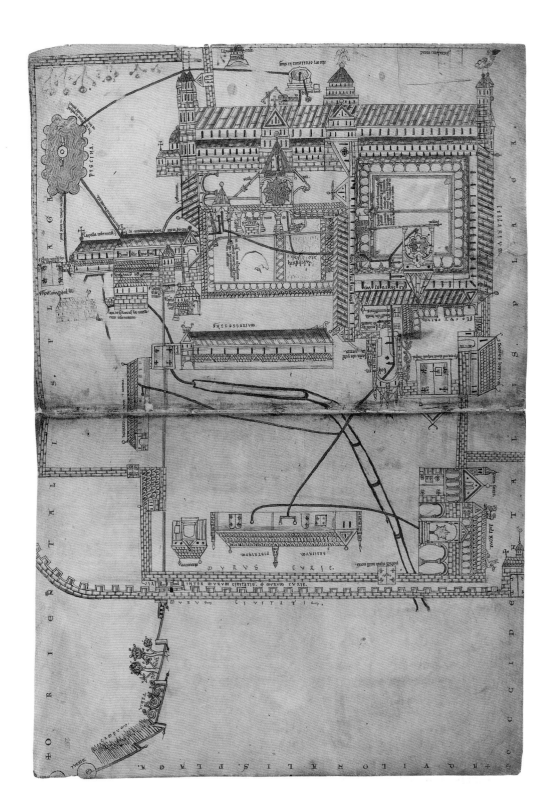

1.15

Plan of Canterbury Cathedral's waterworks and monastic complex, known as the 'Waterworks drawing', in the Eadwine Psalter, *c.*1150 (psalter), *c.*1160–70 (drawing). 66 × 46 cm. Trinity College, Cambridge, MS R.17.1, ff. 284v–285r. At the top of the drawing is the cathedral, with the monastic complex below. Fresh water (green) is pumped into the buildings and used water (red) is pumped out.

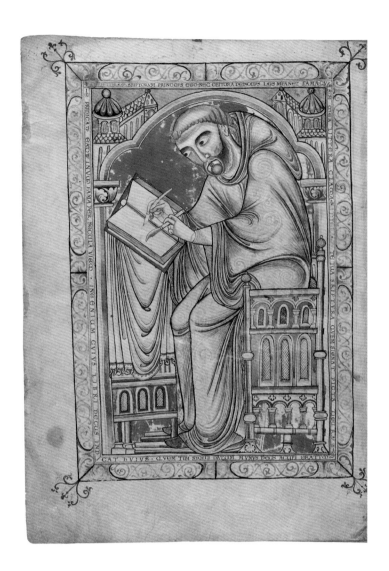

1.16
Portrait of the scribe Eadwine
in the Eadwine Psalter, *c.*1150
(psalter), *c.*1160–70 (drawing).
46 × 33 cm. Trinity College,
Cambridge, MS R.17.1, f. 283v

called the 'Waterworks drawing', produced around 1160, in ink and coloured
with washes of red, blue, green and brown (fig. 1.15).[66] It reveals the scale
and ambition of the monastic complex, mapping out its buildings and
plumbing system, and was later sewn into the back of an impressive book
known as the Eadwine Psalter. Made in the middle of the twelfth century, it
is one of the most extensively decorated manuscripts of the period, offering
an illustrated copy of the Psalms. The manuscript's name derives from a
'portrait' of Eadwine, one of the scribes who worked on it (fig. 1.16). In this
image, Eadwine, shown seated, bends over his desk, holding the tools of his
trade, a scalpel and a quill. A border of text proclaims his identity and skill,

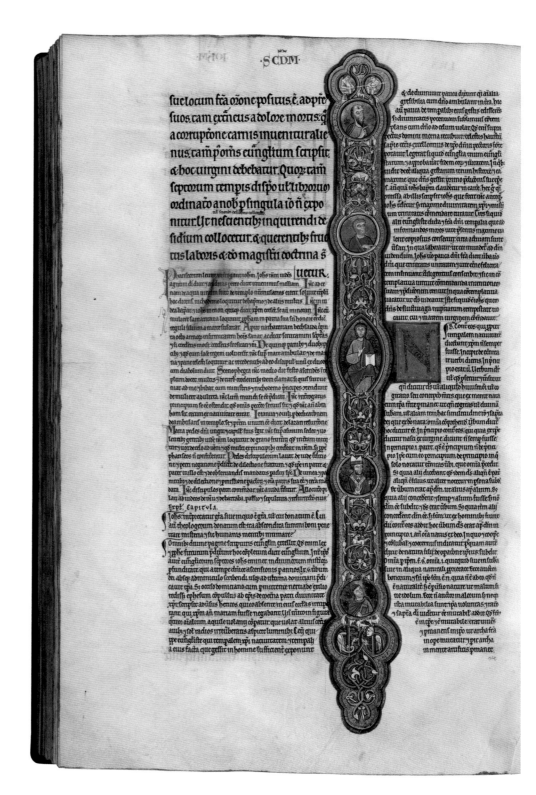

1.17

Glossed book of the gospels, c.1160–70. Trinity College, Cambridge, MS B.5.5., f. 130v. This folio marks the beginning of the Book of John. At the top of the decorated initial are two apostles. Christ sits at the centre on a rainbow. Below him is the bust of a mitred archbishop, possibly Thomas Becket. Underneath this figure is a young man holding a book.

dubbing him 'the prince of scribes … whose genius the beauty of this book demonstrates'.[67] Talented though he was, Eadwine did not work alone. He was assisted in his project by other scribes who shared the task. It is quite likely that Becket at least knew of, or had even met, Eadwine.[68] Several years later, when Becket became archbishop, he commissioned expensive, deluxe manuscripts.[69] He left most of his personal library to Canterbury Cathedral, the contents of which were later recorded by a prior of Canterbury called Henry Eastry (1285–1331). Becket's library contained religious works but also classical ones, including Livy's *History of Rome*, an extremely rare text at the time.[70] He commissioned a number of books from abroad as well as patronising the scribes and artists of Canterbury Cathedral. Several such volumes are thought to have survived. One, a glossed copy of the gospels, measuring 45 cm high, was probably made in France (fig. 1.17). In one illuminated initial, below Christ seated on a rainbow is the bust of an archbishop who may represent Becket (see detail on page 10). Glossed works were intended to supply commentaries and different theological interpretations for each part of the Bible. They were extremely popular in the twelfth century, not least because of their potential as teaching books, and as a sign that modern knowledge was now considered capable of enhancing understanding of even the most sacred texts of scripture. Such glosses would have been suitable for someone like Becket, who was looking for more than the standard text could offer. They were also of practical use and supplied their readers with a useful summary of current scholarly opinion.

England at war

Becket grew up in a period of profound political upheaval. On 25 November 1120, King Henry I (*c.*1068–1135) lost his only legitimate male heir, William (1103–1120), in a terrible accident. Along with many young Anglo-Norman nobles, William was drowned when his boat, the *Blanche-Nef* or 'White Ship', sank off the coast of the Norman harbour of Barfleur. Henry never recovered from the loss of his son and England was immediately plunged into a succession crisis. His reign would be remembered for the sinking of the *White Ship*.[71] An image of Henry from a fourteenth-century genealogy of the kings of England shows him enthroned with a mournful expression on his face, his shoulders sagging

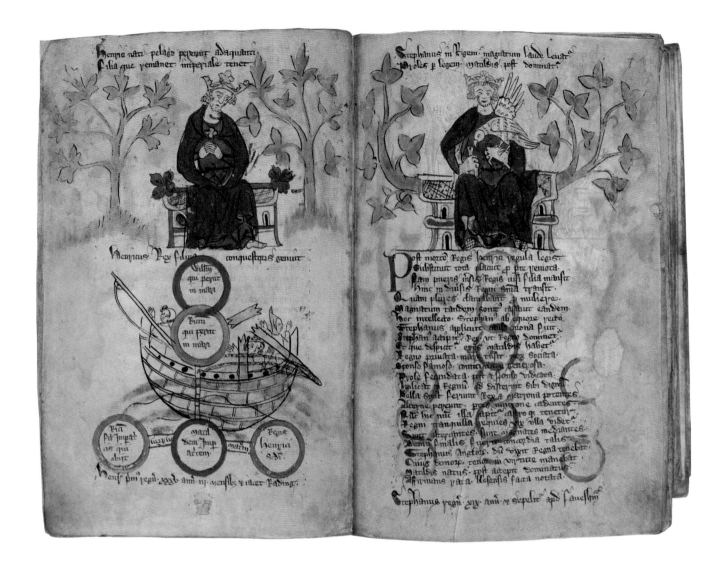

1.18
King Henry I (left) and King
Stephen (right), from a
genealogy of the kings of
England, c.1307–27. Parchment
codex. 23 × 15 cm (closed).
British Library, London, Royal
MS 20 A II, ff. 6v–7r

and his hands clasped (fig. 1.18). Below him a boat made of short wooden planks sinks beneath the waves. Inside it three men, including the crown-wearing prince, look on in panic as a broken mast crashes down. On the opposite page sits a new king who presents a different countenance. This crowned figure proudly holds out a falcon on his wrist and, as the text tells us, is King Stephen of England (*c*.1092–1154). Across these pages the complex political situation is set out as a young Becket would have experienced it: a fractured line of royal inheritance, multiple possible heirs to the throne and the suspicion that Stephen now ruled as an oath-breaker and usurper.

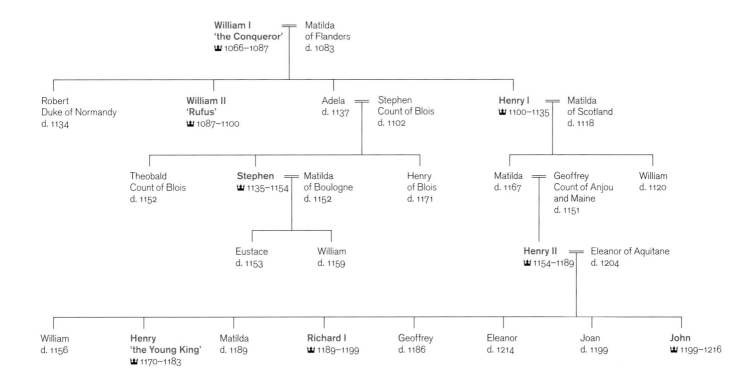

After the disaster of the *White Ship*, Henry's chief concern lay in securing the smooth transition of power to Matilda (1102–1167), his eldest legitimate daughter (fig. 1.19). To do so, he asked his barons to swear allegiance to her as heir to England and Normandy in 1127. One of the lords who took the oath was his nephew Stephen, Count of Blois. It was a promise that he would ultimately break. Several months later, Henry also secured the backing of the powerful county of Anjou by encouraging Matilda to marry Geoffrey (1113–1151), son of Count Fulk of Anjou. Matilda had been a widow since 1125, following the death of her first husband, the Holy Roman Emperor Henry V (1081–1125). She was less than enthusiastic about marrying Geoffrey, who was nearly twelve years her junior.[72] Their relationship was unstable from the start, and it soon broke down completely. Eventually, the couple were reconciled and Matilda went on to give birth to three sons: Henry (the later King Henry II) in 1133 (d. 1189), Geoffrey in 1134 (d. 1158) and finally William (1136–1164). In the meantime, the couple quarrelled with Henry I over several matters.[73] When the king suddenly fell ill and died in 1135, father and daughter were not on speaking terms.[74]

1.19
Simplified family tree showing the descendants of King William I

1.20
Reverse of King Stephen's second Great Seal from a charter, 1152–4. King's College, Cambridge, GBR/22. The Latin inscription reads 'STEPHANVS DEI GR[ATI]A DUX NORMANORVM' (Stephen, by Grace of God, Duke of Normandy). The obverse side of the seal shows Stephen enthroned with a sword in one hand and an orb in the other. The Latin text reads '+ STEPHANVS DEI GRATIA REX ANGLORVM' (Stephen, by Grace of God, King of England).

1.21
Coin of Stephen minted in Dunwich, *c.*1150–4. Silver. Diam. 1.9 cm. 1.5 g. British Museum, London, 1990,0629.73

Despite his attempts to avert a crisis Henry had failed, and the strained relationship with his daughter and son-in-law at the time of his death opened the way for a challenger to the throne. The resulting fight for the crown drew England into an eighteen-year civil war. Stephen of Blois was the first claimant to the throne to reach England, in December 1135. After landing at Dover his retinue marched to Canterbury and then made their way to London, where the citizens declared their support for him. Chroniclers disagree over whether this endorsement was given freely or through bribery and persuasion, but nonetheless Londoners played an important role in securing the crown for Stephen.[75] At this time Becket was a teenager and may have witnessed this assertion of collective civic power.

With help from his brother, Henry of Blois, Bishop of Winchester (*c.*1096–1171), Stephen secured the backing of the Church. He took control of the royal treasury and was crowned in Westminster Abbey on 22 December 1135. By choosing to hold his coronation ceremony in the same church as his three immediate predecessors, Stephen was making a public statement about his legitimacy and lineage. In other practical ways Stephen presented himself in the image of Henry I. He commissioned a new set of seal matrices in order to authenticate documents as King of England.[76] Like almost all royal seal matrices from the Middle Ages, Stephen's no longer survive. Most were destroyed after the king's death. Stephen's Great Seal, which is known only from wax impressions, is large, measuring over 8 cm in diameter, and double-sided, following the form of Henry I's seal (fig. 1.20). In another show of strength he commissioned a new national coinage and authorised more mints to produce these coins (fig. 1.21).[77]

Stephen spent the first years of his reign trying to establish control. In particular, 1139 proved to be a decisive year.[78] Becket's future mentor, Theobald, was consecrated as Archbishop of Canterbury in January. A few months later Stephen grew suspicious that three of his English bishops – Roger, Bishop of Salisbury (d. 1139), and his nephews Alexander, Bishop of Lincoln (1123–1148), and Nigel, Bishop of Ely (*c.*1100–1169) – were plotting against him.[79] He ordered their arrest and in doing so made powerful enemies in the Church. Opposition to Stephen intensified after Matilda crossed the Channel in September to stake her claim to the throne. By this point, Becket was probably immersed in his studies in Paris, but he must surely have heard of the growing tension back in England. Matilda was in an increasingly strong position, having secured the support of a powerful ally, her half-brother Robert, Earl of Gloucester (before 1000–1147), Henry I's favourite among his many illegitimate children. She had also been busy seeking the Pope's guidance, especially to decide whether Stephen's claim was invalid, something on which the Pope refused to adjudicate. Determined to take what she saw as rightfully hers, Matilda landed at Arundel and set off on her campaign for the throne. A turning point in the skirmishes between Matilda and Stephen's factions came at the Battle of Lincoln on 2 February 1141. It was a resounding victory for Matilda and resulted in the king being taken prisoner. Stephen was kept in captivity for most of the year.[80] Theobald's handling of this situation demonstrated the shrewd political judgement needed to survive in these challenging times. He had remained loyal to the king throughout, but now he was asked to swear to serve Matilda and obey the papal legate for England, Henry of Blois, who had turned against his brother.[81] Theobald was in a difficult position, torn between conflicting loyalties. In the end, he agreed to follow the empress, but only if Stephen granted his approval.

With the king in captivity, Matilda's destiny as queen seemed secure, particularly after her supporters declared her to be Lady of the English. Unlike Stephen, Matilda did not have a new seal made to reflect her changing status. Instead she continued to use a smaller single-sided seal. Only a few impressions survive (fig. 1.22). It shows Matilda crowned and on her throne, encircled by a Latin text identifying her as 'Queen of the Romans'.[82] Through her first marriage to Henry V, Holy Roman Emperor, she had been crowned 'Queen of the Romans'. The title of empress, although widely used by her and her supporters, had never officially been granted by the Pope, so her peculiar status continued to be reflected in all of her letters, issued in her capacity as empress yet sealed with a matrix from which the imperial title was conspicuously absent.[83] It was during these years that Stephen's initially tight grip on the country's coinage loosened (fig. 1.23). In a situation unprecedented in England since the immediate aftermath of the decline of the Roman Empire, several individuals now began minting coins in their own name, either in opposition to, or in support of, the king.[84] This diversity of coinage is itself a potent indicator of the political divisions that plagued the realm.

By late 1141 Becket had concluded his studies and returned to London from Paris. The following year, his future friend and king, Matilda's eldest son, Henry, was brought to England for the first time.[85] Aged nine, Henry was taken to his uncle Robert's household in Bristol. His upbringing was a world away from that of Becket. Henry was the son of an empress and via

1.22
Seal of Empress Matilda, attached to the confirmation of a grant to Bordesley Abbey, 1141–3. King's College, Cambridge, SJP/19. The Latin text reads '+ MATILDIS DEI GRATIA ROMANORUM REGINA' (Matilda, by Grace of God, Queen of the Romans).

1.23
Coin of Matilda minted in Oxford, c.1141–5. Silver. Diam. 2 cm. 1.1 g. British Museum, London, 1896,0609.126

his grandmother, Henry I's first queen, could claim direct descent not only from William the Conqueror (*c*.1028–1087) but also from the Anglo-Saxon kings who had preceded the Norman Conquest. As Aelred, the Abbot of Rievaulx (1110–1167), pointed out in a specially commissioned work of genealogy, this made the future Henry II the first king to restore the Anglo-Saxon bloodline to the English throne.[86] Such things mattered, and Henry was raised with full knowledge of his place in the world, far above that of a mere clerk. In time he grew to become a confident and bold young man. Henry's first military expedition against Stephen came in 1149, when he replaced his mother as chief claimant to the throne. Matilda, having never been able to fully take control of the country, had sailed back to France in 1148 and never returned. Around the same time, Becket witnessed the fury of an angry king. Now firmly ensconced in the household of Theobald, he was by the archbishop's side when they, against Stephen's explicit command, stole away to Rheims to attend a church council summoned by Pope Eugenius III (*c*.1080–1153). On returning, Theobald found himself banished from England on royal orders, with his lands confiscated. Here, again, Theobald demonstrated canny diplomacy. Back at the papal council, Eugenius was reportedly about to pronounce a sentence of excommunication (expulsion from the Christian community) against Stephen when Theobald interjected, begging clemency for his sovereign lord. To this, the Pope is said to have declared to all present, 'Regard him, O brethren … loving his enemies and praying for his persecutors.'[87] The archbishop's tact secured his return to England; it was an important lesson from which Becket must surely have learnt a great deal.

By the 1150s Stephen was chiefly concerned with securing the crown for his son, Eustace. This was to lead to further difficulties with Theobald and the Church. In 1152 the king gathered his bishops together and encouraged them to support Eustace's claims to the throne. They refused to comply and Stephen reacted angrily. For the second time Theobald found himself in exile but in much more dangerous circumstances. The archbishop is said to have escaped, pursued down the Thames by armed knights.[88] Becket did not flee with him, but we can imagine the horror that he and the rest of Theobald's household would have felt at the thought of their master being placed in mortal danger. Theobald remained overseas for about four months before returning to play a part in the diplomatic negotiations between Stephen and Henry, the future king.

The rise of Henry II

Back in France, young Henry's fortunes continued to prosper. In 1150 he was recognised as Duke of Normandy, and a year later, after his father's death, he also inherited the title of Count of Anjou. An advantageous marriage to Eleanor of Aquitaine (c.1122–1204) in May 1152 greatly enhanced both his prospects and his future estate (fig. 1.24). Together, they made a formidable pair. Just months previously Eleanor had divorced King Louis VII of France (1120–1180), a decision approved by the Pope on the grounds that they were cousins, which in theory should have prohibited them from marrying in the first place. In reality, the kinship between Eleanor and Louis would not have been raised as an issue save for the fact that husband and wife had grown to detest one another, their marriage fatally undermined by their failure to produce a male heir to the throne of France. Contemporary chroniclers harboured strong opinions of her, both bad and good. One of the most effusive was Richard of Devizes (c.1150–c.1200) who described Eleanor as 'an incomparable woman, beautiful yet virtuous, powerful yet gentle, humble yet keen-witted: qualities which are most rarely found in a woman'.[89] Stretching from the Loire south to the Pyrenees, Eleanor's rich territory in Aquitaine put Henry in a commanding position. In 1153 he once again sailed from France for England, intending to complete the conquest that thus far had eluded him.

This time warfare yielded place to negotiation, with mediators, including Theobald and Becket, working in the background throughout the year to secure a deal. The terms of the agreement included Stephen's acceptance of Henry as his sole heir. It was, perhaps, the deaths of both his wife, in 1152, and his eldest son, Eustace, in 1153, that forced the king's hand. By November, Stephen had formally accepted Henry as his successor. Even so, the king might have lived for many more years. Once again, fate intervened. Stephen fell ill in October 1154 and died within a matter of days. On 19 December, Theobald crowned Henry II and Eleanor as the new king and queen in a lavish ceremony at Westminster Abbey. Henry was only twenty-one. He had nonetheless risen to become one of the most powerful rulers in Europe: King of England, Duke of Normandy and Aquitaine, and Count of Anjou, now ruling territories that stretched from the borders of Scotland to those of Spain.[90] Over the course of his thirty-five-year reign, Henry strengthened this position by adding to his already vast dominions.

'Second in rank in the realm only to the king'

As Theobald's secretary, Becket witnessed Henry's ascendancy at first hand, but little did he know that he was about to become a key player in the new king's administration. One of Becket's biographers describes the mood as Henry took the throne: 'there was no little trepidation in the Church, on the one hand because of the worrying youth of the king, and on the other because of the well-known antipathy of his courtiers towards the Church's right to liberty.'[91] Perhaps because of this concern and the inexperienced king's need for a steadying hand to help him, Theobald recommended Becket for the position of royal chancellor. Henry accepted the advice of his archbishop and within months, possibly even a few days after the coronation, Becket found himself working for the king. This catapulted him into the heart of the royal court, as FitzStephen tells us:

> The chancellor of England is considered second in rank in the realm only to the king. He holds the other part of the king's seal, with which he seals his own orders. He has responsibility and care of the king's chapel, and maintains whatever vacant archbishoprics, bishoprics, abbacies and baronies fall into the king's hands. He attends all the king's councils to which he does not even require a summons.[92]

From the outset Henry and Becket got on well. As head of the royal writing office, or scriptorium, the new chancellor spent most of the next eight

1.25
Coin of Henry II minted
in London, c.1180–9.
Silver. Diam. 1.9 cm. 1.4 g.
British Museum, London,
1902,1204.598

years personally attending to the king's business. Henry was known for his
energy and love of hunting, and chroniclers describe him as someone who
was always on the move, spending much of his time travelling between his
dominions. According to Gerald of Wales (c.1146–c.1223), describing the king
later in life, he was,

> a man of reddish, freckled complexion with a large round head, grey eyes
> which glowed fiercely and grew bloodshot in anger, a fiery countenance
> and a harsh, cracked voice. … Except when troubled in mind or moved
> to anger, he was a prince of great eloquence and … polished in letters.[93]

His first priority as king was to restore the rule of law to what it had been
under his grandfather, Henry I, in the process sweeping away changes made
by Stephen (fig. 1.25).[94] Henry made this clear in his 1154 Charter of Liberties,
also known as the Coronation Charter. In it, he confirmed the liberties of the
Church, according to Becket's later recollection, and placed the document in
pledge on Westminster Abbey's high altar.[95] This determination to restore the
glories of the past can be seen in Canterbury's earliest surviving city charter
(fig. 1.26). Written between 1155 and 1161, this document was witnessed
by Becket, as 'Thomas the chancellor', along with his former mentor,
Archbishop Theobald.[96] It confirmed the privileges of the citizens and on
three separate occasions stressed that these were to be the same as they had
been 'in the time of Henry I'.[97] The king's Great Seal, attached by means
of a silk cord, follows in this same tradition, deliberately mimicking those
of previous English kings, including both Henry I and Stephen. As royal
chancellor, Becket was personally responsible for the king's seal matrices.[98]

Becket's new job was wide-ranging. He was directly responsible for
the scriptorium, where formal documents such as writs and charters were

1.26
Charter of Henry II to the city of Canterbury, 1155–61. Parchment with wax seal. 34 × 21 cm (charter). Canterbury Cathedral Archives and Library, CCA-CC-A/A/1. This document confirms the privileges of the citizens of Canterbury, such as the freedom to hunt in certain lands. Among the witnesses to the charter were Becket and Theobald, Archbishop of Canterbury.

produced on the king's behalf. According to FitzStephen, no fewer than fifty-two clerks now worked for Becket: one for every week of the year.[99] In addition, he oversaw the royal archives and church services at court.[100] Kings had often looked to their leading churchmen to fill the position of chancellor. Becket, by contrast, was largely unknown. A parvenu, he responded to this situation with behaviour and a lifestyle that were widely regarded as both boastful and more worldly than clerical. With his new role came significant wealth. He was now able to maintain his own household, which he kept in great splendour, often playing host to visiting dignitaries. He pursued secular pleasures such as hunting and chess, and dressed in rich, imported silks and fabrics.[101] Becket's most ostentatious display came during a trip to the French royal court in 1158. His mission was to secure the marriage of Henry's eldest son, also called Henry (later Henry the Young King, 1155–1183), to Margaret of France (c.1158–1197), the daughter of Louis VII. FitzStephen writes that Becket 'prepared to display the opulence of England's luxury'.[102] As well as an astonishing twenty-four personal changes of clothes, this included an entourage of two hundred or so mounted members of his household, a menagerie of birds, monkeys and other exotic animals, and eight huge horse-drawn wagons.[103] The wagons carried a vast supply of English beer, intended as a riposte to the French wines in which the court of Louis VII took such pride. It is perhaps no wonder that Garnier de Pont-Sainte-Maxence, another biographer of Becket, characterised him as 'one who lived a life of ostentatious extravagance'.[104] During his tenure as chancellor, he assisted the king in matters of war. In 1159, he led troops as part of a campaign in Toulouse, successfully seizing several towns in the process. Two years later, he again engaged in battle, this time in Gisors. Theobald was reportedly dismayed and wrote to Becket asking him to return to England. Little could he have predicted that his one-time protégé would soon become his successor.

Archbishop of Canterbury

> Upon his consecration he immediately put off the old man, and put
> on the hairshirt and the monk, crucifying the flesh with its passions
> and desires.[105]

In 1161 Theobald died and the archbishopric of Canterbury fell vacant. Henry was keen to appoint Becket but, crucially, he wanted him to continue

1.27

Enamelled plaque showing Henry of Blois, c.1150–71. Copper alloy, gilding and enamel. 9.2 × 17.9 × 1.4 cm. British Museum, London, 1852,0327.1. Bequeathed by Revd Henry J. Crowe. Henry of Blois, Bishop of Winchester, is shown with a crozier and another rectangular object, probably an altar frontal he commissioned. The Latin reads: 'HENRICUS EPISCOP' (Bishop Henry). In the double border there are two further lines of Latin text: '+ ARS AVRO GEMMISQ (UE) PRIOR, PRIOR OMNIBVS AVTOR. DONA DAT HENRICVS VIVVS IN ERE DEO, MENTE PAREM MVSIS (ET) MARCO VOCE PRIOREM. FAME VIRIS, MORES CONCILIANT SVPERIS' (Art comes before gold and gems, the author before everything. Henry, alive in bronze, gives gifts to God. Henry, whose fame commends him to men, whose character commends him to the heavens, a man equal in mind to the Muses and in eloquence higher than Marcus [Cicero]).

as chancellor. With his ally in both positions, Henry saw an opportunity to exercise even greater authority over the Church as well as the State. This decision was not met with universal support: Henry's mother, the formidable Empress Matilda, counselled against the idea.[106] Even Becket was not sure he wanted the archbishopric. It took a visiting cardinal, Henry of Pisa, to convince him to accept. The king's recommendation was put to the vote and after much debate the bishops of southern England and the monks of Canterbury agreed to elect Becket. The promotion shocked many including Gilbert Foliot (c.1110–1187), future Bishop of London, who commented on the king's actions that 'from a secular man and a knight he [had] fashioned an archbishop'.[107] Since Gilbert had himself coveted the job, there was more than a small degree of sour grapes to such remarks. Although Becket had worked for both an archbishop and the king, and was already Archdeacon of Canterbury, he had never accepted ordination as a priest and had shown little inclination for the priestly life. With considerable haste he was now ordained, just twenty-four hours before his formal consecration as archbishop in Canterbury Cathedral. This took place on 3 June 1162 and was presided over by Henry of Blois, brother of the late King Stephen (fig. 1.27).[108] Alongside Henry of Blois were fourteen bishops who oversaw the moment

1.28
Mitre, c.1180–1230. Silk and linen. 23.5 × 33.3 cm (headpiece); L. 70.4 cm (headpiece and lappet with figure). Westminster Cathedral, London, on loan to the Victoria and Albert Museum, London, LOAN:WESTMINSTER.1. This mitre was previously kept at Sens Cathedral as part of a group of vestments thought to be relics of St Thomas, which he left there during his exile. It was given to Nicolas Wiseman, the future cardinal and archbishop of Westminster Cathedral, in 1842.

1.29
Finger ring, 12th century. Gold and sapphire. Diam. 2.8 cm. British Museum, London, AF.1866. Bequeathed by Sir Augustus Wollaston Franks. This ring was reportedly found in 1829 at the tomb of a 12th-century bishop of Verdun.

1.30
Crozier, mid-12th century. Copper alloy, gilding. 76 × 16 cm. Eglwys Gadeiriol Tyddewi / St Davids Cathedral, Pembrokeshire. Discovered in the grave of a bishop in 1865–6, possibly the grave of Bishop Richard de Carew (d. 1280), who chose to be buried with this much older crozier.

when Becket, seated on the episcopal throne, was presented with the symbols of his office including the mitre, the crozier and the archiepiscopal ring. Those given to Becket have not survived, but similar examples, made during or soon after his lifetime, provide some sense of what they might have looked like (figs 1.28–1.30).[109] A later alabaster carving, originally from an altarpiece, shows this grand ceremony (fig. 1.31). Becket sits in the centre, in full regalia, flanked by members of the clergy and overseen by God the Father. Roger of Pontigny, a biographer and friend of Becket's, described the outpouring of joy from those in attendance and 'the devotion and exultation of those who came running up to meet him ... tears flowing from their eyes.'[110]

The final stage in Becket's transformation to archbishop required a journey to Rome. He sent envoys on his behalf to receive a pallium from the Pope. It was a white woollen garment in the form of a circular band worn round the shoulders, with lappets running down the front and back, embroidered with crosses. Only the Pope and archbishops were permitted to wear a pallium, and it represented the conferral of full jurisdiction upon Becket. In accepting it he pledged an oath of obedience to the papacy.[111] But in doing so, he revealed a potentially disastrous clash of loyalties between his two lords, the King of England and the Pope. Whether it was in receiving the symbols of his new office, or in appreciating the immense role he had now taken on, Becket is said to have undergone a spiritual transformation almost immediately after consecration, casting off the worldliness of his former life. To Roger of Pontigny, it was almost as if the archbishop had become another person: 'with the aid of divine grace, he was transformed into another man, he put off the old man with his acts, and put on the new man in righteousness and sanctity'.[112] Henry's plan had been for Becket to maintain his duties as chancellor alongside those newly assumed as archbishop, thereby uniting these two jurisdictions in a single figure capable of enacting the king's will. However, this was not what Becket wanted: very soon after accepting the pallium he resigned his offices at court. He did so against the king's express wishes and turned his attention to the needs of the Church.

1.31
Panel from an altarpiece
showing Becket's
consecration as
archbishop, *c*.1425–50.
Alabaster. 49 × 24 × 4 cm.
Private collection

Henricus natus Matildes regna tenebat.
Sub quo sacratus Thomas murrore radebat.

Henricus Rex filius   Matildis Imperatrix

hen
havene

Fall: exile, murder, canonisation

King Henry saw Becket's about-turn as the ultimate betrayal, and the two friends soon became enemies. The souring of their relationship was a defining feature of Henry's reign and over time numerous artists would try to capture something of the volatility of the moment. Two different versions of the affair convey the tense drama of archbishop and king arguing with one another. In one manuscript, from an early fourteenth-century genealogy of the kings of England, Henry is shown enthroned and debating with Becket (fig. 2.1). Gesticulating, he presses his finger into his open palm. Becket stands alongside with his right hand raised, as if to refute the king's point. Neither is willing to back down. A second image, from the Queen Mary Psalter, a richly illuminated fourteenth-century manuscript, depicts the two men in the middle of a heated quarrel (fig. 2.2). Becket gestures at Henry with a single pointed finger, as if to accuse him, and the king, sitting with sword in hand, answers the archbishop with an outstretched arm. Those gathered to either side of Becket and Henry watch the unfolding scene, mirroring what people across Europe would do.

Very quickly you would turn your heart and favour away from me, which is now great between us, and replace it with the most savage hatred.[1]

Thomas Becket, speaking to Henry II, 1162

2.1
Henry II and Thomas Becket, detail from a genealogy of the kings of England, c.1307–27. Parchment codex. 23 × 15 cm (closed). British Library, London, Royal MS 20 A II, f. 7v

2.2

Henry II and Thomas Becket,
detail in the Queen Mary
Psalter, c.1310–20. Parchment
codex. 27.5 × 17.5 cm (closed).
British Library, London, Royal
MS 2 B VII, f. 291v

The fallout

The reasons for Becket and Henry's dispute at first appear relatively obscure.
Their disagreement centred on the question of clerical immunity from
secular prosecution, and related to clerics who had committed serious crimes
– the so-called 'criminous clerks'. What might on the surface seem to be a
world of bureaucracy and legal administration was in fact set in the context
of radical political thought in twelfth-century Europe.[2] The resurgence of the
study of law had much to do with it. Around 1140, Gratian, a monk and legal
scholar based in Bologna, in northern Italy, completed his great work the
Decretum (also known as 'Gratian's Decretals'). This text is a compilation of
much older Church laws or 'canons', for the most part derived from solemn
papal letters ('decretals'). Intended to resolve discrepancies between the
rulings of successive popes and church councils, it rapidly became a standard
textbook.[3] By creating a definitive collection, Gratian aimed to differentiate
between custom and law, arguing that the latter was for the universal benefit

of all citizens.[4] He was writing at a time when the concept of 'justice' was of considerable interest to scholars of various disciplines, including law and moral philosophy, who sought to define the term and discuss how it could be best applied by those in power.[5] Becket was well acquainted with the *Decretum* and frequently referenced it in his letters and disputations.[6] He had studied law in Bologna and probably had his own glossed copy made.[7] It was through his reading of the *Decretum* and other legal texts, coupled with the advice of those close to him, that Becket developed the view that Henry's actions were in violation of the rights of the Church. At the heart of their disagreement was a question about temporal authority, the proper dispensation of justice, and who could impose it: the king or the Church? Justice was one of the four cardinal virtues, alongside prudence, temperance and fortitude, and like the liberal arts, it was frequently portrayed in different media.[8] The legally minded imagery of the Guennol Triptych, an enamelled reliquary made around the time of Becket and Henry's dispute, reflects a twelfth-century view of justice (fig. 2.3).[9] It points towards God's role as the ultimate arbitrator and depicts the laws of God and of all nations brought together. But whose laws were to be obeyed, those of the Church or the secular ruler? During Becket's lifetime this was a fiercely contested issue.

There has been much debate surrounding Becket's motives in resigning as chancellor. Was it a true moral conversion, was he taking a public stance against the king, or was he heeding contemporary discussions about whether churchmen should be allowed to hold secular office?[10] Whatever the reason, Henry was incensed by this change of heart and his irritation grew throughout the first twelve months of Becket's archbishopric. One chronicler pointed out twelve stages that led to the total breakdown of their relationship, but one issue in particular irked Henry.[11] The archbishop intervened in a number of legal cases to have the culprits, all of whom were clerics, tried in his own ecclesiastical court rather than in that of the king. How exactly clerics such as these who had broken the law should be tried was a question that came to underscore Becket and Henry's increasingly fractious relationship.[12] Clerics were in theory entitled to be tried in ecclesiastical courts, which had a reputation for leniency.[13] The author of the *Leges Henrici Primi* (*Laws of Henry the First*) confirmed this right, stating that 'The bishops should have jurisdiction of all accusations, whether major or minor, made against those in holy orders.'[14] Clerical bodies were sacrosanct and thus violence against them was taken very seriously.[15] Thomas of Chobham (d. 1233/6) went as far as to declare that the killing of a cleric was as bad as killing one's own father.[16] It was argued that the nature of their work provided them with a special status and they were therefore entitled to be treated differently. Furthermore, just as clerics should not be subjected to any violence, neither should they commit any. The situation became tricky when a cleric sullied his own sanctity by committing a crime. William of Newburgh (1136–1198) reported that in the first nine years of Henry's reign more than one hundred murders had been carried out by members of the clergy.[17] To many, including the king, violent crimes committed by clerics, and their perceived lenient treatment in the courts, posed a serious problem. The king and his supporters argued that in such instances the cleric had forfeited the right to be tried in an ecclesiastical court and should instead be brought to justice in the secular courts. Henry desperately wanted to see this matter settled so that he could fully exercise his royal authority.

On this matter, king and archbishop were in separate camps. Becket regarded Henry's position as an infringement of the freedoms and rights of the Church. What exactly constituted these freedoms was of interest to Becket and his circle, and he surrounded himself with scholars with whom he could discuss the finer details.[18] A leading member of this group was John of Salisbury who, having worked for Theobald, continued in the archiepiscopal household after Becket took on the role. John had been thinking about these issues for most of his adult life, and they were discussed by him in his magnum opus, the *Policraticus: De nugis curialium et vestigiis philosophorum* (*Policraticus: Of the Frivolities of Courtiers and the Footprints of Philosophers*), his treatise on statesmanship, completed in 1159, three years before Becket's appointment. It is an electrifying work of political thought, full of controversial and exciting ideas about authority and who should wield it.[19] In it he covers a multitude of topics but focuses on matters of politics and morality.[20] John dedicated the *Policraticus* to Becket, who must have known it well. In the dedicatory inscription John calls him 'The jewel of clerics, glory of the English race, the right hand of the king, and pattern of all good.'[21] A twelfth-century manuscript of the *Policraticus*, now kept in the Parker Library at Corpus Christi College, Cambridge, has long been thought to be Becket's own personal copy, presented to him by the author (fig. 2.4).[22]

The *Policraticus* underscores the reasons why Becket stood up to Henry. A recurrent theme is the proper relationship between Church and Crown. In John's eyes the Crown should look to the Church and churchmen as

2.3

The Guennol Triptych, c.1160–70. Copper alloy, gilding, wood, enamel and rock crystal. 26.9 × 29.2 cm. Private collection. A splinter of the True Cross, now lost, was originally located at the centre of this elaborate triptych. It shows a crowned personification of Justice (*justicia*) holding a set of scales. At her feet, holding up the pans of the scale, are Mercy (*misericordia*) and Piety (*pietas*), and either side of them are figures representing Almsgiving (*eleemosyna*) and Prayer (*oratio*). The people of the world, All People (*omnes gentes*), surround Justice. On its wings are scenes from the Last Judgement with the dead rising from their tombs, awakened by trumpeting angels.

models for instruction and imitation because 'the prince is the minister of priests and their inferior'.[23] He went on to state:

> And not only are men enjoined to take priests as models for imitation, but the prince is expressly sent to the tribe of Levi [i.e. to the clergy] to borrow of them. For lawful priests are to be hearkened to in such fashion that the just man shall close his ear utterly to reprobates and all who speak evil against them.[24]

John also makes a case for the importance of moderation in all things and advises his readers to avoid personal excess and avarice. He is at his most controversial when criticising tyranny.[25] At several points in the *Policraticus* he tackles this topic, especially focusing on the dangers of tyrannical kings. He goes so far as to suggest that 'it is not merely lawful to slay a tyrant but even right and just'.[26] In this case, however, John seems to have reserved the actual slaying for God, or for God's chosen instruments, arguing that although tyrants *ought* to be slain, it was not for mortals to pre-empt the judgement of God. Even so, opinions like this could get a writer into trouble and, as John acknowledged, there had been a move to suppress all debates over tyranny or politics more generally during the reign of King Stephen.[27]

In 1163, Henry attempted to settle the issue conclusively at a gathering of his bishops. Two years previously, in 1161, his royal ancestor St Edward the Confessor (*c*.1003–1066) had been canonised.[28] This was a project in which the king had taken a personal interest, with Becket's assistance as chancellor. On 13 October 1163 St Edward's body was duly 'translated' (that is, moved) into a new shrine in Westminster Abbey. This solemn occasion was attended by many of the country's leading figures including the king, Becket as Archbishop of Canterbury, the Archbishop of York and various English bishops. With so many senior members of the Church gathered in one place, it was an opportunity for Henry to resolve the ongoing matter of 'criminous clerks'. After the translation ceremony the king seized his chance and presented a proposal to a council of churchmen, stating that clerics, even though they might first be tried in the courts of the clergy, should, if found guilty, then be handed over for final judgement and sentencing in the courts of the king.[29] Making his case, Henry declared, 'I am very concerned with peace, and greatly distressed on its behalf, which in my kingdom is disturbed by the wickedness of clerks who perpetrate rapine [the seizure of property] and theft and often murder.'[30] Led by Becket, the bishops immediately rejected the king's proposition. As an alternative, Henry asked the council for a second concession: that the clergy would instead acknowledge the traditional rights of the Crown. In response, those present agreed, but added a caveat that they could only do so if the supremacy of the Church were also acknowledged. The phrase they used in making this oath was 'saving my order', which can be interpreted to mean that they deferred to the king's authority except for their allegiance to the Church, which in theory was deemed to take precedence over the Crown. With these words, in effect, they declared the king to be the Church's subject and hence inferior. It is a phrase that became central to the quarrel between Becket

2.4

John of Salisbury, *Policraticus and the Metalogicon*, after 1159. Parchment codex. 34.2 × 24.7 cm (closed). Parker Library, Corpus Christi College, Cambridge, MS 046, ff. 52v–53r. The text is open on Book 4, chapters 1 to 3. To the right, the red 'H' marks the start of chapter 3. The Latin text reads 'This sword is therefore accepted by the prince from the hand of the Church, although it still does not itself possess the bloody sword entirely. For while it has this sword, yet it is used by the hand of the prince, upon whom is conferred the power of bodily coercion, reserving spiritual authority for the papacy. The prince is therefore a sort of minister of the priests and one who exercises those features of the sacred duties that seem an indignity in the hands of priests.' Translated by Cary J. Nederman.

2.5
Becket in conference with
Henry II and Louis VII at
Montmirail (detail), the Becket
Leaves, *c.*1230–40. Vellum.
30.3 × 22.3 cm (folio). Private
collection, f. 2r

and Henry, cropping up frequently over the next eight years. An image
from the 'Becket Leaves' (part of an illustrated life of Becket, discussed in
detail in Chapter 7) shows the archbishop remonstrating with both Henry
and the King Louis VII of France at Montmirail (fig. 2.5).[31] To the right-
hand side, both kings are shown surrounded by their retinues, who point
and gesticulate at the standing figure of Becket. But rather than backing
down, the archbishop points back and holds in one hand a scroll with the
words 'Oblatis adquiesco salve honore Dei' (saving the honour of God).[32]
This phrase may not seem particularly controversial to us today, but
the words were fundamental to Becket and Henry's falling out. Garnier
de Pont-Sainte-Maxence described how the archbishop interpreted the
king's demands before the assembled churchmen: '"Just see", he said,
"how oppressively King Henry is acting towards us. What he wants is for
bad customs to be imposed on Holy Church. If I agree to them being
established, this brings shame on Holy Church."'[33] Henry was incensed

by the inflexibility of his bishops and the next day he left London in a rage. Realising the strength of Henry's feelings on this matter, Becket's biographers mention the regret of the bishops, many of whom quickly sought to appease the king. In contrast, Becket would not compromise and found himself increasingly isolated.[34] Several meetings followed, with individuals from both sides intervening to repair relations between king and archbishop, including an emissary from the Pope, but things only became worse. On a subsequent occasion, at Woodstock in Oxfordshire, Becket begged Henry to follow the example of saintly kings and, perhaps recalling the *Policraticus*, asked him to condemn 'forever the abuses of tyrants'.[35]

In late January 1164 the king convened a council at Clarendon Palace in Wiltshire, where he once again tried to persuade Becket to accept his terms. The atmosphere at Clarendon must have been tense as intermediaries hurried back and forth between the two men. Eventually, Becket agreed verbally to accept Henry's rights saying, 'I will keep the customs of the realm in good faith.'[36] But he refused to endorse the deal in writing, and when the clerks returned with a charter listing the king's customs, Becket could not bring himself to add his seal, and thus his legally binding endorsement, to the document. Known as the Constitutions of Clarendon, the king's list covered a range of topics, including the issue of 'criminous clerks', but also a clause that forbade any clergyman from leaving the realm without the king's permission. Herbert of Bosham (*c*.1120–*c*.1194), one of Becket's most learned clerks, tells us that the archbishop quickly regretted verbally agreeing to the terms and on riding away from Clarendon wore 'an uncharacteristically sad expression'.[37] Henry, meanwhile, by writing down what he claimed were the customs of the Church under his grandfather, King Henry I, turned what had previously been a bout of shadow-boxing between Church and Crown, with neither side obliged to commit itself to extremes, into something far more serious. Henceforth it became a matter of pride as well as principle, in which neither king nor archbishop was prepared to retreat from what they considered irrefutable positions of right.

Becket's rejection of Henry's Constitutions had dramatic consequences. In October 1164 he was summoned to appear before the king at yet another council, this time to be held in the shadow of the royal castle at Northampton (fig. 2.6). There, over the course of several days, a series of grave charges were laid against Becket, including the misuse of funds while he had been chancellor, and his failure to repay a loan.[38] The frivolity of Becket's secular past now returned to haunt him. The king's intention

2.6
Stained-glass panel
showing Becket before
Henry II at the council of
Northampton, c.1210–20.
Chartres Cathedral, bay 18,
panel 9

was presumably to bully and browbeat, in the hope that Becket might be persuaded either to accept the Constitutions or to resign. Becket saw matters differently, fearing that he was in grave danger of being put on trial for his life. Having heard the complaints against him, and having failed to rally his fellow bishops to his support, Becket fled. Travelling first to Lincolnshire, then via Bedfordshire, disguised as a Gilbertine monk to avoid recognition, he eventually arrived at the Kent coast.[39] Fourteen days after his escape from Northampton, and exhausted, he set sail for Flanders (fig. 2.7). He would not

return to England for six years. On learning the news, Henry is reported to have said: 'We have not finished with this fellow yet.'[40] The archbishop's plan was to head for France and the court of Louis VII, Henry's chief rival.[41] His prolonged time in exile, in the kingdom of France, brought him into close contact with many leading figures and further strengthened his network of international contacts. After his death the shock was deeply felt by many across Continental Europe, but especially by those he had encountered as a wandering refugee.

2.7
Stained-glass panel showing Becket bidding farewell to his supporters and departing England, c.1210–20. Chartres Cathedral, bay 19, panel 10

Exile

Kings and high-ranking members of the clergy often clashed. Becket's escape to France was not unprecedented and a period of exile could sometimes allow red-hot tempers to cool. Theobald, Becket's predecessor, had himself spent time away from England in 1148 when he had fallen from King Stephen's favour. So too had Anselm (c.1033–1109), archbishop from 1093 to 1109. He had been banished twice by his king, William II (c.1056–1100). Becket's own experience was similar to that of Anselm and Theobald, but whereas theirs had ended peacefully, his would culminate in murder.[42] On arriving in France, Becket first made his way to Soissons to meet Louis VII, and then to the Pope, Alexander III (c.1100–1181), himself living in exile in the city of Sens, south-east of Paris. Alexander was embroiled in a major dispute with the Holy Roman Emperor, the German Frederick Barbarossa (c.1123–1190). Rather than accept Alexander as Pope, Barbarossa had recognised an alternative candidate, currently installed in Rome, who was, in the eyes of Alexander, a false or 'anti-Pope'. Against this background, and desperate for whatever support he could secure among the squabbling kings of northern Europe, Alexander was in no position to offer Becket the unequivocal support he craved. Moreover, by courting the advice of Henry II's adversary, Louis, Becket not only fanned the flames of the king's anger but also placed the Pope himself in a difficult position, attempting to appease both kings. In retaliation for the archbishop's perceived treachery, Henry forced his family and household into exile, confiscating their property in the process – an act described by FitzStephen, with deliberate biblical overtones, as 'a distressing exodus' (fig. 2.8).[43] Some of the fugitives joined the archbishop; others sought refuge elsewhere.[44] Several appealed to Henry for clemency. On the Pope's advice Becket took sanctuary in the Cistercian monastery at Pontigny, near Sens. He was established there for almost eighteen months, from the winter of 1164 onwards. In Pontigny, the archbishop and his household settled into a life of quiet study and contemplation. From this place of shelter, he wrote letters and sought the support and guidance of friends from across western Europe.

By 1166 the tone of the dispute had begun to change. Becket, hearing that his enemies in England were conspiring against him, preached against them at Vézelay, south of Pontigny, at one of the greatest shrines of the Christian world, in theory home to the relics of Mary Magdalene. At Vézelay the archbishop railed against the Constitutions of Clarendon, excommunicating a number of the king's followers. It was a deliberately provocative act which

came as a shock to many of his own household. Herbert of Bosham, the loyal clerk who had fled into exile with his master, tells us that 'we were immediately astonished that he had acted in this way without consulting us'.[45] In retaliation, Henry threatened to expel all Cistercian monks from England unless the archbishop left Pontigny. This forced Becket to seek refuge elsewhere, and in November 1166 he and his exiled household moved to the Benedictine Abbey of Sainte-Colombe at Sens, where the Pope himself had previously resided. This became the archbishop's home for the next four years. As Becket remained in protracted exile, Henry, Louis and the Pope were left in a quandary and attempts were made to reconcile king and archbishop.

2.8
Henry II orders Becket's family into exile (detail), the Becket Leaves, c.1230–40. Vellum. 30.3 × 22.3 cm (folio). Private collection, f. 1r

In January 1169 Henry and Louis, accompanied by their courts, met at Montmirail, a frontier town located halfway between Le Mans and Chartres. Their intention was to conclude formal discussions on various matters, leading to a peace agreement. Several days into the conference, Becket came before both kings. It was the first time he had met Henry since fleeing Northampton. The archbishop spoke first, expressing his willingness to observe the English Crown's rights 'saving the rights of the Church'. Henry was furious and could not contain his anger, shouting harsh insults at his one-time friend. Louis, too, was incensed and asked 'Lord archbishop, do you wish to be more than a saint?'[46] Fearing that he would be expelled from France after this outburst, Becket subsequently sought out Louis and tried to appease him. The French king, in a reversal of his earlier behaviour, reportedly burst into tears of guilt, promising to support the archbishop whatever might happen.[47]

Montmirail supplied not peace but further cause for dispute. With tensions escalating, the entire situation came to a head the following year. By early 1170 Becket had been away from England for five years. His absence meant that there was no Archbishop of Canterbury to preside over formal proceedings, such as royal crown wearings or church councils. This created a particularly tricky situation. Henry had decided to have his eldest son, also named Henry, crowned and anointed as king in his own lifetime, not least as a means of securing a clear and undisputed line of succession to the throne. This was an innovation in England at the time, deliberately copying the practices of France. Henry's son, henceforth to be known as the Young King, would in theory wield equal powers of State. In reality, the elder Henry continued to hold the reins of power with the Young King as merely his puppet or subordinate. Meanwhile, the question arose of who could crown the Young King if the archbishop were overseas. Becket knew that one of his ancient rights as Primate of All England was to crown future kings of the realm. On hearing news of a plan to have the Young King crowned by the Archbishop of York, his old adversary Roger de Pont l'Évêque, he sprang into action to prevent the ceremony from taking place. The Pope was asked to forbid it, and appeals to halt the coronation were sent into England. These were ignored, and on 14 June 1170 the Young King was crowned at Westminster Abbey (fig. 2.9). It represented a direct challenge to Becket's authority and demanded swift retaliation. But before the situation could escalate, the Pope intervened on Becket's behalf. Two papal commissioners arranged for Becket and Henry to meet. This time, king and archbishop came together at Fréteval, only a few miles from their previous meeting place at Montmirail. On 22 July they publicly agreed

2.9
Coronation of the Young
King (detail), the Becket
Leaves, c.1230–40. Vellum.
30.3 × 22.3 cm (folio).
Private collection, f. 3r

to a reconciliation. It was reported to be an uneasy truce, particularly as the king refused to grant Becket the kiss of peace, an act of symbolic importance that served as a public guarantee of safety. Its refusal was something that, as Becket prepared to travel back to England, continued to trouble his supporters. Worryingly, in the ensuing months before he could return to England, Becket found that the concessions promised by Henry at Fréteval failed to materialise. One of his final acts before departing for England was to compose a series of explosive letters excommunicating the churchmen who had been chiefly involved in the coronation of the Young King. This last dramatic move proved to be the spark that set the entire dispute ablaze. In late November, Becket and

2.10
Becket lands at Sandwich
(detail), the Becket
Leaves, c.1230–40. Vellum.
30.3 × 22.3 cm (folio).
Private collection, f. 4v

his household set sail from the port of Wissant, between Boulogne and Calais, and landed on Tuesday 1 December 1170 at Sandwich, on the Kent coast (fig. 2.10). With the return of the archbishop to England there must have been high hopes for a lasting peace between Church and State. However, it was not to be. Before the end of the month Becket would be dead, brutally butchered on the flagstones of his own cathedral.

Return to Canterbury

On 2 December Becket arrived at Canterbury. It was the first time he had visited his own cathedral in over six years. His exile and quarrel with the king had seriously damaged his reputation and it was essential for him to rebuild his friendship networks throughout England. An immediate priority was the Young King. His opposition to the coronation did not bode well for their future relationship. After a brief stay in Canterbury, Becket and his entourage set off for Winchester, where the Young King was intending to spend Christmas.[48] Richard of Dover (d. 1184), acting as Becket's emissary, went ahead to seek permission for the archbishop to approach the Young King.[49] Much to the dismay of both Richard and Becket, this was refused and the dejected party returned to Canterbury (fig. 2.11). Becket's biographers tell us that over the next few weeks the archbishop sensed impending danger. On Christmas day he delivered a sermon in the cathedral in which 'he predicted that the time of his death was at hand, and that he would soon leave his people'.[50]

At the same time, and without Becket's knowledge, the bishops he had excommunicated, including Roger de Pont l'Évêque, Gilbert Foliot, of London, and Jocelin de Bohun (1105/10–1184), of Salisbury, made their way to Henry. They travelled to France, where the king was spending Christmas at the hunting lodge at Bur-le-Roi, near Falaise. On their arrival they went straight to Henry to make their situation known. He had already heard by other means of their plight and was in a state of fury when they found him. The king's anger was famous and there is little doubt that he raged when first informed of Becket's excommunication of the bishops. What exactly took place at Bur-le-Roi continues to excite debate to this day. Over time his actual words have been misconstrued and are now often repeated as 'Will no one rid me of this troublesome/turbulent priest?' It is easy to see why. By attributing this phrase to Henry, the blame for Becket's murder could be laid squarely on him. In this version of events the king's wish for the murder is made explicit. However, it is highly unlikely that he ever said these exact words, perhaps first attributed to him as late as the eighteenth century. Becket's biographers provide a rather different version of the king's reaction to the news. Edward Grim (d. *c.*1186) reports that after being told of the bishops' predicament, Henry exclaimed 'What miserable drones and traitors have I nourished and promoted in my household who would let their lord be treated with such shameful contempt by a low-born clerk!'[51] Another account records his description of Becket in slightly different form:

> A man … who has eaten my bread, who came to my court poor, and
> I have raised him high – now he draws up his heel to kick me in the
> teeth! He has shamed my kin, shamed my realm; the grief goes to my
> heart, and no one has avenged me![52]

Whatever his true words, the king's anger must have been fearsome.

Among those present were four knights who would become infamous: Hugh de Morville, Richard Brito, William de Tracy and Reginald Fitzurse. All were high-standing members of Anglo-Norman society with close ties to the Crown, and in most cases with landed estates that neighboured one another in Somerset and Devon. Becket's biographers were particularly keen to stress the knights' closeness to the king, which served to emphasise Henry's culpability.[53] However, three of them (Morville, Tracy and Fitzurse) sprang from families that had prospered under King Stephen, but had then managed to hold on to their gains after Henry's accession to the throne, leaving them with a permanent sense of insecurity lest their recent gains be taken away. As a result, all had a particular incentive to demonstrate loyalty to Henry, well beyond what others may have considered the call of duty.[54] Together they hatched a plan to go to Canterbury, apparently to arrest Becket on the king's behalf and bring him for trial in the royal court. By helping to silence this problematic 'low-born clerk', they hoped to curry royal favour. On 28 December they landed in England and made their way to Saltwood Castle in Kent, where they were the guests of the de Broc family. There was no love lost between Becket and the de Brocs, who had received custody of the archbishop's estate during his period of exile. FitzStephen records that the de Brocs 'laid nocturnal ambushes for him [Becket] at the exit of the roads everywhere around Canterbury, and so as to exasperate him and provoke his men to violence, they hunted without licence in his drive, and caught a stag, and captured and kept the archbishop's own dogs'.[55] As something of a pariah, Becket was not short of enemies and heard daily of the threats against him.

Murder in the cathedral

On 29 December Morville, Brito, Tracy, Fitzurse and their retinue arrived at Canterbury. They issued a proclamation to the townspeople either to aid them in their search for Becket or to stay out of the way. This crowd of armed men must have been a frightening and imposing sight. Yet their very public demonstrations in Canterbury meant that everything that transpired took place in full view. Five eyewitnesses wrote down what they saw and it is because of them that the events can be recounted in vivid detail. Differences do exist between the accounts, from the number of sword blows to identifying particular knights, but they all agree on a core set of facts.

2.11
Stained-glass panel showing the Young King refusing to meet Becket, c.1210–20. Chartres Cathedral, bay 18, panel 18

They were written within a few months or years of the event and, given the mayhem of the day, it would have been difficult to recall precise details. Nonetheless, the authors, all of whom were supporters of the archbishop, shared one purpose: to glorify Becket's posthumous memory.

It was late afternoon when the four knights, accompanied by twelve of their men, arrived at the Archbishop's Palace, which lay in the north-west part of the cathedral precinct, more or less where the modern Deanery stands today. Becket had just finished his dinner and was busy conducting business in an anteroom (fig. 2.12). We can only guess at what the knights' true intentions were: had they come simply to make an arrest or were they preparing for more violent action? They were certainly dressed for battle. All four had arrived in the city fully armed, carrying their swords and shields. But this was not how Becket first encountered them. Before entering the palace they removed their armour and weapons, stashing them behind a tree.

Standing before the archbishop, the knights were silent at first but began to curse Becket once he had greeted them. Any attempts at a calm discussion were soon abandoned, as tempers flared on both sides. Fitzurse accused Becket of wanting to take the Young King's crown away from him and of flouting the king's wishes. It was for this reason, he declared, that Becket must go with them to face royal judgement. Insults and accusations flew across the room until Becket told them that he would not leave. Throughout this quarrel the archbishop's behaviour was perhaps not in keeping with what was expected of a future saint. Far from accepting their threats meekly, he instead stood his ground and argued back, taunting them with provocative questions such as 'Have you come to kill me then?'[56] As the knights turned on their heel and stormed out of the palace, Becket followed them to the door. He called after them and placed his hand to his neck as if showing them where to strike him down.[57]

Tempers were high and with haste the knights went to gather their weapons and put on their armour. To prevent Becket's escape, they positioned soldiers in the palace courtyard, and as a countermeasure the archbishop's men barred the doors. Those around Becket encouraged him to flee into the cloister and from there into the cathedral itself. Perhaps they imagined he would be safe once inside the church. If so, they were wrong. Having been bundled along through the cloister, Becket entered the cathedral via a side door into the north transept. His followers made to secure the entrances, but Becket ordered the doors to be unbarred. In doing so, he left himself undefended and open to attack. He then began to ascend the stairs into the

main body of the choir where the monks were busy singing Vespers (evening prayers). While the cathedral's monks chanted their service, a large body of townspeople mingled in the nave as onlookers to what was about to unfold.[58]

Meanwhile, the knights, locked out of the palace, sought another means of entry. Robert de Broc, who knew the location well, advised them of a way through an upper porch or gallery, and the knights managed to climb in.[59] From here, they hurried through the palace and into the cathedral, calling out 'Where is Thomas Becket, traitor to the king and the kingdom?'[60] For those present it was a terrifying display. These were, after all, trained men of war, and all but a handful of those in the church now abandoned the archbishop and fled to safety. Becket was completely unarmed, but defied the knights nonetheless. Walking back down the steps, he stood between two altars, one dedicated to the Virgin Mary and the other to St Benedict, as he faced the men. At first the knights tried once more to arrest him. Using a sword, one flicked Becket's cap off his head. They then grabbed him and attempted to carry him away, but Becket pushed back forcefully. Cursing the

2.12
Becket confronted at dinner by the knights (detail), mid-1180s. Parchment codex. 32.5 × 22 cm (closed). British Library, London, Cotton MS Claudius B II, f. 214v

knights, he declared, 'You and your accomplices are acting like fools',[61] even going so far as to call Fitzurse a 'pimp'.[62] By now the situation was spiralling out of control. Morville moved back to stand guard, making sure they were not interrupted, as the others advanced again. The exact details of what happened next are not entirely clear, given that it was dusk and in the flurry of activity it must have been difficult to make out the sequence of events. Before the fatal attack Becket knelt down and publicly commended his soul to God, the Virgin Mary, St Denis and, according to one eyewitness, St Alphege too. These last two were episcopal saints: St Denis, patron saint of France, was murdered by decapitation, and St Alphege, a former Archbishop of Canterbury, was likewise murdered in the eleventh century by marauding Danes. Becket's invocation suggests he knew what was coming next.

It is not certain who struck first, either Fitzurse or Tracy, but the sheer force of their blow cut into the top of Becket's head (fig. 2.13). The same strike injured the arm of Edward Grim, a clerk from Cambridge, who had sprung to Becket's defence, and who went on to write an account of the murder. The cut to Grim's arm is said to have been so deep that his forearm was nearly severed in the process. After receiving several wounds to the head Becket lay prostrate on the flagstones. Brito delivered the deciding strike. Bringing his sword down upon the archbishop he sliced off the crown of Becket's head, sending his brain and blood spilling out. Brito used such force that his sword smashed into the floor and shattered at the tip. The final violation was perpetrated by a fifth man, not a knight but a clerk named Hugh of Horsea, who had accompanied the murderers. For his part in this affair he came to be known as Mauclerk, meaning 'bad clerk'. He placed his foot on Becket's neck and, after dipping the tip of his sword into the archbishop's open skull, flicked fragments of brain and blood out onto the floor. After this he turned to the others and made the grim declaration, 'Let's get out of here … this fellow won't get up again.'[63]

Aftermath

Those who were present were filled with horror and fear at what they had just witnessed. The knights, who one biographer described as 'sons of Belial [the devil]',[64] fled, but not before ransacking the archiepiscopal palace. In all likelihood they were looking for incriminating letters from either the Pope or the King of France that might brand Becket a traitor and thereby justify their appalling act of violence. So shocked were they by the deed they had

committed that at every step, so one of them later confessed, they feared the earth might open up and swallow them. There was still, however, a very real possibility that they might take further violent reprisals against the monks and congregation.[65] In the meantime Becket's body was left lying on the floor for hours. None of the monks, clerks or townspeople had any idea of how to proceed. After a while, some came forward to dip their fingers or scraps of cloth into his blood. Such was their eagerness that Benedict of Peterborough (c.1135–1193), a monk who recorded Becket's posthumous miracles, tells us 'there was no one who did not carry away some portion of that precious treasure'.[66] FitzStephen thought that Becket's first miracle happened later that day.[67] One man, a citizen of Canterbury who had witnessed the murder, hastened home to give his wife a small sample of Becket's blood, soaked into a strip of fabric, mixed with water.[68] On drinking the liquid her paralysis was cured. This was Becket's first miracle and, as will be discussed in Chapter 4, it was the first of a large number of cures attributed to the murdered

2.13
Becket's martyrdom (detail), mid-1180s. Parchment codex. 32.5 × 22 cm (closed). British Library, London, Cotton MS Claudius B II, f. 214v

archbishop. Many of these would come from drinking a tincture of Becket's blood mixed with water, known as St Thomas's Water.

That night, Becket's body was carried into the choir and placed before the high altar. At some point, either then or the next day, his soiled clothes were removed and some were dispersed to the poor. These were among the earliest of Becket's relics to circulate in Canterbury. A surprise came, however, when the monks took off the outer layers of his clothing. In his lifetime, Becket had never enjoyed close friendships with the monks of Canterbury. They had elected him archbishop in order to gain favour with the king, but having done so had found themselves led not by a king's friend but by his most implacable enemy. They too had suffered in the fallout, sharing in the hardships that Becket's exile had brought to his church in Canterbury. Although they had always considered Becket a luxury-loving courtier, they now saw to their amazement that beneath his garments the archbishop was secretly clothed in a hair shirt: a coarse garment, worn so long to irritate the skin that it was teeming with lice and vermin. Its presence was viewed by the monks as a sign of Becket's inner humility and austerity.[69] This discovery, along with the earliest miracles, was recorded as evidence of Becket's sanctity.

The next morning, a rushed burial took place. A rumour had circulated that armed men were planning to return in order to carry away Becket's body, perhaps to be burnt or otherwise permanently disposed of. To avoid further conflict, the archbishop was laid to rest in a marble coffin in a chapel in the cathedral crypt's eastern part. It was a hurried affair that dispensed with the required funeral Mass. One of the earliest depictions of his interment recalls the entombment of Christ. It is one of several illuminated pages inserted into a thirteenth-century English psalter (fig. 2.14).[70] At the centre of this striking and emotionally charged image is the recumbent figure of Becket, fully clad in archiepiscopal robes, surrounded by grieving monks. Three of them tend to his body, and their facial expressions display their sorrow and anxiety. One bends to place Becket's crozier into the tomb with him. Above and to the left is a standing figure who leans into the scene and, with his processional cross in hand, raises his fingers to his brow in grief. To the far right, another monk holds something out between his two fingers. This area is damaged but it is possible that the monk is presenting the others with a fragment of Becket's skull or another relic from the murder. Whatever the case, all of the figures convey the sadness and distress of those involved. Once the archbishop had been laid to rest, the cathedral was officially closed. Its sanctity had been desecrated by the sacrilegious spilling of blood and time was required to

2.14
Becket's burial, Harley Psalter, c.1175–1200 (miniatures), c.1200–25 (psalter). Parchment codex. 31 × 22 cm (closed). British Library, London, Harley MS 5102, f. 17r

cleanse the building of this stain. It should have remained shut to the public for an entire year, but the overwhelming desire to view Becket's tomb meant that occasional entry was permitted after Easter 1171, with liturgical services resuming on 21 December that year.

Meanwhile, news of Becket's murder spread like wildfire. Within three days it had reached Henry, who, at least in public, put on a display of great grief, fasting on bread and water for the next forty days. Arnulf, Bishop of Lisieux (1105/9–1184), described his reaction: 'the king burst into loud lamentations and exchanged his royal robes for sackcloth and ashes. … At times he fell into a stupor, after which he would again utter groans and cries louder and more bitter than before.'[71] The Young King had also heard the news within days and is said to have 'grieved bitterly'.[72] After about a month the Pope and those at his court also knew of the murder.[73] To survive the consequences, Henry needed to take control of the new saint's legacy, transforming it from an anti-royal cult into a prop for his own support. Others, however, had the same idea. Seeing an opportunity to unseat Henry, Louis VII wrote to the Pope denouncing the crimes of the English king and encouraging violent reprisals. 'The man who commits violence against his mother [i.e. the Holy Church]', he declared, 'revolts against humanity. … Such unprecedented cruelty demands unprecedented retribution. Let the sword of St Peter be unleashed to avenge the martyr of Canterbury.'[74] Others joined in, calling the Pope to action. William, Archbishop of Sens (d. 1180), wrote urging excommunication for Henry, who he claimed was 'exceeding all the wickedness of Nero, the perfidy of Julian, and even the sacrilegious treachery of Judas'.[75] These were strong words, but would they be matched by strong actions?[76]

In his own letter to Alexander III, Henry showed little remorse for what had taken place, fearing only the political repercussions, and he sought to blame Becket for provocations that had led sadly, but inevitably, to his death.[77] After commissioning legates to investigate the crime, the Pope placed the king's Continental territories, but not England, under papal interdict, and excommunicated the murderers and their accomplices.[78] The four knights are said to have made their way north to Yorkshire, seeking refuge in Knaresborough Castle, a custody held by Hugh de Morville. For around a year, the men remained at the castle, with Henry making little effort to punish them.[79] Behind the scenes, however, he took steps to prevent their male heirs from inheriting property.[80] Exactly what happened to them is not entirely clear. In all likelihood, they visited Rome in order to receive penance from the Pope.[81] This involved their being sentenced to a penitential expedition to the Holy Land. All four are presumed to have died either in Jerusalem or on their way there.[82] Between 1173 and 1174 William de Tracy issued a charter at Cosenza in southern Italy, granting an endowment to the monks of Christ Church in return for prayers for his soul.[83] By 1175 Tracy, Morville and Fitzurse were all probably dead, with the king appointing daughters or female relatives to inherit a share in their property rather than their male heirs.[84]

For his involvement Henry also faced judgement from Alexander, but, unlike the murderers, he got off lightly. On 21 May 1172 he met with papal legates at Avranches in Normandy, situated across the bay from the great monastery of Mont-Saint-Michel.[85] In Avranches Cathedral the king swore upon the gospels that he had not sought Becket's death, agreeing thereafter to conditions set down by the Pope.[86] These terms were something of a posthumous victory for Becket and included the abolition of any new customs Henry had imposed during his reign that were deemed to be harmful to the Church. The king confirmed this again in a public ceremony at Caen, the principal city of western Normandy, on 30 May. By September 1172 Alexander had formally approved their agreement through a sealed bull. With this document, Henry was officially exonerated.

Canonisation

> In the place where Thomas suffered, and where he lay the night
> through, before the high altar awaiting burial, and where he was
> buried at last, the palsied are cured, the blind see, the deaf hear, the
> dumb speak, the lepers are cleansed, those possessed of a devil are
> freed, and the sick are made whole from all manner of disease. …
> I should have not dreamt of writing such words on any account had
> not my eyes been witness to the certainty of this.[87]
>
> John of Salisbury, *Ex insperato*, letter, 1171

Early in 1171, perhaps within months of the murder, John of Salisbury composed a letter recounting what he had witnessed of Becket's death.[88] It was addressed to his friend John of Canterbury, now Bishop of Poitiers, but its details were transmitted far more widely.[89] The letter went beyond a simple or straightforward narration of the facts to praise Becket as a paragon of virtue and a potential saint: 'You know', he writes, 'of the passion of the glorious martyr Thomas, Archbishop of Canterbury, who glorifies not only his own Church but every province of England with his many great miracles.'[90] His letter is possibly the earliest report of Becket's recognition as a miracle worker, and it no doubt formed part of a dedicated campaign by Canterbury for the archbishop's swift canonisation.[91] John of Salisbury went on to compile a fuller biography of Becket, establishing a picture of a man who, from birth, was destined for greatness.

One of the earliest known images of Becket's martyrdom is bound up together with a copy of John's letter (fig. 2.15). It comes from an English manuscript made around 1184, which includes a compilation of Becket's letters put together by Alan of Tewkesbury (d. 1202), monk, and later prior, of Canterbury. This illumination, and subsequent depictions of Becket's death, were closely tied to the details of the witness accounts. Yet there are subtle differences that demonstrate how, in the years following the murder, artists and authors constructed a saintly persona for Becket, drawing parallels with Christ's life and Passion. It is possible that Christ's Last Supper is the shared reference for the upper part of the image, where the archbishop is interrupted at dinner. But it is the scene of Becket's murder that clearly shows the deliberate refashioning of events. Here Becket, and the loyal Edward Grim, are shown attacked by four knights, the first of whom carries a shield with the head of a bear. This identifies him as Reginald Fitzurse, whose last name means 'son of the bear'. Between Thomas and the knights, two objects fall to the ground (fig. 2.15): one, a piece of Becket's severed skull, and the other, a fragment of the broken sword. This differs from the eyewitness reports that describe the sword breaking on the floor of the cathedral and not on Becket's head.

From mid-April 1171, owing to the phenomenal public desire to visit Becket's tomb, the crypt of Canterbury Cathedral was reopened. What began as a trickle of miracles soon became a torrent. To help manage the situation, the monk Benedict of Peterborough was appointed as custodian of the tomb. He also recorded and investigated the myriad miracle stories recounted to him by visiting pilgrims, but it was not all plain sailing. Once the crypt had been reopened to the public, the monks heard news that the de Brocs were plotting to break into the cathedral and drag away Becket's body.[92] To combat this the monks hid the body, 'in order that if the wicked should by any chance prevail they might retire disappointed and confounded on finding that the martyr was not in his sepulchre'.[93] By May, the danger had passed and Becket's remains were returned to the tomb. To guard against

2.15
Illumination with scenes from Becket's martyrdom, mid-1180s. Parchment codex. 32.5 × 22 cm (closed). British Library, London, Cotton MS Claudius B II, f. 341r. At the top, the knights arrive at the archiepiscopal palace while Becket is at dinner. Below, Becket is killed by the knights (left) and pilgrims kneel at his tomb (right).

icera caritati. uto et respondear ma   modamine cuertad. Explicit epla

ne ustucia sua. humilisq; & pmpta   od coruna. Incipit octogesima pma

2.16

St Osmund's tomb-shrine, late 12th–early 13th century. Salisbury Cathedral. This is a rare surviving example of its kind, with oval openings (foramina) in the side allowing access to the inner part of the tomb. Becket's tomb in Canterbury Cathedral's crypt took a similar form.

any future threats, the coffin was placed in a solid marble casing secured with a lid.[94] Two circular holes in the sides of the tomb facilitated access for the pilgrims, so the devout could lean in and touch or kiss the martyr's tomb. The shrine to St Osmund in Salisbury Cathedral shows just such a structure (fig. 2.16).[95] At this point Becket was not yet a saint, but the site of his burial was beginning to achieve shrine-like status. His cult commanded a popular following among lay people, with increasing numbers visiting his tomb. One of his biographers describes this growing fame: 'from the lowliest up to the greatest, few remained who did not come and honour the tomb of the famous martyr. … Equally a great concourse of pilgrims went there from remote regions overseas.'[96] For the monks of Christ Church, Becket's murder was transformational. In life, he had been absent from their community for many years and they had not felt much benefit from his patronage. In death, he became a miraculous healer, drawing in crowds of pilgrims, who were a major source of revenue for the priory.[97]

With Becket's cult booming, former members of his household made their way to the Pope with accounts of his miracles, in order to promote his canonisation as a saint. John of Salisbury and Herbert of Bosham made the case, stressing the manner of his death and his miraculous cures. After a short deliberation, Alexander III officially recognised Becket as St Thomas of Canterbury on 21 February 1173 (Ash Wednesday). It was the networks Becket had cultivated during his lifetime, as clerk to Theobald, chancellor to Henry, and Archbishop of Canterbury, that served to bolster support for his rapid canonisation and the widespread adoption of his saintly cult.[98] Many of his supporters, including John of Salisbury, Louis VII and the Pope, had lost a friend in Becket and these personal connections played a large part in shaping his European legacy.[99] In less than three years he was transformed from disgraced exile to miracle-working saint. At the time, his was among the fastest canonisations in history. It was an internationally significant event, promoting Canterbury Cathedral as one of Europe's premier pilgrimage destinations. His new status meant his name would be entered into the calendar of saints in churches across Latin Christendom.

Relics of the saint were eagerly sought after, and a large number of reliquary caskets can be dated to the first few decades after Becket's murder. A precious silver-gilt box decorated in monochrome, with niello enamelled scenes of the archbishop's death and burial, was probably made in England not long after the event (fig. 2.17). Its interior is divided into two separate compartments; the original contents remain unknown. Most surviving caskets were, however, produced in France in the workshops of Limoges.[100]

2.17
Reliquary casket with scenes from the martyrdom of Thomas Becket (front and back views), c.1173–80. Gilded silver, niello, with a glass cabochon set over a tinted foil. 5.5 × 7 × 4.7 cm. The Metropolitan Museum of Art, New York, 17.190.520. Gift of J. Pierpont Morgan, 1917. On the front, the Latin text reads: 'S[ANCTUS] TOMAS OCCIDIT' (St Thomas is killed). The Latin inscription on the reverse reads: 'I[N]T[INTUS] SANGVIS E[ST] S[ANCTI] TOM[AE]' (The blood of St Thomas is inside).

2.18

Reliquary casket showing
the martyrdom (below)
and burial (above) of
Thomas Becket, c.1210.
Wooden core, copper
alloy, gilding and enamel.
13.6 × 13.7 × 6.5 cm.
British Museum, London,
1854,0411.2

These skilled metalworkers crafted delicate reliquaries consisting of wooden
cores covered in copper-alloy plaques and enamelled in vivid shades of blue,
red and green. Most depicted scenes of the martyrdom and sometimes his
burial (figs 2.18–2.19; see also figs 0.1, 2.21 and 3.16). Nearly fifty such caskets
have survived in locations across Europe, demonstrating the phenomenally
wide reach of Becket's early cult. It was the dissemination of Becket's relics,
along with his canonisation and tales of his death and miracles, that helped
to spread his cult across the Continent. These precious relics were dispersed
through a series of religious and political networks. For instance, in 1176 John
of Salisbury was elected to the bishopric of Chartres and took with him a knife
belonging to Becket and a vial of his blood.[101] Two further caskets attest to
Becket's popularity in northern Europe.[102] The first is a golden reliquary from

Hedalen Stave Church, located around ninety miles north of Oslo (fig. 2.20).[103] It was probably produced in Bergen, Norway, around 1220–50, and is made from hammered sheets of gilded copper held in place around a wooden core. As in the earliest known images of the murder, Becket kneels down to face the oncoming knights, with the top of his head and the broken sword-point falling down in front of him. Edward Grim, standing alongside, receives a blow to his arm from one of the men. It is unmistakably an image derived somehow from Canterbury – and yet, on either side of its lid is an open-mouthed and upturned dragon's head, seamlessly blending aspects of English iconography with Norwegian style.[104] This casket is unique, but another showing Becket's martyrdom, from Trönö, Sweden, shows a similar hybrid approach, with two gilded-metal dragon heads having been added to a Limoges enamelled

2.19
Reliquary casket showing the martyrdom of Thomas Becket (below) and his ascension to heaven (above), c.1200–10. Wooden core, copper alloy, gilding and enamel. 16 × 14.2 × 6.9 cm. British Museum, London, 1878,1101.3. Donated by Lt-Gen Augustus W. H. Meyrick

2.20

Reliquary casket, c.1220–50. Wooden core, copper alloy and gilding. 35.7 × 41 cm (excluding dragon heads and cross). Hedalen Stave Church, Norway. The front of this casket shows Becket's martyrdom, with the Adoration of the Magi above.

box (fig. 2.21). Veneration of Becket was widespread across both countries, as well as in nearby Iceland and Denmark.[105] His popularity in Norway was second only to St Olaf, the national saint, and potentially linked to the presence of a high-ranking Norwegian churchman in England in the years following Becket's murder.[106] Øystein Erlendsson, the Archbishop of Nidaros (1120–1188), had been in exile in England during the 1170s, and surely witnessed the impact of Becket's canonisation on the English Church.[107] Over time the number of pilgrims visiting Canterbury from Scandinavia

2.21
Reliquary casket
with added dragon
heads, c.1210. Wooden
core, copper alloy,
gilding and enamel.
26.2 × 22 × 8.5 cm.
Trönö Old Church,
Sweden

grew immensely. One early pilgrim to Canterbury, whose story was recorded by Benedict of Peterborough, was Sweyn, a canon of Lund Cathedral in modern-day Sweden (at the time part of the Kingdom of Denmark), who was miraculously cured of paralysis by St Thomas.[108] In Bergen, where the golden casket was probably produced, an early lead-alloy ampulla, made to hold St Thomas's Water, was found, no doubt brought back by a Norwegian pilgrim.[109]

In the space of eleven years, Becket had gone from secular and worldly chancellor, to pious archbishop, to exiled pariah, and finally, to martyred saint. No one could have predicted this extraordinary personal journey, least of all his former friend King Henry when he sought to promote his loyal servant to the archbishopric. Despite the steps Henry took to distance himself from Becket's violent death, his connection to the crime endured, as it does to this day. The king would find that, for the rest of his reign, he was not able to evade the long shadow cast by the murder of Thomas Becket.

Reactions, rebellion and the death of a king

As Fortune turns her wheel so changes the fate of the King of England (fig. 3.1). Here, a man hanging upside down falls through a spoke. Another loses his balance and tumbles backwards. A third man pulls himself upwards with all his strength. At the top is the one who wears the crown, stable now, secure, but for how long? The wheel keeps spinning and, as one twelfth-century writer put it, 'men rise one day, only to fall the next'.[2] This image of Fortune's wheel comes from a late twelfth-century copy of Henry of Huntingdon's (*c.*1088–*c.*1157) *Historia Anglorum* (*The History of the English*), in which the author recounts the ups and downs of those who rose to the top of the wheel to wear the English crown.[3] Succession was a messy business and thrones could be lost as easily as they were won, something monarchs knew only too well. Henry of Huntingdon finished his text for the *Historia* as Henry II ascended to the throne of England, but he could hardly have predicted what was in store for the new king. Henry's reign began with the promise of unifying a kingdom pulled apart by civil war, but it would end in bitterness and regret. His legacy was forever tainted by his involvement in the Becket affair. If the archbishop had proven to be a thorn in the king's side during his life, then the events of December 1170 would haunt Henry for years to come. After Henry's public penance at Avranches in 1172, it

The voice of the blood and the cry of the brains spilt and scattered by the bloody swords of the devil's henchmen filled heaven and earth with a great tumult. At the cry of this blood the earth shook and trembled; and the powers of heaven were so disturbed that people rose up against people, and kingdom against kingdom, as if in vengeance for innocent blood — yea, the realm was divided against itself and great signs and wonders were seen in the heavens.[1]

Benedict of Peterborough, *Liturgy for St Thomas's Feast*, December 1173

3.1
Fortune's wheel, in Henry of Huntingdon, *Historia Anglorum*, late 12th century. Parchment codex. 29.8 × 20.3 cm. Parker Library, Corpus Christi College, Cambridge, MS 066, p. 66

seemed that peace had been restored, but the wounds opened by Becket's death were not so easily healed. In 1173 Henry's wife, Eleanor of Aquitaine, encouraged three of their sons, Henry the Young King, Richard (who would become Richard I 'the Lionheart', 1157–1199) and Geoffrey (1158–1186), to rebel against their father, citing Becket's murder as just cause for their actions. They sought to remove Henry as king, by death if necessary, to rule his territories in his stead. Gerald of Wales remembered this as divine judgement for Henry's sinful behaviour.[4] He wrote: 'After the sacrilegious boldness of such a detestable wrong and such a wicked crime, the whirling wheel of fortune began to go down more quickly for him and rise on high more slowly than usual; the royal fate gradually began to diminish; and the strength of his rule began to weaken day by day.'[5] It was an acrimonious business and all the more shocking given that Henry's sons were only eighteen, fifteen and fourteen respectively.

Rebellion, 1173–1174

For that sacred blood was crying out to us.[6]
Henry the Young King, letter to Pope Alexander III, 1173

The coronation of the Young King in 1170 by the Archbishop of York had been a key scene in the final dramatic act of the Becket controversy.[7] The Young King's outrage at the murder placed additional strain on what was an already fractious relationship between son and father. The Young King described Becket positively in a letter, probably written in the spring of 1173, which asked the Pope 'to extend the renown of our former companion, the glorious martyr St Thomas, formerly archbishop of Canterbury'.[8] He made the bold move to go to Becket's tomb in 1172, two years before his father first visited there, and a year before the future saint was officially canonised. Through this act, he committed himself publicly to the developing cult, and thus established himself as a king who supported the rights of the Church, for which Becket was now commonly seen to have died. Certainly, he and his followers would closely associate themselves with the murdered archbishop and would invoke his protection on the battlefield. In 1173 the situation between father and son worsened.[9] Henry II was in the midst of ultimately unsuccessful negotiations with Humbert III, Count of Savoy (1135–1189), intending to marry his fourth son John (1166–1216) (aged just six at the time)

to Humbert's daughter Alice (1166–1178). As part of the marriage settlement Humbert offered substantial territories in Savoy and Piedmont to the young couple, in effect offering the ever ambitious Henry II access to northern Italy and rule over the city of Turin. In return, Henry promised them castles in Anjou, including Loudun, Mirebeau and Chinon. The Young King, who considered these castles his, openly opposed the plan, at the same time demanding that he be allowed a realm to govern as king in more than name alone. His actions speak of his great frustration as 'he had many knights but he had no means to give rewards and gifts to the knights'.[10] Worse still was the fact that his brother Richard was already exercising his authority alongside his mother in Poitou. Without the power or wealth that came from administering territory or receiving fealty, the Young King was still dependent on his father for almost everything (fig. 3.2).

In 1169 Henry II had hatched a plan to divide his English and Continental territories between his sons. To his eldest, the Young King, he

3.2
Henry II (left), Henry the Young King (middle) and Richard I (right), detail from a series of images of English kings, in Matthew Paris, *Historia Anglorum*, 1250–9. Parchment codex. 36 × 24.5 cm. British Library, London, Royal MS 14 C VII, f. 9r

would give England and Normandy, with a few token castles on the Loire. On Richard he would bestow Aquitaine, a decision much favoured by Eleanor as this was her ancestral land and Richard was her favourite son. Geoffrey would be given Brittany. John, the youngest son, was initially offered nothing, acquiring the nickname 'Lackland' as a result. Henry's successful invasion of Ireland in 1171, however, also secured a potential realm for John, who was later recognised as Lord of Ireland.[11] Critics of the king, such as Herbert of Bosham, alleged that his expedition to Ireland was because he was fleeing the anger of the Church following Becket's murder.[12] The division of Henry's estate was intended to appease not only his own family but also his chief rival, Louis VII of France, who feared the threat posed by united Plantagenet lordship across the whole of western and south-western France.[13] Henry's sons assumed they would receive their inheritances soon, all the more so when in 1172 Henry took vows to go on Crusade and thus absent himself from his kingdom. But the promised division did not take place. Instead the king's sons waited with increasing impatience for a time when they might fulfil their ambitions on a truly European stage. Tensions mounted in the royal household and in March 1173, provoked by the new arrangements for John, the Young King fled in fury to the court of his father-in-law, Louis VII of France. Two of his brothers, Richard and Geoffrey, soon joined him in Paris, adding fuel to the fires of rebellion. Henry II now faced mass desertion by his closest family – even by his wife, Eleanor, whom some have identified as chief architect of this crisis. For her part in the revolt, Eleanor was arrested, attempting to flee in male disguise, and imprisoned.[14] She remained Henry's prisoner until his death. These were troubling days for the king, now abandoned by his family and experiencing serious opposition to his authority. In the hope of circumventing further division, he first sent word and gifts to his eldest son and then an official delegation to negotiate peace.[15] But when the embassy arrived it was met with a declaration of war. It was Louis who responded in the place of the Young King, saying: 'Who asks? The king of England. … What nonsense, the king of England is here; his father may still pose as king, but that will soon be remedied, for as all the world knows he has resigned his kingdom to his son.'[16] Apart from the Becket controversy, this was the greatest challenge Henry faced in his reign and in the end he sought the help of St Thomas to save him in his hour of need.

At the instigation of Louis, the Young King had a new seal matrix cut, his first one having been surrendered to his father by his own chancellor.[17] He used this new matrix to authenticate documents as rightful King of England

and grant generous concessions. The Young King also needed additional support beyond the help of his father-in-law, making extravagant promises to gain such assistance. Holding out the prospect of great estates in England and elsewhere, he appealed to the Counts of Flanders, Boulogne and Blois, who were only too happy to join his cause.[18] He was also able to secure the backing of the King of Scotland, William the Lion (*c.*1142–1214), with the offer of Northumberland and Carlisle, pledging to restore the most northerly parts of England that Henry II had only reacquired in the late 1150s after twenty years of Scottish rule. Several English earls openly took the Young King's side, including Robert, Earl of Leicester (*c.*1130–1190), Hugh Bigod, Earl of Norfolk (1095–1177) and Hugh, Earl of Chester (1147–1181). All were promised lands in reward for their allegiance. A number of those who joined the rebellion against Henry had long-standing grievances against the king, who in many cases over the past twenty years had confiscated their lands or castles.[19] The rebellion offered an opportunity to redress these issues and to seize back what Henry had himself taken by force. At the outset of this conflict, Henry could still count on a large number of barons to support him but he remained nervous about his position. He knew full well the possibility that he could be unseated and replaced on the throne by another turn of Fortune's wheel. Warfare spread across England and France and by 1174, according to William of Newburgh, 'there were only a few barons at that time in England who were not wavering in their allegiance to the king and ready to defect'.[20]

Apart from the chronicle accounts, most material traces associated with the rebellion have vanished. However, a sword was found with other material at the site of one decisive battle, near the Suffolk village of Fornham St Martin (fig. 3.3).[21] It was here that Henry II's local commanders destroyed an army of invading Flemish mercenaries. Neither Henry nor his sons were present at the battle, but Reginald, Earl of Cornwall (*c.*1110–1175), his uncle, led the loyalists. In the run up to the Battle of Fornham, the rebel earl, Robert of Leicester, had recruited an army of perhaps 3,000 men, transporting them safely across the sea to Suffolk from where they planned an advance towards the Midlands.[22] What they could not possibly have known was that the Earl of Cornwall and his band of experienced knights were waiting for them. When Robert of Leicester reached the River Lark at Fornham, the loyalists ambushed the rebel troops and, with the support of the townspeople, had many of them drowned in a bog.[23] It was a scene of devastation, with one chronicler describing how across the battlefield 'Crows and buzzards

3.3
Sword, 1150–1200/50. Iron, silver or gilded silver. 107 × 15 cm. Moyse's Hall Museum, Bury St Edmunds, 1978.440. This sword was discovered before 1876 near to the village of Fornham St Martin, Suffolk, believed to have been the site of the Battle of Fornham. The blade is set with Latin text in wire, reading on one side 'SES BENEDICTAS' and on the reverse '+ I NOMINE DOMIN' (Be thou blessed in the name of the Lord).

descend on their corpses'.[24] Various weapons were found here during the nineteenth century but it is not known whether they belonged to rebels or loyalists.[25] Reflecting on the battles that took place during the revolt another chronicler wrote: 'Many a castle and many a town was ruined because of this war and many a fine man … was killed or exiled, impoverished or brought low by this cursed turn of events.'[26] This contemporary description recalls the words of the Canterbury monk and guardian of Becket's shrine, Benedict of Peterborough, who, at the time of the rebellion, was composing the liturgy that would be used for public worship on 29 December for the feast of the martyrdom of St Thomas of Canterbury. Benedict explicitly connected the events of the ongoing war with the martyrdom of Becket, projecting an image of a country mired in turmoil:

> At the cry of this blood, the earth shook and trembled; and the powers of heaven were so disturbed that people rose up against people, and kingdom against kingdom, as if in vengeance for innocent blood – yea, the realm was divided against itself and great signs and wonders were seen in the heavens.[27]

Henry, meanwhile, was busy on the Continent attempting to secure his French territories. He remained in France until July 1174. Then, crossing to England, he headed straight to Canterbury and, for the first time, the tomb of St Thomas.

Henry's Canterbury penance

On 12 July, in the midst of civil war, Henry arrived outside Canterbury intending to do penance for his involvement in Becket's murder.[28] He had already undertaken an earlier papally sanctioned penance, a carefully managed public performance at Avranches in May 1172.[29] Why he waited for a further two years to make his second penance is unknown. Perhaps he hoped that he might never actually need to perform another, particularly at the site of Becket's tomb: kings were not in the business of publicly admitting they were wrong. But the saint could not be ignored. Scores of miracles were being recorded in the crypt at Canterbury, and those rebelling against the king were acting in the belief that they had the glorious martyr on their side. If there was a time for Henry to reclaim Becket's cult as his own, it was surely now.

On the day of his penance the king arrived on horseback at the western outskirts of Canterbury. At the village of Harbledown he dismounted and continued on foot. Having reached St Dunstan's church, outside the city walls (more or less where the Canterbury West railway station now stands), he removed most of his rich outer garments. From here he walked barefoot through the Westgate, down the main thoroughfare and into the cathedral precincts.[30] One of Becket's twelfth-century biographers, Garnier de Pont-Sainte-Maxence, tells us that:

> he wanted to come not as a king but as a beggar. He approached the door humbly and knelt down; and stayed there a long time weeping and praying. Then he entered the church and went to the Martyrdom … and kissed the marble. After that he went to the tomb and made his peace with the martyr.[31]

3.4
Stained-glass panel showing Henry II's penance at Becket's tomb, 15th century. Selden End, Duke Humfrey's Library, Bodleian Libraries, University of Oxford. This panel and another showing Becket as archbishop kneeling before Henry II, also in the Bodleian, originally came from St Andrew's Church, Great Rollright, Oxfordshire. They probably derive from a window dedicated to Thomas Becket, showing scenes of his life, martyrdom and legacy.

Gilbert Foliot, Bishop of London and a one-time enemy of Becket's, spoke at the tomb on Henry's behalf. He addressed the king's guilt, adding that Henry 'declares before God and before the martyr that he did not have Saint Thomas killed or murdered, nor did he command that he should be struck at or killed, but freely admits that he did use such words as were the cause and origin of his being murdered'.[32] After the bishop finished speaking Henry acknowledged his own involvement and put himself at the mercy of the monks.[33] No contemporary images depicting this event are known, but a panel of stained glass, from St Andrew's Church in Great Rollright, Oxfordshire, portrays the discipline that Henry was subjected to by the monks (fig. 3.4).[34] At the tomb itself he suffered scourging with reeds. These would have been less painful than rods, but even so this must have been a humiliating experience for the king. Garnier tells us that 'he had himself disciplined, first by the superiors, and then by over 80 monks'.[35] Henry's penance was a turning point that had a profound effect on the remaining years of his reign. Through this public demonstration he aligned himself and his family with the cult of St Thomas for the remainder of his life. Once and for all, he showed he was willing to make amends for the murder of the archbishop, even though he refused to shoulder any burden of personal guilt. Following punishment by the monks, Henry gave gold coins and silk cloths to the tomb in addition to a grant of £40 per year and a promise to build a monastery in St Thomas's name.[36] In a further act of penance, he went on to found a number of religious houses including Amesbury Priory, Newstead Abbey in Sherwood and various smaller institutions in France, as well as refounding Waltham Abbey.

Back at Canterbury on the evening of his penance, Henry remained praying at the tomb overnight (without, we are told, moving once from the spot for 'natural functions') and then, dressed as a pilgrim, made his way to pay respects to all of the cathedral's other saintly relics.[37] That same day, 13 July, William the Lion, King of Scotland, was defeated and captured at Alnwick by Henry's forces. It was widely perceived that St Thomas had intervened on the king's behalf and effectively brought the English part of the war to an end. A poem written in celebration of Henry's victory proclaims this: '"St Thomas", said the king, "guard my realm for me. To you I declare myself guilty of that for which others have the blame."'[38] Within weeks the entire rebellion had collapsed and Henry was once again secure at the top of Fortune's wheel. In an attempt to avoid another revolt he pardoned most of the rebels, including his sons. The same could not be said for William the Lion, who suffered severe penalties, being obliged to become 'the liegeman of

the lord king Henry against every man in respect of Scotland and all his other lands'.[39] Edinburgh itself and a series of Scottish castles were now supplied with garrisons under the command of the King of England. Becket had a part to play in William's story too. He had known Becket personally and, in 1178, went on to found Arbroath Abbey as the site of his final resting place, dedicating it to St Thomas of Canterbury (figs 3.5–3.6).[40] The townspeople of Arbroath later used the image of Becket's martyrdom on their own seal, further cementing their close association with the cult of the saint. With the saint now treated as a major supporter for the Plantagenet throne, it is not surprising to see that others in the close orbit of the court turned to Becket as their protector. As has been pointed out, with kings 'there was always a political element to their spirituality, and a spiritual element to their politics'.[41] In the decade following Becket's murder several of Henry's courtiers promoted his burgeoning cult by providing for the foundation of a monastic house in honour of the martyred saint. Beauchief Abbey in Derbyshire was established by members of the court, which held a handsome head reliquary of St Thomas. Richard de Lucy (1089–1179), chief justiciar of England,

founded Lesnes Abbey in Kent in 1178, dedicated to St Thomas the Martyr and St Mary. Another early house connected to St Thomas was Langdon Priory in Kent. It was established by the courtier William de Auberville (d. *c*.1195) in 1192. The saint also had an important presence in Ireland through the activity of Henry's steward William fitzAudelin (d. 1205). In 1177 he endowed an Augustinian abbey in Dublin dedicated to St Thomas the Martyr.[42]

After the end of the war Henry made nine separate pilgrimages to Becket's tomb between 1174 and his death in 1189.[43] Through his repeated visits and gifts of money, luxury items and even land, he bound himself to the saint in thanksgiving for bringing the war to a close. It was almost universally acknowledged by chroniclers that St Thomas had intervened on the king's behalf, and Henry's ongoing public largesse at Canterbury only served to strengthen the relationship between the Plantagenet throne and the cult of St Thomas. We can see this in a charter of 1175 by which Henry renewed the privileges to the monks of the cathedral (fig. 3.7). This was possibly placed by the king on the saint's tomb on Maundy Thursday in 1177. Other notable figures followed his lead. In 1179 King Louis VII of France made the extraordinary decision to undertake a pilgrimage to Canterbury to visit Becket's tomb. For a king to travel to a 'foreign' shrine such as this was virtually unprecedented, save in such cases as Rome or Jerusalem, which were regarded as central to the wider history of Christianity. Louis had supported Becket in his lifetime, especially during his exile in France, and now he needed the saint's help. His firstborn son, Philip, whom he had planned to have crowned in August 1179, had fallen so ill that his coronation ceremony had

3.7 (above)
Writ of Henry II with his Great Seal, *c*.1175. Parchment with wax seal. 39.5 × 22 cm. Canterbury Cathedral Library and Archives, CCA-DCc-ChAnt/C/19

3.8 (right)
Dover Castle, Kent

3.9 (opposite)
King Louis VII of France at the shrine of Thomas Becket, altarpiece of St Thomas, late 15th century. St Nikolai Church, Wismar, Germany

been cancelled. In a dream, Louis received an instruction to go to Canterbury. This was a remarkable act both because no King of France had ever journeyed to England, and because by thus trusting to St Thomas, Louis appeared to deliver a snub to the protector of his Capetian dynasty, St Denis, whose shrine was located just north of Paris. Arriving at Dover, and staying at the newly rebuilt castle, Louis was welcomed by Henry II, who personally escorted him to Canterbury (fig. 3.8).[44] The French king spent five days with his 'most dear brother'.[45] He made gifts to the cathedral, mostly unrecorded but certainly including one hundred measures of French wine, intended for use at the cathedral's Masses.[46] The red of the wine, it was supposed, was an appropriate gift to honour one whose own bloodshed was so central to his appeal to pilgrims.[47] Henry later confirmed that the wine could be brought to England free from all customs duties. By the fourteenth century, it was also being alleged that Louis had gifted to the shrine a large red ruby known as the Regale of France, which was said to have been previously owned by Charlemagne (fig. 3.9, where an angel points to the jewel).[48] Remembering Louis's visit, as depicted in a painting now in Wismar, Germany, and his donations, real or otherwise, became a central aspect of Becket's cult. The honour of St Thomas would in due course spread beyond even the Plantagenet and Capetian courts, as Henry's family carried devotion to the saint with them as they married into the ruling dynasties of much of western and southern Europe.

Henry's daughters and the spread of Becket's cult

If Henry II and Eleanor of Aquitaine's sons marshalled the memory of Becket for their own ends, especially during the rebellion of 1173–4, then their daughters played equally pivotal roles in the early development of his cult. There were three daughters: Matilda (1156–1189), Eleanor (1161–1214) and Joan (1165–1199). As was expected at this time, their marriages were arranged for them with the purpose of strengthening their family's political networks and to cement or create alliances with European neighbours.[49] In 1168 Matilda was married to Henry the Lion, Duke of Saxony (c.1129/1131–1195); in 1170 Eleanor wed Alfonso VIII of Castile (1155–1214); and in 1177 Joan married William II of Sicily (1153–1189), and after his death a second husband, Raymond VI, Count of Toulouse (1156–1222). These were illustrious matches made at the height of Plantagenet prestige, guaranteeing Henry II a sphere of influence stretching from northern Germany to the Iberian

3.10
Gospel book of Henry the Lion and Matilda of England, c.1168–89. Herzog August Bibliothek, Wolfenbüttel, Germany, Cod. Guelf. 105 Noviss. 2°, f. 171v. Parchment. 34.2 × 25.5 cm. Henry and Matilda's joint coronation is commemorated by this illumination. At the base of the image, in the centre, they are shown receiving their crowns. Either side are members of both royal dynasties. Behind Matilda, on the right, stands her father, Henry II, and her grandmother, Empress Matilda. Above them are rows of saints surrounding the central image of Christ. Becket, holding a martyr's palm and wearing a mitre and pallium, is directly above Empress Matilda.

3.11

Mosaic, *c.*1180. Central apse, Monreale Cathedral, Sicily. This golden mosaic shows Christ Pantocrator. Below are the Virgin and Child with standing figures of saints either side. In the bottom register, St Thomas of Canterbury is flanked by St Sylvester and St Lawrence. A detail of Becket is shown in the image on the right.

Peninsula and across to the Adriatic. Joan's son by Raymond inherited the county of Toulouse. Matilda's son became the Holy Roman Emperor Otto IV (1175–1218), and Eleanor's nine children by Alfonso provided a strong and stable Castilian lineage for many years.

Given these international networks, it is not surprising that several of the earliest images of Becket made after his canonisation appear in manuscripts, wall paintings and metalwork items from or connected to Spain, Italy and Germany. For instance, the Gospel Book of Henry the Lion and Matilda of England, commissioned between 1168 and 1189 for Brunswick Cathedral, shows an image of Becket holding his martyr's palm above the standing figures of Matilda, her father Henry II and his mother, the formidable Empress Matilda (fig. 3.10). Produced by an illuminator at the Abbey of Helmarshausen in Saxony, northern Germany, Becket is prominently depicted as a protector of the Plantagenet dynasty in this manuscript made for Henry's eldest daughter and her husband. Becket can be found elsewhere too. At the east end of Monreale Abbey, outside Palermo on the island of Sicily, is an apse mosaic of Becket, made around 1180 (fig. 3.11). Labelled as 'St Thomas of Canterbury', he stands positioned between other martyrs, St Sylvester and St Lawrence.[50] Across the Mediterranean, in Spain, further early images of Becket can be seen. A large and detailed depiction of the martyrdom, painted between 1180 and 1190, is located in the church of Santa Maria de Terrassa, in central Catalonia (figs 3.12–3.13).[51]

3.12 and 3.13 (this page and overleaf) Wall painting showing scenes from the life and death of Thomas Becket, c.1180–90. Santa Maria de Terrassa Church, Spain. It is one of the earliest depictions of Becket's martyrdom in continental Europe and was discovered in 1917 during restoration work to the church. Becket argues with the knights on the left of the painting and his martyrdom is shown at the centre. To the right, his body, wrapped in a shroud, is laid to rest as his soul ascends to heaven.

3.14

Reliquary pendant, c.1174–7.
Gold. 5 × 3.1 × 0.7 cm.
The Metropolitan Museum
of Art, New York, 63.120.
Purchase, Joseph Pulitzer
Bequest, 1961. The front of
the pendant, which is now
an open cavity, originally
contained relics of Becket.
The reverse shows Queen
Margaret of Sicily being
blessed by Bishop Reginald
of Bath.

Sicily

Becket developed a close connection with the Sicilian court during his lifetime.[52]
He had been a correspondent of Queen Margaret of Sicily (c.1135–1183),
the mother of Joan's future husband King William II.[53] After the canonisation,
Margaret received a gold reliquary pendant from Reginald fitz Jocelin, Bishop
of Bath (c.1140–1191), containing fragments 'of the blood and bloodstained
garments of St Thomas the Martyr and of his hair shirt, cowl, shoes and
shirt' (fig. 3.14).[54] During the formal discussions to broker the marriage of
Joan and William – which took place in both England and Sicily – news
and gossip must also have been shared, such as reports of Becket's murder,

3.15
Double-seal matrix of Joan, Countess of Toulouse, c.1196–9. Silver. 8.7 × 4.8 cm (each). British Museum, London, 1897,0508.1–2. On the left Joan is shown seated and holding up a large cross of Toulouse. The Latin text reads '+ S IOHA DVCISSA NARb COMTISSA ThOL MARChISIA PROV' (Seal of Joan, Duchess of Narbonne, Countess of Toulouse, Marchioness of Provence). The right shows her standing and crowned, holding a fleur-de-lys in her right hand. The legend reads '+ S REGINA IOHA FILIA QVONDAM h REGIS ANGLORUM' (Seal of Queen Joan, formerly daughter of King Henry of England).

his miracles and intervention in the recent rebellion on Henry II's behalf. Gifts too would have been exchanged, but whether relics of St Thomas were among them is unrecorded. There was, in any case, a steady flow of traffic between the courts of England and Sicily, which included diplomats, clergy, poets, musicians and artists.[55] The ruling dynasties of both kingdoms derived from Norman stock and they considered each other kin. Once the marriage negotiations were successfully completed, Joan was escorted to Sicily in 1176 to be wed to William the following year. On this occasion she was accompanied for part of the way by Richard of Dover, who had been a close friend of Becket's and was now his successor as Archbishop of Canterbury.[56] If anyone had the ability to authorise the gift of a Becket relic from Canterbury to Sicily it was surely Richard. Others in the official party included the Bishops of Evreux and Ely, the Archbishop of Rouen, and Hamelin, Earl Warenne (*c.*1130–1202), Henry II's illegitimate half-brother, who at some time after this trip received a cure at Becket's tomb.[57]

William II died prematurely in 1189 and Joan in due course became Countess of Toulouse. Her double-seal matrix as countess, made in silver, is a testament to her power, authority and nobility (fig. 3.15). On the obverse side it declares that she is 'Queen Joan', daughter of the King of England;

3.16

Reliquary casket showing the martyrdom and burial of Thomas Becket, 1195–1200. Copper alloy, gilding and enamel. 15 × 21 × 9.3 cm. Society of Antiquaries of London, LDSAL 110

on the reverse, that she is 'Duchess of Narbonne, Countess of Toulouse and the Marchioness of Provence'. Double-sided seals were more commonly used by kings; her mother, Eleanor of Aquitaine, was the first woman to use one of this type. Joan was making a bold statement about her status through the seal's form, and her retention of the title 'Queen' recalls her grandmother, Matilda, who continued to be addressed as 'Empress' until the end of her life.[58] Beyond Joan and her court, Becket's cult flourished across Italy, both north and south. The acquisition of an enamelled reliquary casket in southern Italy in the late eighteenth century by the Envoy Extraordinary to Naples, William Hamilton (1730–1803), who served as a British diplomat to Ferdinand I (1751–1825), King of the Two Sicilies, attests to the saint's popularity and wide geographic reach (fig. 3.16).[59] Depicting Becket's martyrdom and subsequent burial, the casket was found stuffed with lead pilgrims' flasks, called ampullae, and relics.[60]

Saxony

Unlike the other daughters and sons-in-law of Henry II and Eleanor of Aquitaine, their eldest daughter Matilda and her husband Henry the Lion both resided in England for extended periods. Henry the Lion faced an ongoing dispute with the Holy Roman Emperor, Frederick Barbarossa, which resulted in his being forced into exile, with Matilda and their children, from 1182 to 1185. By now Henry II had strengthened his personal connection to St Thomas of Canterbury so that there could be no doubt Becket was a Plantagenet saint of the highest order. Henry the Lion and Matilda continued to enjoy a close relationship with Henry II and, given the saint's perceived support for the king during his sons' rebellion of 1173–4, it is not surprising that the couple sought Becket's help with their own conflict. Before returning to Saxony, Henry the Lion made a pilgrimage to Becket's tomb in Canterbury.[61] Perhaps, then, he might have brought relics of the murdered archbishop to Brunswick as early as 1185.[62] Becket's appearance in the Gospel Book commissioned by Henry the Lion and Matilda is, therefore, in keeping with the wider promotion of St Thomas in the 1170s and 1180s by Henry II's daughters.

Early on in their marriage, Matilda of England and Henry the Lion showed a keen interest in early medieval, and especially royal, English saints. Two splendid reliquaries have long been associated with their patronage.[63] The first, now in the Musée du Louvre, Paris, shows the sainted Henry II, Holy Roman Emperor (973–1024), on one side and the Northumbrian king St Oswald (604–642) on the other. Another reliquary of St Oswald, and the more impressive of the two, was made for Hildesheim Cathedral, where it remains today (fig. 3.17). The main part of this reliquary is octagonal and on each of its eight sides there is a niello portrait of an English saint, including the recently canonised St Edward the Confessor (canonised 1161). It is covered by a scalloped roof, on the top of which sits the crowned head of a man, perhaps Oswald himself.[64] This fascination with the saints of pre-Conquest England demonstrates how Henry and Matilda were aware not just of the power of relics but also of their historical importance.

Brunswick Cathedral, of which they were founding patrons, was consecrated on 29 December 1226, a date deliberately chosen to coincide with the feast of Becket's martyrdom. As part of this ceremony the cathedral, which until then had been jointly dedicated to St John the Baptist and St Blaise, was rededicated to St Thomas of Canterbury. From this moment onwards all three saints had equal rank as protectors of both the church and

3.17
Reliquary of St Oswald, *c.*1185–9
(with later additions). Wooden
core, silver, gilding, niello, enamel,
gems, pearls, cameos. H. 43.2 cm.
Dommuseum Hildesheim,
Germany, DS 23

3.18
Reverse of a book-shaped reliquary showing St Blaise (left), St John the Baptist (centre) and St Thomas of Canterbury (right), *c*.1000 (front), *c*.1340 (reverse, shown here). Wooden core, silver, embellished on the front with ivory, gold, pearls, rubies, emeralds, onyx and crystals. 31.6 × 24.4 × 7.5 cm. Cleveland Museum of Art, 1930.741. Gift of the John Huntington Art and Polytechnic Trust

the duchy. A fourteenth-century reliquary from Brunswick Cathedral shows them brought together in this manner (fig. 3.18).[65] Becket's life story and his martyrdom appeared prominently within the church. Located in the chancel of the cathedral is a narrative cycle of paintings, produced around the time of the consecration ceremony, which includes seven scenes from Becket's life, such as his dispute with Henry, his exile, his return to England and the murder.[66] These form part of a larger cycle documenting the stories of the other patron saints. It was Henry, Duke of Saxony (*c*.1173/4–1227), son of Matilda of England and Henry the Lion, who took the decision to rededicate the cathedral. Here he followed in the footsteps of his parents, who were responsible for the foundation of the church and, as has been discussed, were active promoters of Becket's cult.[67] In rededicating the cathedral to St Thomas of Canterbury, Henry was continuing their work, and thus promoting his dynastic link to an English king through his mother.

The death of Henry II

> From the Devil he came and to the Devil he will surely go.[68]
>
> Bernard of Clairvaux (1090–1153) on Henry II, from Gerald of Wales,
> *De principis instructione*

Henry II died on 6 July 1189, aged fifty-six, at the castle of Chinon on the Loire. He had not passed the final years of his life peacefully, whiling away his days, but in attempts to maintain his authority over what he saw as his insubordinate and squabbling children.[69] Just months before his death, in a move reminiscent of the rebellion of 1173–4, his son Richard conspired with the new French king, Philip II (1165–1223), to wage war on him. Henry, the battle-weary king, is said to have remarked: 'My children will never do anything that is good; all they will do is destroy me and themselves; they have always done me harm and injury.'[70] Richard's behaviour came as little surprise, given his past actions, but some days before Henry died news reached him that his favourite son John had also joined the rebellion. This, it is said, broke the old king's heart, with Henry exclaiming, 'Is it true that John, dear to me as my own heart, whom I have loved above all my sons, and for the sake of whose advancement I have endured all these evils, is it true that he has deserted me?'[71] Henry was buried in the nearby Abbey of Fontevraud, alone, with none of his ancestors around him. Gerald of Wales called the choice of location 'a place so obscure and unsuitable for so great majesty'.[72] His effigy had to wait until its patron, his estranged wife, Eleanor of Aquitaine, committed funds to its construction (fig. 3.19). In it we see Henry not as an older man brought down by a lifetime of war, but as a strong and stately ruler, who managed to weather the storms brought about by the murder of Thomas Becket, retaining his position as one of the most powerful rulers in Europe. These dual legacies of shrewd statesman and hot-headed tyrant endure to the present day.

And yet, on occasion, when some medieval sculptors and painters turned their attention to representing Becket's murder, they implicated Henry as the instigator of the martyrdom. Not surprisingly, it was away from England that this was most pronounced. Around 1191, shortly after Henry's death, a

new font was commissioned for the parish church of the village of Lyngsjö, in the south of modern-day Sweden (fig. 3.20). Around the upper part of the bowl is a representation of Becket's martyrdom alongside a series of Christological images.[73] St Thomas was immensely popular in Denmark, Sweden, Norway and Iceland, and – more locally to the font – a relic of his was recorded at the nearby church of Gumlösa as early as 1191, where, as it happens, there is another font carved by the same mason who made the example in Lyngsjö.[74] At first glance the Lyngsjö font appears to be a relatively standard image of the martyrdom. It shows three heavily armoured knights advancing upon the archbishop, who falls down in front of one of them and is struck in the head by a sword. Above Becket, Edward Grim is shown reaching out with his cross, only to be struck in the arm by another of the knights. To the left of this scene, however, is an unusual addition. Here, Henry II sits enthroned with sword in hand, conversing with a fourth knight. The king is easily identified by an unfurled scroll that projects from his right hand, reading 'REX:HRICVS' (King Henry). Although Henry had made penance for the role he played in the archbishop's death, he emphatically distanced himself from the actions of the knights. But here, on this font, he is

3.19
Tomb effigies of Henry II and Eleanor of Aquitaine, c.1200 (Henry) and c.1204–10 (Eleanor). Fontevraud Abbey, France

3.20
Baptismal font showing
scenes from the life of
Christ and the martyrdom
of Thomas Becket, *c.*1191.
Limestone. H. 78.5 cm.
W. 69 cm (bowl). Lyngsjö
Church, Sweden. It was
possibly made by Master
Tove, a stonemason whose
name is carved into the font
at nearby Gumlösa Church;
a third font located in the
same area has also been
attributed to him.

explicitly shown as the instigator. Images like it can be found elsewhere, also on the Continent. In Treviso, Italy, a thirteenth-century wall painting from the Bishop's Palace, probably from his private chapel, shows such a scene (fig. 3.21).[75] Henry is shown enthroned, inside his palace wearing full regalia and, with an outstretched arm, he gestures to a figure holding a sword who looks towards the viewer with an uneasy expression. To the left of the king, Becket's martyrdom takes place in a multi-domed church, where a knight strikes his head in front of a collective audience of clerical onlookers. Above, two angels lift his soul into heaven. In the imagery of the Lyngsjö font and the Treviso wall painting Becket's murder and Henry's involvement take on a new dimension. Henry had attempted to control the narrative of Becket's death and subsequent cult by binding himself to the saint through his devotion. But this could not save him from being implicated in the murder. Through continued reinterpretation of the details, Becket was transformed into an ecclesiastical figurehead who was murdered with the full backing of the king and died in defence of the Church. It was this powerful and enduring aspect of the Becket story that remained central to his legacy for many centuries to come.

3.21
Wall painting showing the martyrdom of Thomas Becket, c.1250–75. 162 × 337 cm. Museo Diocesano di Arte Sacra, Treviso, Italy, inv. no. S690112. In 1960, during restoration work taking place in the bishop's palace of Treviso, this painting was discovered along with another showing Christ's descent into limbo. They possibly decorated the Bishop of Treviso's private chapel.

Canterbury Cathedral transformed

Between the hours of 4pm and 5pm on 5 September 1174 a fire broke out in Canterbury.[2] From across the city people rushed to extinguish the blaze, which was localised to three cottages near the entrance of the cathedral precinct. There were high winds that day and without the knowledge of those present, who were distracted by the fire, a few inconspicuous embers drifted over the tall walls and worked their way in between the lead coverings of the roof, firmly lodging themselves in the cathedral's old rotting beams. Disaster struck. From these glowing embers a fire spread. Encouraged by the strong winds, the now raging blaze devoured the entire roof, destroying much of the east end of the mighty Romanesque church. On an earlier visit to Canterbury, the chronicler William of Malmesbury (d. *c.*1143) described the outstanding beauty of this interior, writing 'nothing like it could be seen in England, whether for the brilliancy of its glass windows, the beauty of its marbled pavements or the many coloured pictures'.[3] Understandably, the monks were devastated by the fire and the Christ Church monk and chronicler Gervase of Canterbury (d. in or after 1210)

Great and very wonderful things were being worked every day around the tomb of the martyr.[1]

Benedict of Peterborough, *The Miracles of St Thomas of Canterbury*, 1173

Detail of fig. 4.4

recorded with profound sadness that most of the structure had burnt down and needed to be rebuilt.[4] In the end, significant sections of external masonry from the choir were retained in the subsequent reconstruction but almost all of the internal decoration was lost. Yet in its destructive wake the fire provided an opportunity for the monastic community to rethink the east end and restore the church on an even greater scale than before.[5] Such ambitious plans centred on Thomas Becket, their hugely popular new saint, and the future building would grow to become one of the largest churches in Europe. Since the frenetic days immediately following Becket's murder, his body had been kept in a tomb in the crypt underneath the Trinity Chapel. Within the space of just a few years his cult had burst onto the international stage, attracting followers from all over Europe. Unprecedented numbers of pilgrims had been arriving at the cathedral and crowding into the crypt to visit the martyr's tomb. It was widely recognised that St Thomas now deserved a more appropriate shrine and, as part of the 1173 canonisation process, the Pope had decreed that Becket should be moved to a better and more prominent location.[6] There had been insufficient time and funds to carry out this wish, but now, with the east end gutted by fire, the priory possessed a relatively blank canvas on which to project a new vision for the building.

Rebuilding Canterbury Cathedral

Given Canterbury Cathedral's heritage and ancient primatial status nothing but the best was acceptable and the monks employed the finest masons, glaziers, metalworkers, painters and sculptors to undertake this colossal task. Construction of the architectural shell took roughly ten years and the project was overseen by two master masons. The decoration of the building, including its elaborate stone pavement, magnificent shrine and multi-coloured stained glass, took longer to complete (figs 4.1–4.2).[7] It culminated in a lavish ceremony during which Becket's body was moved from the crypt to a new chapel above. This event, called the 'translation', took place on 7 July 1220 and was orchestrated by Stephen Langton, Archbishop of Canterbury (c.1150–1228). His pivotal role in this process and the reasons for a delay in the translation of Becket's relics are discussed in Chapter 5. As part of the rebuilding the monks still required ample room in the choir to conduct the Divine Office but new enlarged spaces would also be associated with

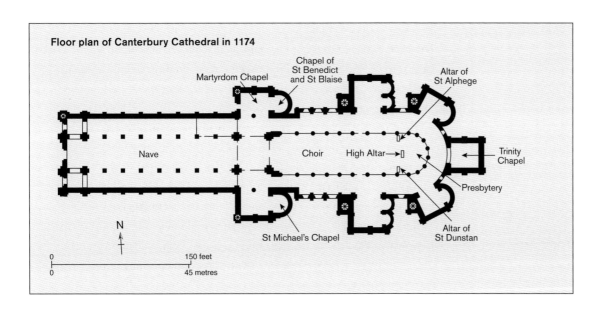

Floor plan of Canterbury Cathedral in 1174

Martyrdom Chapel

Chapel of
St Benedict
and St Blaise

Altar of
St Alphege

Nave

Choir   High Altar →

Trinity
Chapel

Presbytery

St Michael's Chapel

Altar of
St Dunstan

N

| 0 | | 150 feet |
| 0 | | 45 metres |

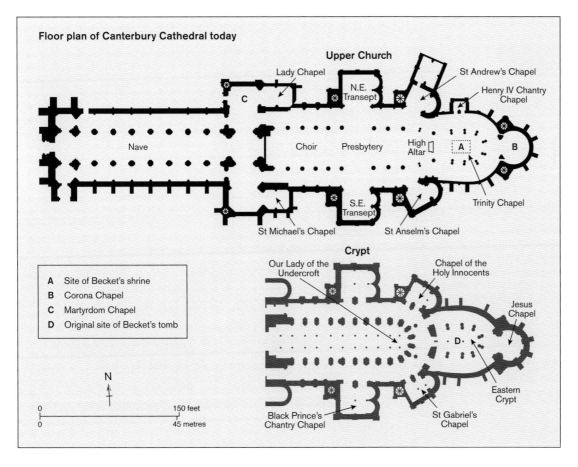

Floor plan of Canterbury Cathedral today

Upper Church

Lady Chapel

St Andrew's Chapel

N.E.
Transept

Henry IV Chantry
Chapel

C

Nave

Choir   Presbytery   High
Altar

A

B

S.E.
Transept

Trinity Chapel

St Michael's Chapel

St Anselm's Chapel

Crypt

Our Lady of the
Undercroft

Chapel of the
Holy Innocents

Jesus
Chapel

D

Eastern
Crypt

Black Prince's
Chantry Chapel

St Gabriel's
Chapel

A   Site of Becket's shrine
B   Corona Chapel
C   Martyrdom Chapel
D   Original site of Becket's tomb

N

| 0 | | 150 feet |
| 0 | | 45 metres |

4.1
Floor plan of Canterbury
Cathedral before the fire
of 1174

4.2
Floor plan of Canterbury
Cathedral today

St Thomas. These were: his purpose-built shrine at the centre of the Trinity Chapel (A on the plan; destroyed in 1538); the Corona Chapel, where a fragment of the top of his skull was displayed (B); a refurbished chapel called the Martyrdom, near to the place of Becket's death (C); and an extended crypt space, where his first tomb was situated (D). Funding the project was, on the whole, no problem for the cathedral. It was one of the wealthiest institutions in England. Generous grants made to them by Henry II and other important visitors, combined with donations from the steady flow of pilgrims already making their way to the church, meant that the cathedral coffers were overflowing.[8] By the time of the 1220 translation, the cathedral's east end resembled heaven on earth. Its soaring vaults were held aloft by a symphony of polished, coloured stone columns, and its myriad jewel-like stained-glass windows served to enhance the magnificence of both the saint's cult and the priory's status. No visitor to Canterbury could have been in any doubt of Becket's divine credentials as a miracle-working saint. The complex design was brilliantly conceived and meticulously planned to incorporate the varied functions of the church in a glorious architectural harmony, but its construction was not straightforward.

For a period when detailed descriptions of construction works are practically non-existent, it is remarkable that there is a surviving contemporary guide to the rebuilding, in the guise of Gervase of Canterbury.[9] Gervase witnessed and recorded the build at first hand. He explains that, following the fire, Canterbury Cathedral employed a master mason called William of Sens (d. 1180) to design and oversee the reconstruction of the church.[10] William, as his name suggests, was not a native Englishman but hailed from the French city of Sens, where Becket had lived in exile for several years. Gervase writes that in the early days after the fire, William, and several other French and English master masons, came to Canterbury to consult on the building's condition.[11] Eventually the others were dismissed and William was chosen because of his 'lively genius and good reputation'.[12] His selection was probably also due to the fact that he had expert knowledge of cranes and other ingenious devices that improved the logistics of the build, making it quicker and more efficient. He surveyed the damage and convinced the monks to support his plans for their beloved church.[13] William set to work coordinating the newly planned structure, preserving the outer walls of the old church and ensuring they were properly supported by the crypt below. His aim was to rebuild the choir, so that the monks could resume their essential function of celebrating the Divine Office there as soon as possible.

It took four years, working from west to east. Relics of numerous saints also needed to be permanently rehoused in this space. Among the most important of these were two previous Canterbury archbishops, St Dunstan and St Alphege, whose remains had been located to either side of the high altar before the fire and occupied the same position in the new east end.[14]

Stylistically the rebuilt east end of Canterbury Cathedral was a fusion of local traditions with Continental ones derived from the building boom that was taking place in and around the Île-de-France.[15] The architectural references of William's church are eclectic, and it provoked a revolution

4.3
Canterbury Cathedral crypt, located directly beneath Trinity Chapel. Becket's tomb was situated between the two central Purbeck columns.

in English architecture that continued well into the following century, but William did not see his work completed. In September 1178, at the beginning of his fifth year overseeing the project, he suffered a violent injury, falling 15 metres from wooden scaffolding. For a time, he directed the ongoing work from his sickbed, but soon returned to France.[16] In his stead the monks appointed another master mason, also named William, an Englishman who had probably been trained in France. This new William made some alterations to his predecessor's design, including expanding and lifting up the floor space of the Trinity Chapel, which extended it significantly beyond the easternmost limits of the earlier church.[17] He thereby created an unusually spacious and lofty crypt, and ensured that the proportions of the columns in the Trinity Chapel approximated to classical prototypes (fig. 4.3).[18] Gervase writes that William the Englishman worked at Canterbury from 1179 to 1184, during which time the building must have been mostly finished. In his first year of work he began the large extension of the Trinity Chapel, which would be dedicated to St Thomas. The earlier incarnation of the chapel was of special significance to Becket during his lifetime, as it was here that he had performed his sacred duties as archbishop. Gervase elaborates on this connection, writing that in the Trinity Chapel Becket had

> celebrated his first mass, where he was wont to prostrate himself with
> tears and prayers, under whose crypt for so many years he was buried,
> where God for his merits had performed so many miracles, where
> poor and rich, kings and princes, had worshipped him, and whence
> the sound of his praises had gone forth into all lands.[19]

It was during William the Englishman's tenure as master mason that Alan of Tewkesbury, the prior of the cathedral, secretly prepared the translation of a number of other saints whose remains were also in the crypt. Becket's body was, however, kept downstairs to await a grander occasion, as Gervase says: 'only … the translation of St Thomas was reserved until the completion of his chapel. For it was fitting and manifest that such a translation should be most solemn and public.'[20] Gervase's account of the rebuilding project demonstrates the importance of Becket's translation ceremony for the entire community at Canterbury, which was working tirelessly towards the completion of the Trinity Chapel. It was to be the cathedral's crowning glory and the monks were clearly eager to see the work finished as soon as possible.

The Trinity and Corona Chapels

Sixteen steps connect the Trinity Chapel to the choir, raising it into a prominent position behind the high altar which, until the sixteenth century, was flanked by the shrines of St Dunstan and St Alphege. This was a dramatic departure from what had existed before the fire. The previous Trinity Chapel was significantly smaller, most likely of a similar scale to those either side of it, which were dedicated to St Anselm and St Andrew. In addition, it was the same height as the choir. By lifting up the new, much larger chapel in this way, William introduced a unique design for the east end of an English cathedral. It does, however, find a parallel away from England in the new east end that Abbot Suger built at St-Denis, Paris, completed over thirty years before in the early 1140s.[21] Around the raised east end and central shrine space both churches contain ambulatories (semicircular aisles) with stained-glass windows set very low into the walls. Suger spent vast sums on the rebuilding of his abbey church, which was on the site of the legendary final resting place of St Denis, the protector saint of the kings of France. It is unsurprising that Canterbury looked to such an esteemed building as a prototype for the location of St Thomas's shrine. The architecture of the Trinity Chapel also shows an explicit desire to exploit the visual language of the classical past, with the paired shafts echoing the arrangement of much earlier churches such as Santa Costanza in Rome, built in the fourth century.[22] Classical references, like Corinthian-style capitals, endow the site of Becket's shrine with the authority of an ancient Roman martyr's church.[23]

The Trinity Chapel is arranged in three stories made up of an arcade (the lowest range, at floor level), triforium (the middle range) and clerestory (the upper level containing stained-glass images) (fig. 4.4). The central part of the chapel, where Becket's shrine was to be positioned, was encircled by an ambulatory, allowing pilgrims to walk around the space. Projecting from the easternmost end of the Trinity Chapel is a smaller chapel, named the Corona, where Becket's 'crown', a piece of the top of his skull sliced off in the murder, was kept. From the fourteenth century onwards, it was housed in a reliquary which took the form of a golden bust of St Thomas himself.[24] It is not known exactly what this reliquary looked like, but it was recorded as being richly decorated with precious metals, gems and jewels.[25] Along with all the other shrines dedicated to Becket, this too was destroyed in the sixteenth century and, although pilgrim badges depicting the bust were not intended to be seen as faithful representations of it, they probably provide

4.4
Trinity Chapel, Canterbury
Cathedral

the best indication of its original appearance (fig. 4.5). William employed different materials to mark a meaningful transition between the choir and the Trinity Chapel. In the choir, the upright structural supports or piers are made of pale limestone with trimmings in dark Purbeck stone. In the Trinity Chapel, limestone is used again, but here it is combined with paired columns of cream and rose-pink marble. The combination of white and pinky-red materials in the columns surrounding Becket's shrine is thought to be of particular significance.[26] Six of the medieval accounts of the murder focus on the symbolism of the colours red and white in relation to his blood and brain, spilled on the floor of the cathedral.[27] Five of these specifically link the blood and brain to red and white flowers, especially roses and lilies. One account of the murder states: 'in such a manner is beautified the bright

4.5
Pilgrim badge of a bust
of Thomas Becket with
fragments from an
architectural frame,
14th century. Lead alloy.
8.9 × 4.6 cm (excluding
frame). British Museum,
London, 2001,0702.1.
It was discovered in
Billingsgate, London.

countenance of this martyr and confessor through the glorious death for holy Church, that the blood brightened from the brain, and the brain reddened from the blood, as if the rose and lily were beautifully blended together'.[28] The symbolic lily and the rose come to life in architectural form through the colours of the polished stones used in the Trinity Chapel.[29] These colours had a further connection to Christ; in his *Ecclesiastical History of the English People* the Venerable Bede (*c*.672/3–735) described the colouring of Christ's tomb in Jerusalem as being 'white mingled with red'.[30] Several of Becket's biographers linked the spilling of his blood at the martyrdom to that of Christ's at his Crucifixion, labelling him 'the Lamb of Canterbury' in evocation of Christ as 'the Lamb of Bethlehem'.[31] In this way, the materials in the Trinity Chapel were allegorical. It became a place to engage with the violence of Becket's murder and contemplate the sanctity of his martyrdom. With the enshrined body of Becket at its centre, the skull fragment in the Corona Chapel, and the red and white marble columns symbolising his blood and brain, and perhaps

4.6
Aerial view east of the shrine
area towards the Corona
Chapel. Trinity Chapel,
Canterbury Cathedral

also the colours of Christ's tomb, those behind the planning and construction
of the Trinity Chapel evoked the martyrdom scene in the architectural details.

The pavement and marble floor of Trinity Chapel

As with the columns in the Trinity Chapel, a similar language of rare materials
was used for the flooring (fig. 4.6).[32] The majority of the floor was made up of
large slabs of Purbeck stone, in a dark blue-green hue. Underneath the area
where Becket's shrine was originally located, these Purbeck slabs were framed
by flagstones made of the same rose-pink marble as the column shafts. To
the east and west of the shrine these took the form of rectangular slabs and
to the north and south they were arranged in rows of seven lozenge shapes.
Some of the marble pieces that can be seen in the floor today were reset after
the sixteenth-century destruction and originally formed part of the shrine's

4.7
Aerial view of the mosaic pavement. Trinity Chapel, Canterbury Cathedral

podium.[33] This selective placing of rare materials in the Trinity Chapel emphasised the importance of the site of Becket's bodily relics. To the west of the shrine area, moving towards the choir and high altar, there is another marble pavement of extraordinary rarity and complexity (fig. 4.7). Arranged as a series of interconnected and overlapping shapes, the pavement is made up of thousands of tiny pieces of predominantly purple and green porphyry, and white marble. These stones were imported from Italy, where the manufacture of pavements like the one at Canterbury had long been thriving.[34] It may even have been made before the fire of 1174, perhaps in the early twelfth century, and was possibly located near to the cathedral's high altar.[35] This line of argument maintains that the fragments of the pavement were retained and reset in front of Becket's shrine as a form of contact relic, owing to the fact that the saint had spent the night following his murder lying in front of the high altar where his blood dripped onto the floor. This may well be the case, as contact relics were preserved in other areas of the cathedral. Becket's

4.8
Cosmatesque mosaic
pavement located in front
of the high altar, 1268.
Westminster Abbey, London

tomb in the crypt was preserved *in situ* even after his body was transferred
to his new shrine in 1220, and pilgrims continued to visit this tomb until its
destruction as a consequence of the Reformation. The end of the sword that
broke on the floor during the murder was also preserved at the martyrdom site,
at what became known as the Altar of the Sword's Point. Evidence for such
repurposing of materials and objects can be found elsewhere. At Peterborough
Abbey two altar stones were created from slabs of the paving on which Becket
was slain, and swords that were believed to have been used in the murder
were recorded at Carlisle Cathedral and Temple Church in London.[36]

To either side of the mosaic there is a series of stone roundels carved with
the signs of the zodiac, the labours of the month and personifications of the
Virtues and Vices. Six patterned roundels in the same style, and perhaps of
the same date, are also located on the eastern side of the shrine area, towards
the Corona Chapel. Over the course of time these roundels were moved
around and reset, possibly more than once, but there is little doubt that
they were originally made for the site of Becket's shrine. All of the Trinity
Chapel flooring was probably laid at some point between the 1180s, when
the building was almost complete, and 1220, when the translation ceremony
took place. It is likely, given the limited availability of some of the materials,

particularly the rose-pink marble, that the majority of the work was carried out around the same time the major architectural work was finished, or soon after. In any case, Becket's shrine was located on top and in front of one of the most sumptuously decorated floors in all of England,[37] rivalled only by the Cosmatesque mosaic pavements at Westminster Abbey commissioned by Henry III (1207–1272) in 1268 (fig. 4.8).[38] These were produced by Italian craftsmen, who were brought to England for the installation, and are located around the shrine of St Edward the Confessor and in front of the high altar. The example in Canterbury is, however, the earliest surviving in England, and may well have inspired the later work at Westminster Abbey.

Canterbury Cathedral's east end was the most prestigious example of early gothic architecture in England. Its impact and influence can be felt across many of the large-scale architectural projects built in the century following its completion. These include nearby great churches, such as Rochester Cathedral, but also ones located further afield: Chichester Cathedral, Salisbury Cathedral, Lincoln Cathedral and Westminster Abbey.[39] A shared interest among these same institutions was the glorification and promotion of their saintly relics through new building works: St Richard for Chichester, St Osmund for Salisbury, St Hugh for Lincoln and St Edward the Confessor for Westminster.[40] Canterbury was fast becoming the major English pilgrimage destination, and the fact that these other esteemed institutions looked to Christ Church for inspiration speaks to the pivotal role Becket's martyrdom had in transforming the architectural landscape of England.

The shrine

> But the magnificence of the tomb of St. Thomas the Martyr, Archbishop of Canterbury, is that which surpasses all belief. This, notwithstanding its great size, is entirely covered over with plates of pure gold; but the gold is scarcely visible from the variety of precious stones with which it is studded, such as sapphires, diamonds, rubies, balas-rubies, and emeralds; and on every side that the eye turns, something more beautiful than the other appears. And these beauties of nature are enhanced by human skill, for the gold is carved and engraved in beautiful designs, both large and small, and agates, jaspers and cornelians set in relievo [*sic*], some of the cameos being of such a size, that I do not dare to mention it: but everything is left far behind

by a ruby, not larger than a man's thumb-nail, which is set to the right of the altar.[41]

Anonymous Italian visitor to England, c.1500

Becket's shrine was almost entirely obliterated in 1538, which makes reconstructing its original appearance a challenge.[42] What is known is that it comprised two principal parts: first, a large stone base made out of the same rose-pink marble as the columns and paving slabs; and second, on top of this, a golden reliquary casket resplendent with precious jewels that held the saint's remains. This casket was covered by a wooden box that was raised by means of ropes and pulleys to reveal the gilded casket within.[43] Medieval descriptions of the base are rare, but Henry d'Avranches (d. c.1262), writing in 1220, provides tantalising evidence, saying: 'near to the altar there rises a catafalque [tomb] of sculpted marble, borne aloft on marble columns. In the midst there is a tomb made of marble.'[44] Most contemporary descriptions of the shrine focus on the golden casket, which was the most eye-catching element. Matthew Paris (c.1200–1259), the monastic chronicler of St Albans Abbey, states that it was 'of the finest refined gold and most precious stones'.[45]

Although the entire shrine assemblage was destroyed early in the English Reformation, it appears that a number of fragments of the shrine base have, amazingly, survived: eleven have so far been found.[46] Among the larger pieces, two small fragments are held in Canterbury Cathedral's collections and a further four, comprising three partially complete capitals and a fragment, are kept in Canterbury's Beaney House of Art and Knowledge (fig. 4.9).[47] Those in the Beaney were discovered in 1984 on the bed of the River Stour. While there is no absolute proof that the fragments are from the shrine, they are sculpted in the same rose-pink marble that was used for the column shafts in the Trinity Chapel and are in a similar late twelfth-century style to the capitals in the choir. This rose-pink marble is rare. Aside from the Trinity Chapel column shafts, it was not used elsewhere in the cathedral, nor anywhere else in England.[48] It has been suggested that the stone came from Belgium, possibly Stavelot or Philippeville, but the source remains a mystery.[49] Perhaps there was only a single opportunity to import it, or it was originally available in limited quantities. Whatever the case, these stone fragments are all that is left of Becket's shrine, which countless pilgrims journeyed to see over hundreds of years.[50]

When exactly the shrine was built is another question that remains unanswered. Was it constructed in two phases, with the base being put

together in the 1180s, during the major building work, and the precious metal casket added later, at the time of the translation? Or, was the entire structure, comprising both base and casket, assembled simultaneously in preparation for the 1220 translation? Matthew Paris records the names of two men, Walter of Colchester and Elias of Dereham, who worked on the shrine to make it ready for the translation ceremony.[51] Paris goes as far as to praise Elias as an 'incomparable artificer', but there is too little surviving documentary evidence to say whether or not the focus of Walter and Elias's work was just the precious metal reliquary.[52] It is, however, likely that each man was responsible for different sections. Elias is known for his contribution to major architectural projects, including the building of Salisbury Cathedral, and it seems appropriate to think he was brought in to finish or refresh the architectural shrine base. Furthermore, Elias had a long-standing connection to Canterbury. He had previously worked for Archbishop Hubert Walter (c.1160–1205) and was closely connected to the subsequent archbishop, Stephen Langton, the mastermind behind the translation ceremony.[53]

4.9
Fragment of a double capital, probably from Thomas Becket's shrine base in the Trinity Chapel, c.1180–1220. Rose-pink marble. 49 × 27 cm (approx.). Canterbury Museums and Galleries, CANCM 1984.32.1

4.10
Pilgrim badge showing the shrine of Thomas Becket, 14th century. Lead alloy. 7.5 × 5.6 cm. Museum of London, BC72[55]<1555>

However, given that the first stage of the rebuilding campaign, between 1174 and 1184, was directed towards the rapid translation of Becket's relics, there is a strong possibility that some of the preparations for the shrine took place then. With the architecture and the flooring almost certainly completed by 1184, the stone base must surely have come next.

Medieval representations of the shrine in manuscripts, badges and stained glass cannot be relied on for accuracy. This was not the intention of those who produced these images.[54] However, souvenir badges of the shrine, sold to pilgrims visiting the cathedral, remain the best indicator of what it might have looked like (fig. 4.10). Several of the best-preserved badges depict the shrine base as a series of repeating quatrefoils with pointed arches above, similar in style to a number of thirteenth-century shrines, such as that of St Frideswide in Christ Church Cathedral, Oxford.[55] An incongruous aspect of this badge is the recumbent effigy of Becket at its centre. This makes the structure appear to be more like the traditional tomb of an archbishop than a saint's shrine, and it is improbable that such an effigy of St Thomas was ever present at Canterbury. Instead, the badge is probably an idealised image of the shrine, and Becket's reclining figure was included to demonstrate the goal of every pilgrim: physical proximity to the body of St Thomas, which remained out of sight and reach.[56] The key visual information that the badge conveys is similar to what many who described the shrine chose to focus on – namely, the magnificence of the golden casket. In all of the badges depicting this structure it is shown covered in gems, with the largest, the so-called Regale of France, at its centre. Many of these souvenirs include an angel, or a small sculpted figure, pointing to the jewel. Given that this visual information appears on other representations of the shrine, such as the altarpiece from Wismar (see fig. 3.9), we can assume that it was a feature of the decoration.

During the Middle Ages, Becket's shrine was internationally famous and its renown lived on long after it had been dismantled. John Stow (c.1525–1605), an antiquarian writing in 1592, over fifty years after its destruction, described the shrine as having

> jewels of gold set with stone, wrought upon gold weir [wire], then again with jewels, gold as brooches, images, angels, rings, 10 or 12 together, cramped with gold into the ground of gold, the spoils of which filled two chests such as six or eight men could but convey out of the church.[57]

Antiquarians were committed to recording whatever information they could about the past. Objects such as Becket's shrine fascinated them. A curious drawing of the structure, made long after its destruction, from a manuscript in the library of Sir Robert Cotton (1571–1631), piqued the interest of men like Stow. It was reproduced as an engraving by Robert Vaughan (c.1620–c.1660) for inclusion in Sir William Dugdale's (1605–1686) *Monasticon Anglicanum*, first published in 1655 (fig. 4.11). It shows what was considered to be the form of the shrine of Thomas Becket at Canterbury. The image depicts a stone structure, with a series of repeating arched niches along the base, upon which sits a gable-ended box topped with three foliate finials. Beneath this is a series of objects, laid out on a plinth, which the text describes as Becket's bones and skull. However alluring, the image bears little resemblance to what is known about the shrine, and, given its date, the anonymous artist of the original drawing almost certainly never saw it

4.11
Robert Vaughan, *The Shrine of Saint Thomas of Canterbury*, c.1655. Engraving after a drawing in MS Cotton Tiberius E VIII, f. 278v, British Library, London. 27.2 × 15.1 cm. British Museum, London, Q,7.153

in person. Nevertheless, its reproduction in the seventeenth century merits attention as a key example of the continued interest in the true appearance of St Thomas's lost shrine at Canterbury.

Becket's miracles and the stained-glass windows at Canterbury Cathedral

Becket's collected miracle stories were the principal source for the imagery of the glass that surrounded his shrine. These were dramatic tales of the wondrous events that took place in the days, weeks and years following his death. They describe how pilgrims drank St Thomas's Water, a mixture of Becket's blood and water that the monks freely dispensed to pilgrims. It was the consumption of Christ's blood as part of the Mass that signalled his sacrifice for all humanity, and in a similar way, Becket's martyrdom was re-enacted by pilgrims through the consumption of his blood. Before Becket's death, medieval pilgrims had often acquired and drunk water containing scrapings from a saint's tomb, or water that had come into contact with an object possessed by a saint, but the ingestion of blood was an unusual new direction for a cult to take. It had no precedent or parallel aside from the Eucharist itself. For some days and weeks, the idea of drinking Becket's blood made the monks of Canterbury uncomfortable.[58] However, the more miracles that resulted from the water's use, the more amenable they became to this innovation, and within a short period of time, pilgrims coming to Canterbury could count on receiving doses of this water for their personal use or to take home with them.

Powerful as drinking or washing with St Thomas's Water was thought to be, it was just one way to seek a miracle. Some people came to Becket's tomb, some went to locations where he had stood or slept, while others hunted out objects or clothing that he had handled. The easiest method was simply to ask Becket for help, and this was probably the most common way his aid was sought. At first, and owing to the fraught political situation, it was dangerous for pilgrims to visit Becket's tomb. Henry II had attempted to suppress the cult and his men had threatened to seize and desecrate Becket's body. To safeguard his tomb and the relics, the monks of Canterbury barred the doors to the crypt. After Easter 1171, in part due to pressure from people seeking miracles, they opened the crypt and allowed free public access. It was after this that the numbers of pilgrims coming to Canterbury in search of miracles, or reporting miraculous cures that had happened to them elsewhere, started to

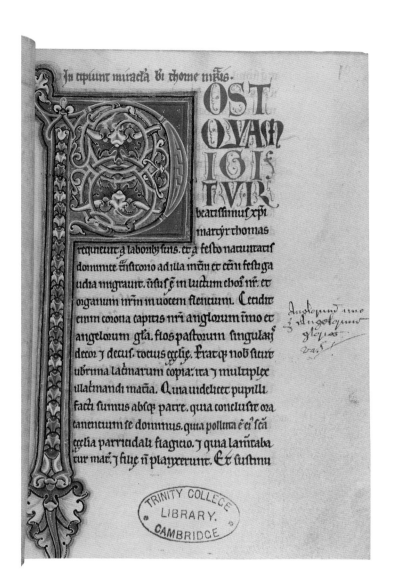

4.12
Opening page of Benedict of Peterborough's *Miracles of St Thomas of Canterbury*, late 12th–early 13th century. Vellum. 18.5 × 14 cm. Trinity College, Cambridge, MS B. 14. 37, f. 1r. The first sentence translates as: 'After the most blessed martyr of Christ, Thomas, rested from his labours, and migrated from the transitory festival of the Nativity of the Lord to the joys of the inner and eternal festival, our dancing was turned into mourning and our organ into the voice of those who weep.' It was produced at St Augustine's Abbey, Canterbury, where it probably remained until the English Reformation.

rise. In connection with this flurry of activity, Benedict of Peterborough began to investigate the authenticity of the myriad miracle stories he heard about or witnessed in connection to Becket's death.[59] He was kept busy, telling his readers that 'great and very wonderful things were being worked every day around the tomb of the martyr'.[60] In two to three years, between about the middle of 1171 and the end of 1173, Benedict assembled around 275 stories, wrote an account of Becket's passion (the final stages of his life and death) to preface this compilation, and also composed the liturgical office that would be used to celebrate Becket's feast day across Europe (fig. 4.12). Benedict complained that he could not write fast enough to keep up with the number of miracles he was being told, and from June 1172 a second monk started collating the miracle stories as well. His name was William of Canterbury. William had taken up residence at Canterbury just a few days before Becket was murdered. He worked on his independent collection for around five years and wrote an even longer version than Benedict's, compiling about 425 stories, but he too stated there were many more that he failed to record. Benedict's collection, the first to be completed, proved to be much more popular than William's, perhaps in part because it did not take as long for a scribe to copy the text. It was Benedict's work that was read aloud in the cathedral's chapter house and was widely circulated; nearly twenty full copies, along with various manuscripts containing partial extracts, survive to this day. On its completion, a volume of William's collection was presented to Henry II as a gift. Today, only two full copies of his text survive.[61]

Throughout their collections, both Benedict and William stress the curative function of St Thomas's Water. Its importance is also attested to by Becket's biographers. William FitzStephen describes how this healing liquid was 'distributed to the pilgrims of St Thomas in tin ampules to be carried back for the health of their infirm. I myself saw the inscription on many phials, *Bottle containing blood of Thomas mixed with water.*'[62] Garnier de Pont-Sainte-Maxence went further, explaining how these vessels formed an important type of souvenir that pilgrims could purchase and take home with them:

> Kings have sought him [Becket] in pilgrimage, princes, barons, dukes
> with their nobles … they take phials home with them as a sign of their
> journey. People bring a cross back from Jerusalem, a Mary cast in lead
> from Rocamadour, a leaden shell from St James; now God has given
> Saint Thomas this phial, which is loved and honoured all over the
> world. It is doubly honoured, for health, and as a sign.[63]

In the early days, as Benedict relates, pilgrims tried to take away St Thomas's Water in little wooden boxes known as pyxides, but these were unreliable, prone to leaking, cracking and breaking apart altogether.[64] To combat this issue, a layman thought of producing small metal containers. These watertight vessels, made out of a cheap and malleable lead-tin alloy, soon superseded the wooden pyxides. Known as ampullae, these decorated flasks were on sale outside the cathedral and have survived in large quantities. They replicate, in terms of material and shape, pilgrim ampullae from the

Holy Land, but the variety and inventiveness of the Canterbury ampullae far exceeded anything that had come before.[65] A number of Becket ampullae have been discovered on the banks of the River Thames in London, but they have also been found more widely in England, Scotland and Ireland, as well as further afield in France, the Low Countries, Scandinavia and beyond.[66] Various designs were employed, from tiny containers with a scallop-shell design to detailed three-dimensional forms with figures projecting from their surface. The sheer variety of types is astonishing. Some included text around their rim. The most common inscription speaks to the hopes that many would have had as they took their ampullae away with them (fig. 4.13). It reads (in translation): 'Thomas is the best doctor of the worthy sick.'[67] Others were elaborately made and required a complex casting process from a series of moulds. In one example, where St Thomas is depicted in a ship, his hands are extended in prayer, projecting from the main body of the ampulla (fig. 4.14). By the time the decorative programme in the Trinity Chapel was complete, the acquisition of an ampulla filled with St Thomas's Water would have been an essential part of many people's pilgrimage to the cathedral. Those visiting would have seen in the stained-glass windows images of monks mixing St Thomas's Water, followed by pilgrims like themselves receiving it. Among the earliest

4.15

Stained-glass window
showing Becket
addressing a crowd of
onlookers from a pulpit
(detail), *c.*1210. Sens
Cathedral

miracle windows in the Trinity Chapel are images showing pilgrims being sold
ampullae before entering the church. It was in the glass surrounding his shrine
that Becket's life and miracles were displayed on a monumental scale.

The miracle windows

The east end of Canterbury Cathedral is one of the greatest places in the
world to view late twelfth- and early thirteenth-century stained glass *in
situ*. This includes the choir, Trinity Chapel and Corona Chapel. What is
all the more remarkable, given the sheer quantity of glass, is the fact that

almost all of it was made and installed in less than fifty years. This glazing programme took place between the time that the post-fire building work had been completed, around 1184, and Becket's translation in 1220.[68] In the Trinity Chapel the windows revealed the story of Becket's life, death and miracles, demonstrating his transformation into the renowned miracle worker St Thomas of Canterbury. Some of the scenes are missing or out of order, having been subject to destruction, removal, reorganisation, restoration and theft over the centuries, but an impressive amount of original glass has survived.

These windows are uniquely important as they show the only known series of Becket miracle stories to be found in glass or any other media.[69] Stained-glass windows depicting narrative cycles from Becket's life can be seen in four French cathedrals: Sens, Chartres, Coutances and Angers.[70] All were produced in the first half of the thirteenth century, but do not portray his miracles and instead concentrate on his life story, murder and burial. Each cathedral's imagery is different, demonstrating how Becket's story was adapted in a variety of places to suit the local or national agenda of those involved. The earliest surviving depictions of the saint in stained glass outside Canterbury are at Sens, where the glazing took place between c.1207 and 1213 (fig. 4.15). Here, special attention is given to Becket's role as a prelate, with panels showing him performing ecclesiastical duties such as celebrating Mass and preaching.[71] As might be expected, there is also a focus on the part played by Louis VII as a mediator in Becket's disagreement with King Henry. Given Louis's personal connection to Sens, his brother-in-law being the archbishop from 1169 to 1176, the glass can be interpreted as a carefully managed piece of political spin. At Chartres, like Sens, there is a focus on the diplomacy involved in the Becket dispute, including the roles of Pope Alexander III and Kings Henry II and Louis VII, as well as senior members of the clergy.[72] Compared with these windows in France, the Canterbury miracle windows are markedly different. The cycle is far larger and in what survives a greater emphasis is placed on Becket's miracle-working aspect rather than his biography. It highlights the people who came into

4.16
Stained-glass panel showing Becket enthroned and receiving a delegation, mid-1180s. Diam. 71.5 cm. Harvard Art Museums/Fogg Museum, 1924.108. Gift of Professor Arthur Kingsley Porter. It was originally inserted in one of the first three miracle windows in the north aisle of Trinity Chapel, Canterbury Cathedral, but was removed, probably in the late 19th or early 20th century.

4.17
Stained-glass panel showing a group of pilgrims travelling to Canterbury, mid-1180s (later restorations, mainly mid-19th century). Miracle window nV 13, north aisle of the Trinity Chapel, Canterbury Cathedral

4.18
Stained-glass panel showing a figure distributing ampullae to pilgrims in Canterbury Cathedral, mid-1180s (later restorations, mainly mid-19th century). Miracle window nV 14, north aisle of the Trinity Chapel, Canterbury Cathedral

contact with the saint and the importance of Canterbury Cathedral as a holy place of veneration. The windows also mark a visual shift in the type of miracles being recorded in England during the course of the twelfth century. Whereas in earlier collections of English miracle stories priority was given to ecclesiastics, with Becket's miracles we find more relatable stories about everyday folk with commonplace issues that continue to trouble people today. The windows demonstrate Becket's power in working miracles for the entire spectrum of medieval society – infants, children, adolescents, adults and the elderly, priests and monks, as well as the laity, men and women, knights, nobility and the wealthy, along with peasants and the impoverished. The vast majority of stained glass at the time was devoted to the stories of biblical figures, royalty or the saints; at Canterbury, the focus moved to the lives of ordinary individuals.[73]

The sequence begins on the north side of the Trinity Chapel ambulatory, at the ground-floor level. It progresses in a clockwise direction around the edge of the chapel, skipping the Corona Chapel, where the windows contain an incomplete typological series. The windows themselves are on the ambulatory level and although each window is over 6 metres high they are set remarkably low down into the wall. Crucially, this meant that the images themselves would be easily visible for visitors to the Trinity Chapel.[74] No medieval glass has survived in the first two windows, but it is highly likely these told the story of Becket's final days and murder. One extant panel, now at the Fogg Museum, Harvard University, fits perfectly into the iron frame (armature) of the first window and matches the rest of the original glass stylistically (fig. 4.16). It shows Thomas Becket as archbishop, enthroned, surrounded by monks and receiving a delegation, which must be a scene from his life rather than from his posthumous miracles. By the third window in the series the story has moved past Becket's death and on to early pilgrims journeying to visit his shrine. Some panels from this window, previously thought to be modern replacements, have recently been identified as medieval originals and include what is the earliest image of a group of pilgrims travelling to Canterbury (fig. 4.17).[75] They represent people from all parts of society, some riding on horseback and others simply walking. The figure at the back of the

4.19
Two panels showing the miracle of William of London, mid-1180s (restorations early 20th century). Miracle window nV 6-7, north aisle of the Trinity Chapel, Canterbury Cathedral. The panel on the left shows a priest having a vision and receiving a message regarding William's cure. The panel on the right shows William, in the centre, at Becket's tomb, receiving St Thomas's Water from two monks.

4.20
Stained-glass panel showing
Adam the Forester being shot
in the neck by a poacher, early
13th century (later restorations,
mainly mid-19th century).
Miracle window sII 1-25, south
aisle of the Trinity Chapel,
Canterbury Cathedral

4.21
Stained-glass panel showing
William of Kellet's accident,
early 13th century (later
restorations, mainly mid-19th
century). Miracle window sII
30, south aisle of the Trinity
Chapel, Canterbury Cathedral

group points their way forward with a stick and the person at the front leads them forward. In the opposite panel, a man welcomes pilgrims to Christ Church (fig. 4.18). He holds ampullae in one hand and a cup in the other, standing before the visiting pilgrims eager to receive the water. It is from here onwards that the miracle stories begin. The first is that of William of London, a priest, who after drinking a mixture of blood and water from Canterbury regains the use of his paralysed tongue (fig. 4.19). From the fourth to the twelfth window, the miracles are told across multiple scenes. Here, dozens of stories are portrayed, nearly all of them drawn from Benedict of Peterborough's miracle collection. It is only in the seventh window, the first one on the south side of the chapel, that stories from William of Canterbury's miracle collection can be found, both of them depicting men suffering injuries.[76] In the seventh window of the series, for example, two different miracles are shown across several scenes, both of which illustrate labouring men who are inflicted with bodily injuries (figs 4.20–4.21). One man, a forester called Adam, has been shot in the neck with an arrow by a poacher. The second, William of Kellet, is a carpenter who has accidentally cut into his own leg with an axe. Each man is healed by Becket's intervention but by different means. Adam is cured by drinking St Thomas's Water, and William receives a vision of Becket in a dream. Both, however, are then shown visiting Canterbury to give thanks and offerings in return for their new-found health.

Together the construction, design and decoration of the Trinity Chapel and its furnishings served to enshrine Becket's body and glorify him. It was a scheme that was decades in the making, and by the time of the translation in 1220, it was unveiled as one of the most ambitious and magnificent spaces in Europe. Today, the chapel still reveals the splendour in which Becket's relics once lay, despite the loss of many central features, not least the shrine and bust reliquary, as well as the numerous changes and restorations that have been made over time. It is particularly fortunate that the glazing has survived in such great quantity and has been preserved *in situ* (fig. 4.22). As a result of the changes and losses it has experienced through the centuries, there has been much debate regarding the original arrangement of the panels and which precise miracles these depict. To understand the glass's complexities, it is necessary to know more about its history and to investigate one window in detail, arguably the finest of the series, to explore the richness of its imagery.

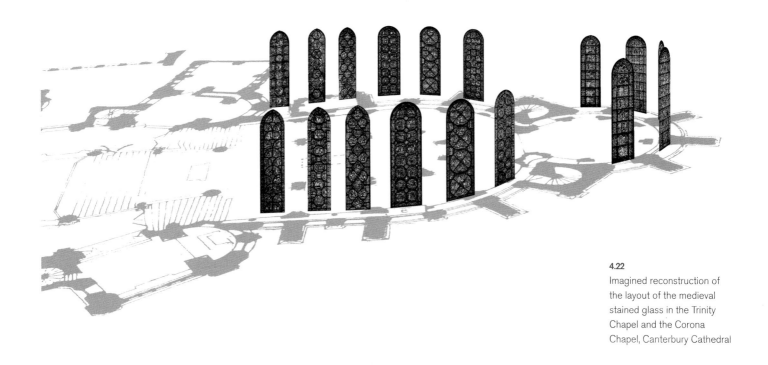

4.22
Imagined reconstruction of the layout of the medieval stained glass in the Trinity Chapel and the Corona Chapel, Canterbury Cathedral

The fifth window of Canterbury's Thomas Becket cycle: new readings

Rachel Koopmans

The fifth window in the ambulatory around Becket's shrine is a masterclass in medieval artistry. Its iron framework, or armature, divides the window into four massive circles. Within the circles are beautiful flower-like petals, and outside them, along both sides of the window, are flanking half-circles. The painting on the glass is extraordinarily delicate and sensitive, the faces and bodies of the figures showing a remarkable range of emotion and movement as they act out Becket's miracles. The glaziers chose an eye-catching colour scheme of deep blues, multiple greens, bright reds, and cool whites and purples, and also lavished attention on the design of the window's sinuous floral ornament. The artists who made this window probably came from France. Stained glass was the most expensive decorative element of any medieval building, and the monks of Canterbury spent generously to get the best possible artists and materials for Becket's chapel (fig. 4.23).

Of the twelve windows devoted to Becket's life and miracles in the ambulatory, medieval viewers especially admired this one. A remarkable thirteenth-century pilgrim's ampulla provides the evidence (fig. 4.24). In miniature form, the ampulla's decoration unmistakably replicates the design of the fifth window. Tiny figurative scenes closely echo those found in the windows, and the verse inscription on the ampulla's frame

4.23
The fifth miracle window, early 13th century (later restorations, mainly mid-19th century). H. 610 cm. Miracle window nIII 28, Trinity Chapel, Canterbury Cathedral

4.24
Pilgrim's ampulla, *c.*1220.
Lead-tin alloy. 9.8 × 8.1 cm.
Musée de Cluny, Paris, Cl. 18063

4.25
Engraving of the Trinity Chapel, 1807, in
Charles Wild, *The Metropolitical Church of
Canterbury*, London: W. Bulmer, 1807, plate 11

comes from another of the windows in the series. Surviving examples of this vessel can be found in France and Norway (see Chapter 4), demonstrating that pilgrims who purchased these were able to take home a memento reminding them of the glories of Canterbury's glass, a practice not dissimilar to the purchase of souvenirs on sale at tourist sites today.

Some mysteries remain about when exactly the window was designed and installed, but it seems most likely that this took place between 1213, when the monks of Canterbury returned from a lengthy exile in France, and 1220, when Becket's relics were translated into his shrine. The majority of the glass present in the fifth window can therefore be dated to the early thirteenth century, but it is important to note that owing to loss

and repair over the centuries, it also contains some glass from the late twelfth century (perhaps inserted into the window in the seventeenth century) as well as from a mid-nineteenth-century restoration campaign. Despite appearances, not everything seen in this window originally belonged to it. Victorian restorers were skilled at creating convincing imitations of medieval glass, so there is a need to tread carefully.

The earliest evidence for the window's pre-restoration state comes from an engraving made in 1807 (fig. 4.25). It shows that all of the north aisle windows in the Trinity Chapel, including the fifth window, had at some point in the past lost their lowermost panels. Although this glass might have been destroyed during the Reformation, it was most likely smashed when Puritan iconoclasts ransacked Canterbury Cathedral in December 1643. Their motivations for attacking only the lower panels remain unknown, but what was left afterwards needed speedy attention. In the 1660s the cathedral's surviving glass was subject to a rough-and-ready restoration, with additional leads soldered onto the original medieval lead matrices to hold the panels together more securely. Most of these repairs were superseded in the course of later restorations, but traces of the buttressing repair leads can still be seen on some pieces of the window glass. It is possible that these restorers were responsible for moving a scene from the third window, dating to the late twelfth century, into the fifth window (now panel 5).

By the nineteenth century there was heightened interest across Europe in the conservation and restoration of stained glass. In 1857 the most extensive repair work on the fifth window took place, and it was the Canterbury glazier and restorer George Austin Jr (1821–1891) who turned his attention to it. He reported that the window was 'in a very precarious state from the great age and decay of the lead work'.[1] To save the glass, he dismantled the entire window, discarded what remained of the original medieval lead matrices and the seventeenth-century buttressing leads, and put the window back together with new leads. Before re-leading, he substituted new pieces of glass for ones that were missing, broken or badly corroded. Every panel in the window was subject to this kind of repair work.

Shaded pieces in figure 4.26 show where Austin's repairs are found in the central panel of the 'Lame Sisters' narrative (fig. 4.27). His replacements include most of Becket's tomb (the low rectangular structure on the right), the monk's clothing and his book, and three heads – those of both sisters and that of a male onlooker – along with ornamental pieces in the border. Fortunately, Austin did not feel that the head or any of the pieces making up the figure of Becket needed repair, meaning that Becket in this panel consists entirely of early thirteenth-century glass. By the standards of the time, Austin's restorations were sensitively carried out. It appears he sought to keep the panel's iconography intact, while also trying to ensure his replacements looked similar to the original medieval glass.

In addition to re-leading and replacing pieces within the window's medieval panels, Austin created four entirely new panels to replace what had been destroyed. Three of these can be found in the second roundel from the top (nos 7, 8, 9), and the fourth is at the very base of the window (no. 22). Rather than inventing imagery for these four panels, Austin simply copied iconography from nearby miracle windows in the Becket cycle. He imitated medieval painting styles and utilised techniques to make the glass itself look older than it was, all to help his panels blend in with the originals.

Alongside this restoration work, Austin also undertook a major reordering of the glass. He recognised that the window was meant to tell stories of Becket's miracles, and realised its panels were badly mixed up, making it very difficult to read. It is likely the confused order was a legacy of the rough repair work done in the 1660s. Austin replaced and reordered the glass in the fifth window 'so as to bring into Harmony the different phases of the Stories illustrated'.[2] His arrangement of the narratives remains in the window today, and although it was carefully thought out, there are still some issues regarding the original medieval layout of the glass and whether all the panels that are now alongside one another actually belong together.

A notable and ingenious aspect of the fifth window's design is that its panels are intended to be read in arcs. All of the other stories from the Becket cycle can be read in straight lines, from left to right, but the narrative in this window is presented in a dynamic and inventive way. Most of the stories are told in arcs of three panels (see, for instance, the Lame Sisters narrative, nos 10, 11, 12), but one, Eilward of Westoning's story, was designed to be told across six panels. Inscriptions describing the stories were supplied for each panel in rhyming Latin hexameters. These were placed under each narrative scene. Verse poetry of this type was popular among the learned at the time, but could only be enjoyed by those literate in Latin. Notably, the glaziers designed the window to be read from the top down, like a book, rather than from the bottom up, which was far more common in French cathedrals of the same period.

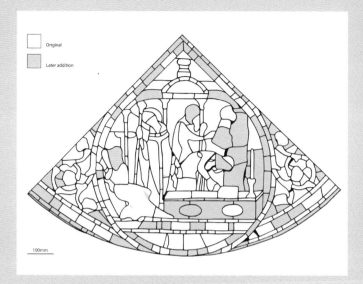

4.26
George Austin Jr's repairs (shaded)
to panel no. 11, the second scene of
the 'Lame Sisters' narrative. Miracle
window nIII 28, Trinity Chapel,
Canterbury Cathedral

4.27
The second scene of the 'Lame Sisters'
narrative (panel no. 11), early 13th century
(later restorations, mainly mid-19th
century). Miracle window nIII 28, Trinity
Chapel, Canterbury Cathedral

All of the stories in the fifth window are derived from the miracle collection compiled by Benedict of Peterborough between 1171 and 1173. By the time the viewer arrived at this window, the overall narrative told by the windows cycle was well advanced. Becket's life and death were portrayed in the first two windows. The third was devoted to the earliest events and miracles occurring after the murder. The fourth pictured miracles of local men and women from Canterbury and Kent, most of which happened at Becket's tomb. It is in the fifth window that the story is first taken further afield, with miracles in England more broadly, including Yorkshire, Northumberland and Bedfordshire. Many of these miracles feature visions. In four of the window's surviving panels Becket appears as part of such a vision. Another notable aspect is the frequent use of St Thomas's Water, the mixture of his blood and water that pilgrims drank or applied to their bodies in the hope of a cure. A wide variety of people experienced miracles in connection to Becket, either at his tomb or elsewhere, and

those depicted in the fifth window are no exception. In it we see men and women, the religious and the laity, all being cured by St Thomas of Canterbury. Several of the other windows in the cycle show miracles involving children and the elderly. They helped to emphasise the universality of Becket's healing power.

The curing of Eilward of Westoning is by far the most prominent story in the window and the single most famous miracle of Becket's early cult. Eilward was a peasant living on a royal manor outside Bedford who was sentenced to blinding and castration for a minor theft. Many of the pilgrims who came to Canterbury for the translation ceremony of 1220 may well have known the story of Eilward and sought it out in Canterbury's stained glass. The survival of so much of the fifth window's original glass allows us to see what medieval pilgrims saw. There is perhaps no more direct or visceral way to connect with those pilgrims and understand what drew them to Canterbury than to contemplate the stories pictured within this glorious window.

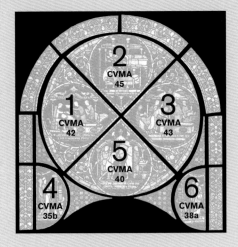

In the uppermost panel (no. 2, and see pages 244–5), Becket bursts out of a golden shrine to come to the aid of a sleeping man. This is the most famous image of the window. It was singled out by the restorer George Austin Jr, who believed that it 'without doubt' pictured Becket's shrine.[3] However, the modest shrine here does not correspond with descriptions of the actual shrine's scale and magnificence. It is a shrine seen in someone's vision, not the real shrine. Philip, an ailing clerk of Alnwick, had a vision in which he 'thought he was lying in a church near the shrines of two saints. The blessed and glorious martyr Thomas rose from one of the shrines and spoke to him', assuring him that he would be cured.[4] This nicely matches the imagery of the panel, with one notable exception: the sleeper has a bandage wrapped round his head, and Philip did not suffer from a headache or head injury. A better explanation is that the sleeper is the famous Eilward of Westoning, the subject of panels 13, 15, 16, 17 and 18. Eilward did suffer a head

injury (he was hit over the head by a large whetstone), and this panel, showing Becket's blessing on Eilward before he underwent blinding and castration, fits neatly into the sequence of panels relating his story.

Panels 1 and 3 portray the story of a leper named Ralph. Panel 14, discussed in more detail below, is the middle panel of Ralph's story. In panel 1, Ralph sits near Becket's tomb. Painted dots representing leprous pustules are visible on his legs (Ralph's head, on which no pustules are visible, is a modern replacement piece). Ralph had already committed himself to a leper hospital when he heard of Becket's miracles. He went to Becket's tomb seeking a cure, and there made numerous vows, including one to go to Jerusalem. For each of the nine days he remained at Canterbury, Ralph drank St Thomas's Water and washed his body with it. This treatment is pictured in panel 1. As Ralph left Canterbury, he was cleansed of his leprosy, the scene of panel 14. A month later, Ralph returned to Becket's tomb, at which point he was 'most whole, healthy, handsome, and without a mark', as pictured in panel 3. Note that the head of the bending 'woman' in no. 3 is a mistaken restoration: this figure represents Ralph giving thanks at Becket's shrine. Ralph stayed at Canterbury for months in perfect health, but when he left to go to Jerusalem, he became terribly leprous again, possibly, the miracle collector suggested, because he had committed a sin. This part of the story is not pictured in the window, although the two winged creatures along the top of panel 3 may well symbolise Ralph's later deterioration.

Panels 4 and 6 picture a woman cured of dropsy, almost certainly the miracle of Goditha

of Hayes. Dropsy was a common affliction in the medieval period. Its symptoms consist of excessive water retention and swelling, and Benedict wrote that in Goditha's case, 'all the beauty of the human form had been removed from all her limbs'.[5] The woman closest to the city gate in panel 4 has an enlarged midriff, and the inscription for the panel reads, 'She who comes sick is all swollen with dropsy.' The story would have had a large central panel picturing the swollen Goditha drinking the water relic, but this scene has been replaced by one from another window (discussed below). Panel 5 does, however, retain its original inscription: 'The one with distended skin tastes [St Thomas's Water], and by the tasting is cured.' The last panel in the sequence (no. 6) shows Goditha, now cured and swelling-free, leaving the city along with her travelling companion. Benedict wrote that Goditha left 'wholly slimmed down'.[6]

In the centre of panel 5, a man in a doorway gives away an article of clothing to a half-naked man. These two figures are noticeably larger than any others depicted in the window, revealing that this glass originated elsewhere. The scene pictures a servant of the monks of Canterbury distributing some of Becket's blood-spattered clothing to the poor for the benefit of the archbishop's soul immediately after the martyrdom. Items of Becket's clothing were greatly prized as miracle-working relics, and the monks later regretted their decision to give away some of these priceless items. Canterbury's glaziers devoted the third window of the cycle to very early post-martyrdom events. It is highly likely this scene came from there.

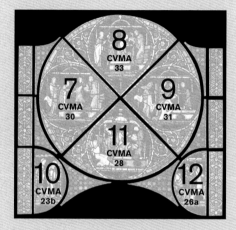

Panels 10, 11 and 12 tell a fascinating story of sibling rivalry. Benedict of Peterborough described how two sisters, the daughters of a man named Godbold from the Kentish village of Boxley, had both relied on crutches to walk since their infancy.[7] In panel 10 the sisters are on crutches near a city gate, above an inscription reading, 'The sisters born with an equal fate come on pilgrimage to be healed.' The medieval glaziers carefully distinguished the sisters by the colour of their dress. The one to the rear, the younger of the two, is wearing rose-purple, while the elder, who is shown looking over her shoulder, leads the way and is in white. As Benedict's story goes, Becket first visited the elder sister in her sleep and told her that she would be healed. On the left of panel 11, she reclines in a chair while Becket gazes down at her. This figure of Becket is worth special attention as it is one of the few in the miracle cycle to be untouched by modern restoration. Meanwhile, the younger sister props herself up on her crutches as she bends over Becket's tomb. Benedict described how she wept and railed and 'blamed the saint' for her lack of healing when she saw that her elder sister was recovered.[8] The next night, Becket visited and cured her too. In panel 12 the younger sister receives a vision of the saint, while the older sister stands at Becket's tomb, now without her walking aids. The inscription reads, 'The first night brings health to the elder, the second to the younger.'

Panels 7, 8 and 9 are replacements crafted by George Austin Jr in 1857. When he had gaps to fill, Austin copied panels he found in other windows of the miracle cycle rather than creating his own imagery. Here, he selected three scenes portraying women's miracles, no doubt inspired by the Lame Sisters narrative immediately below. He based panels 7 and 8 on two panels in the cycle's fourth window that tell the story of Etheldreda, a woman from Canterbury suffering from fevers. In panel 7 a monk at Becket's tomb mixes up the St Thomas's Water for Etheldreda, and in panel 8 she drinks it from a bowl held by the monk. Austin derived panel 9 from another panel in the fourth window, this one showing Saxeva, a woman from Dover who suffered from a painful arm and a stomach ache, making an oblation at the tomb in thanksgiving for her cure.

The glaziers devoted all of the panels in this section to the miracle of a blinded and castrated man named Eilward, a peasant who lived on the royal manor of Westoning near the city of Bedford. His sensational story was the most widely known miracle of Becket's early cult and is Benedict of Peterborough's longest tale by far.[9]

The story begins in panel 13. Eilward has his hands bound behind him and a bundle strapped on his back. It contains the items that he supposedly took from a neighbour in repayment of a debt after a drunken quarrel in a tavern. He confessed to taking some but not all of the items, and a judge, pictured on the left, sentenced him to a trial by the ordeal of water. Eilward failed his ordeal, meaning that he floated rather than sank when immersed in a pool of water, and was condemned to blinding and castration. In his account of the story, Benedict portrays Eilward as being framed by the neighbour and undeserving of punishment.

Panel 14 is misplaced. It is the middle scene of the story of a leper named Ralph, the story begun in panel 1 and concluded in panel 3. After using St Thomas's Water, Ralph, still leprous, left Canterbury. It was at this point that he was healed. Benedict writes: 'and it happened that as he went, he was cleansed'.[10] Nearly all of the original glass of this panel is intact, making this scene of Ralph leaving Canterbury one of the most striking in the window. For the scene occupying this spot in Eilward's narrative, see no. 2 above.

The violent scene of Eilward's blinding and castration is graphically depicted in panel 15. A judge on the left points at Eilward, who lies bound and prone with a plank across his chest to pin him to the ground. The man tasked with blinding him kneels on the plank and directs a knife into his eyes. Eilward's tunic is drawn up and his nether garment down to expose his genitals. A man wielding a knife kneels on Eilward's legs and reaches down to perform the castration, while another man holds up cords, probably meant to represent those placed around Eilward's genitals. Four other men look on and gesticulate wildly. This is the earliest known image of a castration in medieval art.

The next scene, no. 16, depicts the blinded and castrated Eilward lying in bed with Becket standing beside him, holding a staff pointing down towards his face. According to Benedict, ten days after his punishment, Eilward fell asleep and in a vision he saw Becket 'marking the sign of the cross with his pastoral staff on his forehead and eye-sockets'. Unfortunately, the faces and much of the clothing of both men are later restorations, but Becket's hands and staff are original. The largely intact inscription refers to a gradual swelling up and regrowth, which was thought to have happened both to Eilward's eyes and his genitals after he had this vision. Becket's miraculous intervention on Eilward's behalf could be seen not just as a particularly 'marvellous and unusual miracle', as Benedict put it, but also as a commentary on the harshness of the king's justice.

Panel 17 pictures Eilward on pilgrimage. Benedict wrote of how Eilward's 'fame preceded him and roused everyone to meet him' as he went to Canterbury.[11] He gestures with his left hand to his eyes, and gives alms to a disabled man sitting near him. Five bystanders look on in wonder, one of whom, on the left, points to Eilward's genitals. The tree that grows up between Eilward's legs and above his head is an unmistakably phallic image indicating that his genitals have miraculously regrown. Benedict writes that when he was on his pilgrimage, Eilward 'did not deny those who wished to feel them', that is, to feel his restored genitals to confirm that a miracle had occurred. There was such a buzz over Eilward's miracle that the monks at Canterbury heard about it long before he arrived. To affirm that it happened, the Bishop of Durham, who saw Eilward once he arrived in London, sent a messenger back to Bedford to investigate. A letter from the burgesses of Bedford verifying the miracle was transcribed and preserved in Benedict's collection.

Panel 18 concludes the narrative. Eilward bows in thanksgiving at Becket's tomb as two men look on. We know from other records that Eilward stayed in Canterbury for many days telling his remarkable tale to other pilgrims. By the time the fifth window was made in the early thirteenth century, Eilward was long gone from Canterbury and had probably died, but the monks immortalised his story in the glass, making it possible for generations of pilgrims to see the amazing miracle for themselves.

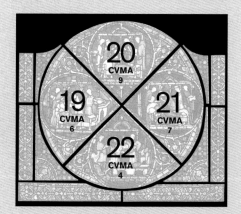

The roundel at the base of the window holds three medieval panels, nos 19, 20 and 21, and one modern replacement by George Austin Jr, no. 22. The medieval panels tell the story of Hugh, a Cistercian monk who fell ill at Jervaulx Abbey in Yorkshire.[12]

In no. 19 Hugh is shown ailing in bed, with an inscription reading, 'The doctors, his father [abbot], his brother [monks], and friends despair.' A doctor wearing a white cap leans over Hugh and offers him medicine from a narrow rectangular container. The doctor's assistant stands to the right, while to the left Jervaulx's abbot and a monk look on. Benedict of Peterborough wrote that Hugh 'trusted in the power of herbs', or medicines, but they did

him no good. After 'much time, much expense in medications, and much zeal and labour, the doctor left Hugh in a desperate state, showing all the signs of approaching death'.[13]

In the second panel (no. 20) the abbot takes the doctor's place. He holds up his hand in blessing and looks down at Hugh, who is sitting up and tipping the contents of an ampulla into his mouth. Benedict writes how the abbot, named John, had cured a number of people suffering from fevers by the use of St Thomas's Water, and implored Hugh to try it himself. At last he did, and this event takes place here. The doctor, who holds his hands up as if in protest, and his assistant are on the left side of the panel.

Benedict states that after Hugh drank the water, 'with a sudden and violent pouring out of blood from his nose, he became well'.[14] Hugh's sip of St Thomas's Water, in other words, provoked a flow of blood that brought his humours back into balance and thus cured him. In panel 21 the glaziers depicted Hugh turned on his side with blood gushing from his nose down the side of the bed and onto the floor. Abbot John leans over Hugh, his hand stretched out in wonder, while the doctor with his white hat looks on in acknowledgement of the miracle. As noted above, a number of ampullae from Canterbury contain text

that reads: 'Thomas is the best doctor of the worthy sick.' For Hugh, the miracle-working liquid proved to be a better treatment than the medicine supplied by the doctor, and without the payment he would have demanded.

Facial features and other details in the panels devoted to Hugh's miracle appear faded and indistinct because a significant amount of the medieval paint has flaked or abraded off the glass. This unfortunate loss, which could be put down to a number of factors, serves as a reminder of how critical the painter's art was in the creation and look of medieval stained-glass windows.

The replacement panel below Hugh's story (no. 22) was created by Austin to fill a gap. We do not know what was originally pictured here. Austin copied an image found in the cycle's fourth window that depicts the miracle of the elderly knight William of Dene. William, whose legs were paralysed, was carried to Becket's tomb and there regained the use of his limbs. In his copy, Austin adjusted the appearance of the central figure, making him into a clean-shaven monk (note the tonsure). Austin's idea seems to have been to supply the viewer with an image of Hugh giving thanks at Becket's tomb. The written account of Hugh's miracle does not indicate whether or not he went on a thanksgiving pilgrimage to Canterbury.

pulta sunt ꝛ uiuent noia eoꝛ
in eternum. iɓ. ix̃. cap̃.
Apiam scoꝛ narrabit
omes popli ꝛ laudem eoꝛ pro
nunciet omis eccta scoꝛ. Ceta
de coi aplon ad hac oꝛoem Deus
qui... dexta.
...tistacõe
...scm̃   nꝛ
...ao. us̃. sup
...pos fꝛz. ꝛ.

Noest

...nꝛis optata tistacio que dum̃i
munis fulger bñficio gaudeam̃
ꝛ psallam ad honoꝛe psibus ut u
tutem ꝛ salutem suis prester famut
cast Omis pontifex. ꝛ. Die
...Martyr dei. p̃. Gla

li m̃ fiat ser̃ie de
sꝛ pos fꝛ z. Iste ses
ꝛ Iace granum.
psa. Clangat past
ij Martyr dei. p̃
ꝛ pastor ethis. p̃.
q̃ nobis. m̃e de ap
mat inuit ij. ae
a ceta oĩa sic in ali
om Deus qui
sꝛ pos fꝛ z. Gra
Ihu bone. Et ceta
psto ppa ɫ festu ñ
Vbi... uere
tistati tistferat m
ij Martyr
Onus hum
heriur sic fulger m

Becket's shadow:
England in the aftermath
of the murder

On 7 July 1220, almost fifty years after Becket's murder, the great and the good of England, accompanied by foreign dignitaries, gathered at Canterbury Cathedral. Those present included the thirteen-year-old king, Henry III, and church leaders from across Europe, as well as a Hungarian archbishop, the Archbishop of Rheims and the papal legate Pandulf Verraccio (d. 1226).[2] Together they witnessed the translation of St Thomas's relics, a ceremony in which his remains were carried from the crypt up to the Trinity Chapel and placed in a purpose-built shrine. Several days before, the monks had opened the saint's tomb and removed his relics in preparation for this event.[3] The timing of the translation was no accident. It took place on a Tuesday, the weekday associated with many notable events in Becket's life, which was also likely to be the anniversary of the Fontevraud burial of Henry II, who had died on 6 July 1189.[4] The date was set by the Archbishop of Canterbury, Stephen Langton, who, like Becket, had spent a lengthy exile in France in dispute with his king. Langton calculated that the translation should be marked by a jubilee year, following Old Testament scripture stipulating that every fiftieth year should be a special year of celebration, remission of sins and granting of pardons. His idea came from

At the same season the body of the blessed Thomas, Archbishop of Canterbury and martyr, was raised out of its marble sarcophagus in the crypt of the church of Canterbury by the Archbishop of Canterbury, Stephen, of glorious memory, who thought that it was an undignified position for him to lie as it were in the basement of the church and in stone.[1]

Matthew Paris, *Historia Anglorum*, 1250–5

Detail of fig. 5.17

the Book of Leviticus, which states: 'And ye shall hallow the fiftieth year, and proclaim liberty throughout all the land unto all the inhabitants thereof: it shall be a jubile[e] unto you.'[5]

By evoking a biblical jubilee, Langton sought to charge Becket's translation with the authority of an Old Testament precedent. The powerful words from Leviticus invoke peace and prosperity across a kingdom after a period of turmoil, where its people are free and land has been returned to the dispossessed. Becket's jubilee-year translation served the same symbolic purpose, after a significant delay caused by a complete breakdown in the relationship between Church and Crown.[6] But why did it take such a long time to move Becket's body from the crypt to the Trinity Chapel? This must be considered both in terms of national politics and in light of Becket's cult and how different factions sought to control his legacy.

Disruption and discord: 1170–1220

The period between Becket's martyrdom and his translation was turbulent. England's throne passed from Henry II to his sons, first Richard I and then John, followed by his young grandson Henry III. In the course of these fifty years, European politics was dominated by the Third, Fourth and Fifth Crusades, with both King Richard and Baldwin, the Archbishop of Canterbury (c.1125–1190), leaving England to join the fray in 1190.[7]

Further destabilisation occurred during King John's reign: a bitter war with France led to the loss of most of his Continental territories, comprising Normandy and Anjou. England and Wales were also placed under a papal interdict, and the Pope personally excommunicated the king in 1209, a sentence that lasted until 1213.[8] The interdict, in theory, halted the administration of the sacraments of the Church, and the excommunication barred the king from all churches and religious ceremonies. In an effort to bring an end to his woes, John handed England over to the Pope as a papal fiefdom, a loss of sovereignty that was hugely unpopular with both bishops and nobles. If this were not enough bad news for the king, in 1215 a group of disaffected barons raised a rebellion that culminated in their drawing up Magna Carta. Through this charter the barons sought to limit unrestrained royal power and promote their interests. Within months, the terms of the document were denounced by the Pope and civil war ensued. John's sudden death in 1216 brought further insecurity and his nine-year-old son, Henry, was crowned in a hurried ceremony. A new king coming to the throne provided Langton, who had been Archbishop of Canterbury since 1207, with the opportunity to reconcile Church and Crown. He had witnessed the effects of John's rule on the English Church and had personally felt the danger of his royal anger. Becket's translation was Langton's way of bringing the two institutions together, both ceremonially and practically. To appreciate the historical significance of Becket's cult and its relationship to these events, it is necessary to review the broader political background from the perspective of late twelfth-century Canterbury.

Taking control of Becket's body: the archbishop versus the monks

In the first few years following Becket's murder, the monks had to adjust to a new life and learn to accommodate the extraordinary number of pilgrims arriving at the cathedral. The position of archbishop remained vacant until 1174, when Richard of Dover, who had been a close associate of Becket's during their time in Archbishop Theobald's household, was appointed. Although he was not Henry II's first choice, they maintained good relations.[9] Given the fragile relationship between the Church and the Crown, Richard needed to tread carefully, and it is likely he was selected because he was an uncontroversial candidate.

Richard had relatively few restrictions placed on him and, after the end of the 1173–4 revolt against the king, he was able to travel to the Italian town of Anagni, south-east of Rome, for his consecration and to receive the pallium, a vestment that conferred jurisdictional authority upon him, from the Pope. At the same time, he was also appointed papal legate to England, which granted him further authority to act on the Pope's behalf. It is possible that on this occasion he took a relic of St Thomas with him.[10] Becket is honoured in several different areas of Anagni Cathedral.[11] In the crypt, an oratory chapel dedicated to the saint is decorated with a painted cycle including four scenes of his Passion.[12] These paintings, which date to the late twelfth or early thirteenth centuries, may have been commissioned to commemorate the gifting of a Becket relic.[13] In the cathedral treasury a sumptuous Limoges enamelled casket and a mitre decorated with fine embroidery using silk and precious metal threads, known as *opus anglicanum* or 'English work', demonstrate the popularity of Becket's cult in Anagni in the decades following his martyrdom (figs 5.1–5.2).[14]

5.1
Reliquary casket showing
the martyrdom and burial of
Thomas Becket, c.1195–1200.
Wooden core, copper alloy,
gilding and enamel. 25 × 21
× 7 cm. Anagni Cathedral
Treasury

5.2
Mitre showing the standing
figures of Becket (left)
and St Nicholas (right),
13th century. Embroidered
textile. Anagni Cathedral
Treasury

Archbishop Richard was also a chief early promoter of Becket's cult in England, particularly at Canterbury. He hosted a number of important visitors to the cathedral, including Henry II and Louis VII of France, as well as various other foreign dignitaries. As one of the king's advisers he was charged with sensitive royal duties such as escorting Henry's daughter Joan for part of her journey to Palermo, Sicily, for her marriage to King William II in 1177.[15] Alongside maintaining good royal relations, Richard supported the monastic community at Christ Church, Canterbury. The priory was a Benedictine foundation. As Richard was a Benedictine monk, himself trained to follow the Rule of Saint Benedict, he had an affinity with and sympathy for the aims of the Christ Church monks. He was also archbishop during the period when most of the cathedral's construction work following the fire of 1174 took place, and, although much of the activity was probably supervised by the prior, as was traditional – first by Benedict of Peterborough until 1177 and then by Alan of Tewkesbury – Richard must have taken a special interest in such an important project. There is no evidence to suggest he was anything other than supportive of the plan to move Thomas's body into the Trinity Chapel as soon as the site was ready. A letter from the prior to Henry II, calling for a better shrine to be built for Becket's remains, indicates that they were already preparing for the translation at this early date.[16]

After Archbishop Richard's death in 1184 circumstances changed dramatically for the Canterbury monks. The Cistercian abbot Baldwin of Forde was nominated Archbishop of Canterbury by Richard I.[17] He was less amenable to priory plans, and relations with the monks of Christ Church soon deteriorated as Baldwin began what was essentially a politically motivated dispute with them.[18] This became a bitter disagreement that lasted for nearly twenty years and effectively put a temporary halt to the translation of Becket's relics. Being a Cistercian rather than a Benedictine, Baldwin's sympathies did not lie with the monks. Cistercians rejected overt luxury, instead promoting a life of austerity, and it is possible that Baldwin found Canterbury's new east end too ostentatious. These considerations aside, Baldwin had other, earthly matters in mind. He was planning to establish a collegiate church (a religious foundation run by members of the clergy who were not monks) away from Canterbury. First it was proposed for Hackington, Kent, but later changed to Lambeth, opposite the city of Westminster. Baldwin did this because, in a situation peculiar to England, a great number of cathedrals were also Benedictine monasteries.[19] Most cathedrals in Continental Europe were secular foundations staffed by canons, who were not confined to a life of monastic devotion and were thus usually more worldly. The powerful monastery at Canterbury had created problems for previous archbishops, on issues often concerning property and finance, so Baldwin sought to resolve these by founding a new church – one not run by monks, over which he could exercise greater control.

Baldwin also probably hoped that the canons of his new foundation would support him in his dealings with the nobility and monarchy, rather than promote the rites of their own institution, as the Canterbury monks were inclined to do.[20] A little later, in the 1190s, a similar situation developed at Coventry Cathedral, where, in the end, the monks were physically expelled from the church and temporarily replaced by canons.[21] At Canterbury, however, the monks sensed the threat posed by Baldwin and opposed his plans with all their might. They were angry that his project proposed to use funds from offerings given to Canterbury. Added to this, they feared the building of a new church, jointly dedicated to St Thomas and St Stephen, would mean the archbishop might have Becket's body removed from the cathedral and permanently relocated to his new church. Reported visions of St Thomas soon multiplied among the worried monks.[22] He appeared to several of them in their dreams, which were interpreted as warnings against any rash decisions regarding his relics. The battle raged on, the papacy taking the monks' side and Richard I and the bishops supporting Baldwin. It was a stand-off that brought the monastic community to its knees and, as a result of the archbishop's interventions, the priory's wealth rapidly declined.[23] Without funds to pay the glaziers and masons who had been working on the building in preparation for the translation, the project stalled. Inevitably, with the Trinity Chapel works delayed, Becket's body remained, almost in limbo, in his tomb in the crypt. Such was the monks' dire predicament that they were even forced to rely on the townspeople of Canterbury to bring them food.[24]

The onset of the Third Crusade brought the monks some temporary respite. Two years before becoming king, Richard had taken up the cross and sworn to go on Crusade. Once crowned, in 1189, he was more determined than ever to fight in the Holy Land and requested that the Archbishop of Canterbury join him. Both men left England in 1190 but Baldwin did not spend long in the Holy Land. Just over a month after his arrival in Acre, north of Jerusalem, he fell ill and died on 19 November.[25] In his absence, no decisions could be made on how to proceed with the building work in Canterbury and the cathedral remained incomplete. With his death, there was a chance that the dispute might come to an end.

The Third Crusade also brought a new dimension to Becket's legacy, as the saint became linked with the activities of English knights fighting in the Holy Land, who wished to set up a military order for the care of the crusaders. With the support of Richard I, they founded a hospital dedicated to St Thomas the Martyr in the city of Acre.[26] It remained active until the city was recaptured by the Mamluk sultan Al-Ashraf Khalil (c.1260s–1293) in 1291. Becket's role as the patron saint of this hospital order was also established back in England. In 1227–8 Thomas, son of Theobald de Helles, the son or nephew of Becket's sister Agnes, donated land believed to be the site of Becket's childhood home on Cheapside to the Knights of St Thomas of Acre to use as a London base (fig. 5.3).[27] From the fourteenth century onwards, this same property played host to meetings of the Worshipful Company of Mercers. In the 1500s the Company built its first chapel and hall on the site, and to this day it celebrates its link with Becket.

After Baldwin's death, there was a three-year delay until his successor, Hubert Walter (fig. 5.4), was appointed archbishop. Walter had been in the Holy Land with Baldwin and the king and, much to the monks' dismay, he reignited his predecessor's plan to build a collegiate church at Lambeth.[28]

5.3
Seal of the hospital of St Thomas of Acre, showing Becket handing a cross to a kneeling figure, 1515. Wax. The Mercers' Company, London. The matrix from which this impression was made probably dates to the thirteenth century.

5.4
Seal of Archbishop Hubert Walter, from the Lambeth Arbitration Award, 6 November 1200. Wax. Canterbury Cathedral Archives and Library, CCA-DCc-ChAnt/L/130. The matrix from which this impression was made was probably produced for Walter when he was appointed archbishop in 1193.

A renewed appeal was sent to the Pope. Like Becket, Walter had risen through the ranks by way of royal appointment in secular affairs, rather than starting his career in the Church as a monk. Lavish objects discovered in his tomb in 1890 demonstrate that, again like Becket, he enjoyed a luxurious life (figs 5.5–5.9).[29] His grave goods, which are a rare survival for a burial from this time, include a silver-gilt crozier set with reused Roman gems, a gold finger ring, probably a signet, containing a green plasma stone engraved with a serpent-like beast and Greek inscription, as well as a silver-gilt chalice and paten. Along with these precious items of metalwork, he was buried wearing the finest imported Islamic silks. These objects testify to

5.5–5.9
Copper-alloy crozier with reused gems, gold ring set with engraved plasma gemstone, silver-gilt chalice and paten, and silk embroidered slippers, late 12th century. Canterbury Cathedral Collections, 01456, 01427, 01426.1–2, 00187.1–2. These objects were discovered in the tomb of Hubert Walter when it was opened in 1890.

5.10
Lambeth Arbitration
Award, 6 November 1200.
Parchment with wax seals.
58 × 43 cm. Canterbury
Cathedral Archives
and Library, CCA-DCc-
ChAnt/L/130

the type of luxury to which Becket himself was accustomed while holding
archiepiscopal office. During his tenure as archbishop, Walter managed to
maintain a generally good relationship with the two kings he served, Richard
and John. In turn, both kings supported Walter, rather than the monks of
Christ Church, over the fraught issue of the building of the new church at
Lambeth. Early in John's reign, a delegation was set up to arbitrate in this
matter and resolve the conflict once and for all. The commission was packed
with keen supporters of the archbishop, including the Bishop of Ely and the
Abbot of Bury St Edmunds. Their decision was something of a certainty
and those present found in Walter's favour. This official agreement took

5.11
Counterseal of Archbishop
Hubert Walter, from the Lambeth
Arbitration Award, 6 November
1200. Wax. Canterbury Cathedral
Archives and Library, CCA-DCc-
ChAnt/L/130. The Latin legend
reads 'MARTIR QUOD STILLAT,
PRIMATIS AB ORE SIGILLAT'
(By the primate's mouth the martyr
puts his seal to the words that are
distilled here).

the form of a document, dating to 1200 and still preserved in Canterbury Cathedral's Library and Archives (fig. 5.10). Its size and lavish production were intended to enhance the legitimacy of its contents. Attached to its lower edges by an array of expensive coloured cords is an impressive display of sixteen individual wax seals, each representing the agreement of one of the members of the delegation. At the centre of the group is Walter's large archiepiscopal seal, reminding the beholder of his power, authority and primacy. On its reverse is an impression of his exceptional counterseal, which shows how Walter marshalled Becket's memory for his own ends (fig. 5.11).[30] A translation of the Latin text reads as: 'By the primate's mouth the martyr puts his seal to the words that are distilled here.'[31] From Theobald onwards, archbishops of Canterbury had regularly used a recycled Roman intaglio gem for their counterseals, but Walter departed from this tradition by opting for an engraved image of Becket's martyrdom. Together, the image and text made the powerful statement that the saint endorsed the decisions of the incumbent archbishop. All those who received personal correspondence from Walter would be reminded that the contents of the letter were symbolically sealed with the blood of St Thomas's martyrdom.[32]

In the end, however, the display of collective ecclesiastical authority wrought by the Lambeth Arbitration Award was unsuccessful. Not surprisingly, the monks rejected the ruling and Walter abandoned the project to build a new church.[33] For almost twenty years the archbishop and the monastic community had been locked in a ferocious battle. At its heart, this had been a dispute about who held authority at Canterbury and, for the monks, the importance of protecting the relics of St Thomas. After the conflict was resolved, the two parties began to repair their damaged relationship. Their public reconciliation resulted in the commissioning of new objects for the cathedral. The monastic accounts for 1201–4 show that the priory was preparing a new throne for the archbishop at great expense.[34] Carved from slabs of Purbeck stone, the throne symbolised the renewed connection between the priory and its prelate (fig. 5.12). Today it sits in its original location, at the top of the steps of the choir in front of where Becket's shrine once stood. In both function and placement, it serves as a visual link between archiepiscopal authority in England, now symbolically tied to Becket's legacy, and the ancient site of Canterbury Cathedral. After Walter's death in July 1205, he was buried in a grand Purbeck stone tomb near to his former throne (fig. 5.13).[35] His was the first burial in the new Trinity Chapel. Such a privileged location close to Becket's intended shrine was surely sanctioned by the monks, and was probably due to his decision to renounce the

plans for a church at Lambeth.[36] The position of Walter's burial also indicates that they were once again preparing for the removal of Becket's body from the crypt and its reinterment in the new chapel. Evidently the monks felt that the chapel was ready to receive important tombs, but there were still further delays to the translation. These were caused by events that would shake the entire kingdom to its core.

5.12
The archbishop's throne (known as St Augustine's Chair), 1201–4. Canterbury Cathedral

5.13
Tomb of Hubert Walter, c.1205. Canterbury Cathedral

King John, the interdict and Magna Carta

> In the first place, [we] have granted to God and by this our present charter have confirmed, for us and our heirs in perpetuity, that the English church is to be free, and is to have its rights in whole and its liberties unharmed, and we wish it so to be observed.[37]
> Chapter 1 of Magna Carta, 1215

In 1199, following the death of his brother Richard, John was crowned king. During his reign, John had one of the worst relationships with the Church of any king of England.[38] However, he recognised the value of public demonstrations of piety and followed in his father Henry II's footsteps by making pilgrimages to Becket's tomb, as well as to other major English shrines such as those of St Edmund (c.841–869) at Bury St Edmunds and St Edward the Confessor at Westminster Abbey.[39] John had inherited his brother's choice, Hubert Walter, as Archbishop of Canterbury, but he was mistrustful of the prelate's significant power and influence. He was keen to select his own man and Walter's death presented an opportunity to do so. Matthew Paris, the monastic chronicler, records the king's words, on learning of Walter's death, as 'now for the first time I am king of England'.[40] Despite this, John's wish to control the appointment was hindered by the opposition of both the Canterbury monks and the Pope. This rupture grew into one of the defining features of his reign as both parties sought to nominate different candidates to the position of archbishop. John's selection was the loyal John de Gray, Bishop of Norwich (d. 1214), while the monks opted for their own subprior, Reginald.[41] A delegation of worried monks travelled to Rome to make their case to Pope Innocent III (c.1160–1216). He was less than enthused by either candidate, and advised them to elect an outsider, Stephen Langton, a respected scholastic theologian and cardinal, who had spent the majority of the last twenty-five years teaching in Paris, where he shaped a whole generation of churchmen.[42] Langton was born in Lincolnshire and may have left England in the same year that Becket was killed.[43] Beginning his own studies in Paris around this time, he would have been acutely aware of the murder and its after-effects, which were no doubt being discussed at length.[44]

The monks duly followed Innocent's advice and elected Langton to the position. But for John, this new man was an unknown quantity whose allegiances, he feared, surely lay outside of England. There was, however, little he could do to stop the process. On 17 June 1207 Langton was consecrated as archbishop by the Pope at Viterbo, Italy.[45] In retaliation, the king took swift action. He barred Langton from entering England, reportedly with the threat of hanging, and sent the monastic community of Canterbury Cathedral into exile.[46] On hearing of this, Innocent sent John a sharp rebuke in which he reminded him of Becket's martyrdom:

> To fight against God and the Church in this cause for which St Thomas, that glorious martyr and archbishop, recently shed his blood, would be dangerous for you – the more so, as your father and brother of illustrious memory, when they were kings of the English abjured that evil custom at the hands of legates of the Apostolic See.[47]

By preventing Langton from travelling to Canterbury to take up his position John had effectively sent his archbishop into exile, no matter that had he not actually set foot in England. This had echoes of Becket's treatment under Henry II, and Gerald of Wales, writing near the time, remarked on the fact, stating that Langton was the first true successor to Becket.[48] Langton himself was all too aware that what turned into a six-year exile had recent precedent and, in imitation of St Thomas, he journeyed to the same Cistercian abbey in Pontigny where Becket had also lived.[49] The parallels were not lost on Langton's contemporaries, and one political song compared the two men and their experiences:

> Complain, O England! And suspend the melody of thine organ, and more especially thou, Kent, for the delay of thy Stephen. But thou hast another Thomas; thou hast again a second Stephen, who putting on fortitude beyond that of man, performs signs among the people.[50]

Like Hubert Walter before him, Langton elected to use an image of Becket's martyrdom on his counterseal (fig. 5.14). Langton's choice of words for the legend reveals his attitude to the saint. In a Latin rhyming couplet, it reads: 'May the death portrayed without | be for thee a life of love within.'[51] While the text of Walter's counterseal emphasised Becket's endorsement of his episcopal authority, Langton's seal was, in more of a scholastic tone, a public declaration of his devotion to the martyr.

Medieval perceptions of John's reign, both in England and abroad, likened him to the tyrannical kings of the Old Testament, many of whom barred the doors of the temples and suppressed religion for their own benefit.[52] In his *De principis instructione* (*Instruction for a Ruler*), begun in the 1190s and completed around 1216, Gerald of Wales was deeply critical of tyranny.[53] His preface tells the reader that it was his disillusion with the behaviour of rulers that motivated him to write the book: 'For which ruler today does not apply the power that has been granted from above indiscriminately to every whim of his mind, to every desire and indulgence of the flesh and to every atrocity of wicked tyranny?'[54] Gerald had long admired the archbishop and his explosive criticism casts light upon contemporary attitudes towards the relationship between John and Langton.

The situation between king and archbishop – like that between Henry II and Becket – quickly spiralled out of control. In 1208, because of John's perceived infringements of the rights of the Church, the Pope

5.14
Counterseal of Archbishop Stephen Langton showing Becket's martyrdom, *c.*1213–15. Wax. 5.5 × 2.2 cm. The National Archives, Kew, DL 27/4. The matrix from which this impression was made was probably produced for Langton in *c.*1207, when he was appointed archbishop. The Latin legend reads 'MORS EXPRESSA FORIS | TIBI VITA SIT INTVS AMORIS' (May the death portrayed without | be for thee a life of love within).

placed England and Wales under an interdict. In the following year he excommunicated the king.[55] These verdicts had serious implications for the whole country. Not only was John forbidden from attending Mass and receiving the Holy Sacrament, but the interdict also led several senior members of the clergy to leave their churches and join the archbishop in exile.[56] Moreover, the people of England and Wales were deprived of the Mass, as well as baptisms, weddings and even burials in holy ground.[57] This was not just inconvenient; it threatened their immortal souls. Bringing the activities of the Church to a halt was catastrophic and this dramatic power play by the papacy had serious and long-lasting consequences for the relationship between Church and Crown.

John was already suffering with problems elsewhere in his reign, and these rulings made his position worse. Earlier, in 1204, he had lost most of his Continental territories in a war with Philip II of France. Beyond the embarrassment of losing these lands, his failure in the war also effectively kept him largely confined to England, limiting him to mounting expeditions to his remaining lands in Poitou and Aquitaine, which he attempted in 1206 and 1213–14. Before this, English kings had roamed their Continental domains, sometimes being away for many years at a time. John's new-found isolation prompted him to turn his attentions to Wales, Scotland and Ireland and also brought him into closer contact with his leading English barons, who were increasingly unhappy with the state of affairs. Added to this was the continuing threat posed by the French king, who waited on the sidelines ready to take advantage of the chaos and invade at any moment. To avoid further troubles, John needed to make peace with Innocent III, which he did in 1213.[58] His settlement was an extraordinary surrender of sovereignty. John gave England over to Innocent on the proviso that he would remain in charge and his successors would inherit the kingdom, which they would hold as a fiefdom on behalf of the Pope. He also agreed to terms that allowed Langton to return to England with all of the bishops who had joined him in exile. In July 1213, six years after his original appointment, the archbishop arrived back in England, where he made his way to Winchester to personally repeal the king's excommunication.

Although John's arrangement had restored the Church to England, and the interdict was finally lifted in July 1214, it did little to restore the barons' faith in the king. His renewed attempts to gain the upper hand on the Continent culminated in failure, later that same month, with the disastrous Battle of Bouvines. There, English forces led by the king's half-brother

William, Earl of Salisbury (*c*.1176–1226), along with the forces of the Holy Roman Emperor Otto IV and the Counts of Flanders and Boulogne, were roundly defeated by King Philip's troops.[59] Although John was not present at Bouvines, his parallel campaign in Poitou was also forced into retreat, leaving him to return to England in 1214 a diminished ruler about to suffer the outcome of the oppression of his subjects in his efforts to finance these failed campaigns. The result of these battles solidified the French king's position and left John more vulnerable than ever.

These circumstances, along with unpopular taxes and distrust of several royal officials, culminated in rebellion by a faction of English barons. They did not want to remove John from the throne, but to make him reform.[60] Robert Fitzwalter (*c*.1180–1235), who had long held a grievance against the monarch, was among the leaders of the group. His surviving seal matrix shows him as a powerful knight in full armour, mounted and with his sword drawn and ready. It is the image of a man at the height of his power (fig. 5.15).[61] A virtuoso piece of medieval metalwork, it is made of solid silver, and dates from a period when he was a key player in England's political arena. The device incorporates the coat of arms of one of his main allies, Saer de Quincy (d. 1219), demonstrating their close connection and unified opposition to the king. Together, they were joined by many leading figures including barons, earls and knights. Aiding them in their cause was Langton, who acted as a negotiator between the rebels and the Crown.[62] Langton's experience in this dispute would influence his approach to Becket's translation ceremony.

In 1215 matters escalated as the rebellious barons sought the help of Louis (1187–1226), son of John's greatest enemy, Philip of France. On 5 May they formally renounced their loyalty to the English Crown. All-out civil war was fast becoming a prospect and just weeks later the rebel barons submitted their terms of agreement to King John. These were crystallised in the famous charter known as Magna Carta, which John was effectively forced to adopt. On 15 June, at Runnymede, near Windsor, he endorsed the charter by means of his wax seal, which was attached to various copies of the document. These were distributed across the country, and one went to Canterbury Cathedral.[63] Here, again, the memory of Becket's murder loomed large. The original Magna Carta included sixty clauses (or chapters), the first of which was to protect the liberties of the English Church, and was without doubt included at Langton's insistence.[64] He was listed in the charter as the first of several advisers to the barons and played a key role in shaping the formation of the text, especially the first chapter. Those present were well aware of the relevance of Becket's

5.15
Seal matrix of Robert Fitzwalter, *c*.1213–19. Silver. Diam. 7.4 cm. British Museum, London, 1841,0624.1. The Latin legend reads: '+SIGILLVM: ROBERTI: FILII: WALTERI' (Seal of Robert Fitzwalter).

murder to that clause. Many of them, like the king himself, had grown up in the long shadow cast over England by the archbishop's death.

Almost immediately after issuing Magna Carta, John appealed to the Pope to nullify the document and punish the barons.[65] By the autumn, everything was in flux: Innocent had declared the charter invalid, the barons were waging war against the king and Langton was making his way to Rome to face the Pope's judgement for his involvement in the proceedings. John would not see peace in his lifetime. Before the struggle was over he

5.16
Effigy of King John with St Oswald and St Wulfstan, 1230s. Worcester Cathedral

contracted dysentery and, on 19 October 1216, he died. His was a lonely burial. Instead of being reunited with his kin at Fontevraud Abbey in France, he was laid to rest in Worcester Cathedral, in the west of England (fig. 5.16), becoming the first and only king to be buried there. Henry III, John's son, and the heir to the throne, was just nine years old when his father died. He went on to have the longest reign of any medieval ruler. During the years he was king, Magna Carta was reissued and ratified on three separate occasions and, alongside these new versions, Becket's position as one of England's most important saints was solidified.

The translation

Nor was there ever seen on earth a translation so largely attended and so magnificent, where so many honoured personages of different nations took part. For all thought it proper to honour in common Christ's holy martyr, who did not fear to shed blood for the universal church, and was in no wise afraid to stand for its freedom to the death.[66]

Matthew Paris, *Historia Anglorum*, 1250–5

Nine days after John's death, Henry III was crowned King of England in a ceremony that was anything but traditional. With the Archbishop of Canterbury still in Rome, and the Archbishop of York also out of the kingdom, proceedings were led by the Bishops of Exeter and Worcester with a small audience in attendance. Furthermore, the ceremony was held at Gloucester Abbey rather than at Westminster Abbey, as was customary. In the midst of such instability, the process was rushed through in order to confer legitimacy on the young king. Given that Henry was a mere child and the country had been engulfed by war for several years, prospects for a peaceful start to his reign did not look good. Those around the young king, particularly his advisers William Marshal, Earl of Pembroke (*c*.1146–1219), the papal legate Guala Bicchieri (*c*.1150–1227) and Hubert de Burgh (*c*.1170–1243; Earl of Kent from 1227), were able to win most of the barons back to the Crown and crush the threat posed by Prince Louis, son of the French king, who had a claim to the throne. They did this by reissuing Magna Carta in 1216 and 1217, and winning two crucial military victories at Lincoln and off the coast of Sandwich.[67] By 1217 the war had come to an end and in the wake of these events it was necessary to smooth over the instability of Henry's early years on the throne. First was the coronation. On 17 May 1220 Henry III was crowned for a second time. Unlike the Gloucester ceremony, this was a sumptuous occasion held at Westminster Abbey and overseen by Archbishop Langton, who had been away from England at the time of the earlier coronation.[68] On the same day as the ceremony, the king laid the first stone for a new Lady Chapel at Westminster Abbey, thus beginning a rebuilding project that occupied him for the rest of his life and bound him in lifelong devotion to St Edward the Confessor.[69]

Next came the translation of St Thomas's relics, which, having been delayed since the 1170s, were now scheduled to take place in the Trinity Chapel on 7 July 1220. As with the coronation, Langton was responsible for orchestrating this event, and he set his sights on bringing together Church and Crown, which had been at odds with each other for so long. He had been planning the ceremony for some time, possibly even since his return from exile six years earlier.[70] A series of letters exchanged between the archbishop and the new Pope, Honorius III (1150–1227), during 1219 shows how the two men were preparing for this occasion. They discussed the granting of indulgences in connection to the translation and Honorius permitted Langton to use offerings given at Becket's tomb to complete the rest of the building work, so that the translation could take place.[71] Since the mid-1180s, construction at the east end of Canterbury Cathedral had been postponed. Now, with the translation ceremony imminent, the project needed to be finished. Stained glass, architecture, flooring and painted vaults all required attention, but the shrine was the centrepiece.[72] At vast expense, Langton employed two men to complete the shrine, Elias of Dereham and Walter of Colchester, whose work is discussed in Chapter 4.

The translation ceremony was a truly international affair, with one chronicler recording that 'such a number of people poured in to this festival, that the city of Canterbury and the neighbouring towns and the district round could scarcely take the multitude in'.[73] Fresh from his coronation, Henry attended in great splendour and was joined by his justiciar Hubert de Burgh, seventeen English bishops and important foreign dignitaries, including the papal legate.[74] Langton was responsible for much more besides the ceremony. He played a key part in formulating a newly written translation liturgy, which explicitly references the recent political instability in England. The words focused on reconciliation, especially St Thomas's role in bringing together Church and Crown: 'The year of peace is present, the terror of war is gone. Peace grows in the world and an abundance of things everywhere. …

After the translation of Thomas all prosperity follows.'[75] The event also marked the creation of a new feast day on 7 July dedicated to the saint. This provided him with two major feasts in the ecclesiastical calendar: his martyrdom, which was already celebrated on 29 December, and now his translation too. An illuminated initial from a fourteenth-century copy of the translation liturgy shows Langton himself presiding over the ceremony (fig. 5.17). Standing at the centre with his crozier in hand, he blesses the perfectly preserved bodily remains of Becket, carefully handled by figures on either side.

After the translation ceremony a sumptuous feast was held in the nearby Archbishop's Palace, which had recently been completed under Langton's supervision. He also made sure to provide food for the poor of Canterbury and wine for all the townspeople. His aim was for this event not to be forgotten by any of those in attendance. A chronicler noted that Langton paid for these refreshments personally, writing, 'the lord archbishop himself, throughout his manors and estates, to the utmost extent of his means, had ordered with wonderful largesse and lavish generosity preparation to be made for men and animals, and to be offered to all comers both in Canterbury and in the neighbourhood'.[76] Fortunately for Langton, the Pope decreed that the whole year was to be Becket's jubilee and pilgrims flocked to Canterbury in greater numbers than ever before.[77] According to the fragmentary records that survive, this period had the highest offerings of any year during Becket's cult.[78]

Langton spent the remainder of his life actively involved in national politics. He preserved the memory of St Thomas, particularly through composing and preaching sermons, and even presented a relic of the saint to the Pope.[79] He also returned to Magna Carta. Although the 1215 issue had been quickly suppressed, Henry and his advisers reissued versions of it in 1216 and 1217 in order to win the loyalty of the rebellious barons. However, as the king was a child when these charters had been authorised, they represented the will of his minority government. By 1225 Henry had turned eighteen and he was more personally involved in what became the conclusive version of Magna Carta (fig. 5.18). Unlike the 1216 and 1217 iterations, copies of this new charter bore his own Great Seal and included a statement that clarified his position on the contents, which he had agreed to 'of our own spontaneous goodwill'.[80] Again, the legacy of Becket's murder can be felt in the opening clause, which confirmed that the English Church was free and that its rights and liberties would be protected. Langton was the chief architect of

5.17
The Stowe Breviary, c.1322–55. Parchment codex. 29 × 18.5 cm. British Library, London, Stowe MS 12, f. 270r. The illuminated initial shows the monks attending to the body of Becket with Archbishop Langton standing above (see page 148). Although the breviary was made in the 14th century, and in Norwich rather than Canterbury, it demonstrates Langton's long-standing connection to the translation ceremony and his role in constructing the liturgical office.

5.18

1225 Magna Carta. Parchment with wax seal. 106.6 × 71.2 cm. The National Archives, Kew, DL 10/71. This is one of four surviving issues of Magna Carta from 11 February 1225. It has been damaged due to exposure to damp and portions of the text have been lost. The coloured cords at the base of the document originally bore a wax impression of Henry III's Great Seal; what little of this remains is held in place by a plastic casing. Two of the other copies, at Durham University Library and the British Library, still retain their wax impressions of the royal seal. The full provenance of this version is unknown but, as has been proposed by Nicholas Vincent, its origins in the deeds of the Duchy of Lancaster, on long term loan to The National Archives, suggest it might come from somewhere in the Duchy lands, such as the Midlands or Lancashire.

the 1225 charter, and along with his fellow ecclesiastics declared that those who contravened its terms would face excommunication.[81] In effect, this theoretically put an end to the dispute that had destroyed the relationship between Henry II and Becket. Langton's death, just three years later, brought to a close the life of a key figure in the development of St Thomas's cult. During his tenure as archbishop, he had aligned himself with Becket and honoured him as a saint with genuine devotion. Through his close involvement in the planning of the translation, Langton finally completed a project begun some fifty years before. In doing so, he made it abundantly clear that Becket's relics would always remain at Canterbury under the supervision of the monastic priory.

Becket's translation ushered in a century of episcopal canonisations, including those of St Hugh of Lincoln (1220), St William of York (1227), St Edmund of Abingdon (1246), St Richard of Chichester (1262) and St Thomas de Cantilupe (1320).[82] The latter's cult was intentionally styled on Becket's own and it is no coincidence that both he and St Hugh were canonised in years that marked St Thomas's jubilee celebrations. The immense draw for pilgrims of Becket's relics at Canterbury, and the financial rewards that resulted, encouraged numerous major churches to rebuild on a hitherto unprecedented scale. The thirteenth century was an age of phenomenal artistic and architectural patronage in England. It saw the completion of vast and ambitious projects, such as the relocation of Salisbury Cathedral by Richard Poore, Bishop of Salisbury (d. 1237), from its site at Old Sarum to a new home around two miles away (fig. 5.19). The foundation stone was laid in the same year as Becket's translation. A poem commissioned for the occasion stressed that the new building was wrested from the grip of the castle, with which it had formerly shared the same walled enclosure.[83] Both physically and symbolically, the relocation of Salisbury Cathedral represented the Church taking steps to free itself from the authority of the Crown – something for which Becket was now a figurehead.

5.19
Salisbury Cathedral from the west front, consecrated in 1258

'A wonderous tale': Becket as legend

From the moment of his death, St Thomas's legend took on a life of its own, and each new interpretation reflected the values of those who sought to comprehend the violent murder, and its backstory, in their own age and in their own way. The earliest accounts of the saint's life and death come from those who were present in the cathedral at the time of his murder. As different versions circulated they were rewritten, enlarged, condensed or recast, authors keeping the basic structure intact but often fabricating new elements, as they creatively drew on a variety of other literary traditions to reframe Becket's story.[2] One of the first non-eyewitnesses to compose a biography was Herbert of Bosham, the archbishop's loyal clerk. He was sent away from Canterbury two days before the murder and regretted his absence for the rest of his life.[3] Having known Becket personally, he provides intimate details of the archbishop's character and personality, and gives a first-hand insight into his transformative years in exile. Herbert's text was written in Latin, a clear sign of the exclusive audience it was intended for. However, several biographies in vernacular languages including English, French and even Icelandic survive, serving as a testament to the popular and international nature of the saint's cult. One of the earliest French accounts, from 1174, was written by Garnier de Pont-Sainte-Maxence.[4] Like Herbert, Garnier was not present at the murder, but he later travelled to England to interview those who had

Listen, lords, both great and small,
I shall you tell a wonderous tale,
How Holy Church was brought in bale
[into sorrow]
By a great wrong.

The greatest cleric in all this land,
Of Canterbury, you understand,
Slain he was with wicked hand,
By the power of the devil.[1]

Fifteenth-century song for St Thomas

6.1
Becket's martyrdom,
c.1425–50. Alabaster
with paint and gilding.
38.5 × 28.4 × 4.5 cm.
British Museum, London,
1890,0809.1

6.2

Becket meeting the Pope in Sens, c.1425–50. Alabaster with paint and gilding. 42.3 × 24.7 cm. Victoria and Albert Museum, London, A.166-1946. These two panels come from the same altarpiece and were donated to the Victoria and Albert Museum together. Originally, there would have been at least three other panels showing scenes from Becket's life and death, but their whereabouts are now unknown.

6.3

Becket landing in Sandwich, c.1425–50. Alabaster with paint and gilding. 45.5 × 24.3 cm. Victoria and Albert Museum, London, A.167-1946

been and met with Becket's sister Mary, who had recently been made Abbess of Barking. As Garnier informs us, his account was more easily understood by everyday people and was even read out publicly near the saint's tomb.[5]

St Thomas's story inspired new interpretations throughout the Middle Ages. This continuous renewal of the narrative invigorated his saintly cult. For instance, John Grandison, Bishop of Exeter (1292–1369), completed a Latin life of Becket that he sent to Pope Benedict XII (1285–1342) in early 1335.[6] Grandison was a passionate defender of the Church's liberties and had a particular devotion to St Thomas. Beyond his written account, he commissioned two ivory triptychs showing Becket alongside other saints such as Peter, Paul and Stephen.[7] Exeter had a long-standing connection to the saint's early cult. Bartholomew (c.1110–1184), who was bishop at the time of the murder, participated in Canterbury Cathedral's first Mass following its reopening in 1171.[8] It is likely he transferred relics of the martyr to Exeter that were recorded in a twelfth-century list.[9] For his written life of Becket, Grandison drew inspiration from the earliest biographies and acknowledged this in a letter to the Pope, stating that his work was drawn 'from many writers newly edited by me'.[10] Some of these were probably available to him in Exeter's library but he may also have consulted manuscripts in Canterbury Cathedral.[11]

The vast majority of people across Europe had no access to, and were unable to read, any of the Latin biographies of St Thomas. Even those in vernacular languages circulated in relatively small numbers. Instead, church sermons, written in Latin but delivered in the vernacular, were an important means by which Becket's story reached the general population.[12] These focused more on his virtues than his miracles. For those who were literate, more widely available texts provided general familiarity with the story. St Thomas features in several of the most popular books of the Middle Ages, including *The South English Legendary* (late thirteenth century), the *Golden Legend* (*c*.1260) by Jacobus de Voragine (*c*.1230–1298), printed by William Caxton (*c*.1422–1491) in 1483, and the *Nova legenda Anglie* (an expanded version of an early fourteenth-century compilation) printed by Wynkyn de Worde (d. 1535) in 1516.[13] These were large compendiums containing shortened accounts of the lives of saints. There were also more popular tales that brought Becket's story to life, several of which suggest a close relationship to the Virgin Mary, who, it was said, took the time to mend his hair shirt.[14] Furthermore, musical renditions comprising plainchant, polyphony, ballads and carols were composed in his honour.[15] One fifteenth-century carol, possibly sung as part of a procession, describes the efficacy of Becket's blood to set the Church free:[16]

Seynt Thomas honour we,
Thorgh whos blod Holy Chyrch ys made fre.

Al Holy Chyrch was bot a thrall
Thorgh kyng and temperal lordys all,
To he was slane in Cristys hall
And set all thing in unite:
Hys deth hath such auctorite.[17]

For those who were not able to read there were thousands of images of Becket's life and martyrdom, often prominently displayed in churches: he could be found in stained glass, wall and panel paintings, textiles and floor tiles.[18] Alabaster altarpieces made up of rectangular panels representing stories from the life of Christ, the Virgin Mary and the saints were produced in the English Midlands and exported across the Continent. Becket's martyrdom was among the most popular images in alabaster, often depicted alongside those of saints Stephen, Lawrence and Erasmus, but surviving panels also show scenes from his exile and return to England (figs 6.1–6.3).[19]

6.4
Finger ring with an engraved image of Becket's martyrdom, 15th century. Gold, diamond. Diam. 2.5 cm. British Museum, London, AF.899. Bequeathed by Sir Augustus Wollaston Franks. The opposite side of the ring shows an image of the Virgin and Child.

6.5
Reliquary pendant showing Becket as archbishop, 15th century. Gold. 5 × 4.2 cm. British Museum, London, AF.2765. Bequeathed by Sir Augustus Wollaston Franks. The reverse shows an image of St John the Baptist.

They demonstrate that, while St Thomas's primary relics remained in Canterbury, his image proliferated widely. He appears on more portable, personal objects too, such as rings and pendants (figs 6.4–6.5). On one occasion, Becket was even served up at the dinner table. In 1443, at the feast for the installation of John Stafford, Archbishop of Canterbury (d. 1452), two sculptures made from sugar were presented after the second and third courses, including 'the trinity sitting in a sun of gold with a crucifix in one hand. Saint Thomas on one side and Saint Andrew on the other', and, later, 'A godhead in a son of gold glorified above … Saint Thomas kneeling before him with the point of a sword in his head.'[20]

Becket and the historians

Becket's story was retold by medieval historians, who were captivated by his opposition to royal tyranny. Historical chronicles, such as Ranulph Higden's (d. 1364) *Polychronicon* or John of Canterbury's *Polistorie*, were vast compilations of knowledge wherein world events were recorded for posterity.[21] For the churchmen who wrote these chronicles, Becket's rise to power and his falling-out with Henry II served as key moments to prompt reflection on the virtues of good and bad kingship, an issue that remained relevant throughout the Middle Ages. In the thirteenth century, the historian Matthew Paris, who had connections to the Crown, demonstrated in word and image the continued power of Becket's legacy. Paris was a Benedictine monk and scholar based at St Albans Abbey. He was probably present at Becket's translation, where

6.6 (below and detail, right) The martyrdom of Thomas Becket, in Matthew Paris's *Chronica majora*, c.1240–55. Vellum. 26 × 19.5 cm. Parker Library, Corpus Christi College, Cambridge, MS 026, f. 132r

he witnessed the extraordinary reconciliation between the Church and the Crown masterminded by Archbishop Stephen Langton.[22] During his tenure at St Albans, he created a series of illustrated histories that drew on the work of his predecessor, the monk–historian Roger of Wendover (d. 1236). When he came to illustrate the largest of his projects, a universal chronicle called the *Chronica majora*, Paris copied Wendover's description of Becket's murder but included his own pen-and-ink drawing of the event (fig. 6.6).[23] It is a lively and dramatic rendering of the scene, which shows St Thomas kneeling at the altar but facing the oncoming knights.[24] Here, Becket crosses his arms as he falls to the floor and Edward Grim leaps towards the knights in his defence, a sword blow injuring his arm in the process.

Paris probably saw an image like this in one of the now lost Becket miracle windows at Canterbury, or on Stephen Langton's seal, whom he knew well.[25] Nevertheless, Paris's version of the martyrdom is markedly different from comparable scenes from the first half of the thirteenth century – for example, in the Carrow Psalter, from Carrow Priory, Norwich, Becket is shown being attacked from behind and Grim recoils in horror (fig. 6.7). Regardless of where Paris came across an image of Becket's murder – he could, of course, simply have invented it himself – he would have been well aware of the violent details of the event. Becket was a major figure of veneration at St Albans. Two painted images of him survive at the abbey, one on a column in the nave and another situated in a privileged position behind St Alban's shrine.[26]

Paris produced a number of illustrated saints' lives in Anglo-Norman French, including one of Becket. His *Life of St Alban*, now in Trinity College Dublin, has an inscription on the flyleaf in his own handwriting, which confirms that he had written a life of St Thomas, then in the possession of Isabel de Warenne, Countess of Arundel (1226/30–1282).[27] A group of similar fragments, called the Becket Leaves, has had a long-contested authorship. Although they are unlikely to be by Paris, their importance cannot be overstated: they are the only surviving examples of an illustrated life of Becket.[28] It is unclear exactly how large the manuscript was when it was originally made and bound, some time around 1230–40.[29] Of the four leaves, or folios, that remain, the images and text begin with Becket's exile at Pontigny, in France. The missing pages probably focused on his early life, his time as chancellor, his final weeks in England and the climactic scene of his murder.

The text is in rhyming couplets, beginning with several lines in red ink (the rubric) providing a summary of the page. Across the folios a number of

6.7
The martyrdom of Thomas Becket, in the Carrow Psalter, c.1250. Parchment. 24.7 × 17.6 cm. Walters Art Museum, Baltimore, W.34, f. 15v. Acquired by Henry Walters

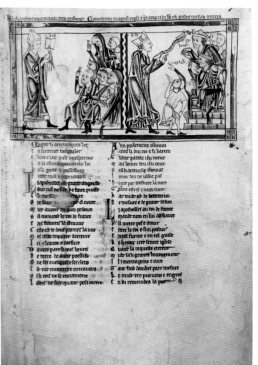

the most dramatic moments of the story play out and the key characters are depicted.[30] Both the imagery and text are unambiguously anti-monarchical. Henry's actions, combined with the fact that he is repeatedly called a tyrant, contrast with those of the archbishop, who is portrayed as steadfast and saintly. In the first image, on the left the enthroned Henry angrily orders Becket's family and followers into exile (fig. 6.8; see also fig. 2.8). His knights, brandishing swords, push and kick a group of people of varying ages out of the court. It is a chaotic scene as one of the knights climbs over a woman on the floor who clutches her baby. Here, Henry is akin to Herod, the biblical king who used violent force against his people.[31] On the right, Becket reclines sick in bed in Pontigny while he consults with a physician. As the text states, it is pious fasting and prayer that have made him ill, as well as the worry of his dispute with Henry. On the reverse of this folio, Pope Alexander III leaves France to return to Rome, embracing Becket as he departs (fig. 6.9). The following leaf shows two contrasting scenes. On the left, Becket preaches a sermon to the people in which he announces a sentence of excommunication against his enemies. On the right, the archbishop again stands before a group but this time he is arguing with Henry and Louis VII of France at the meeting at Montmirail, on 6 January 1169 (fig. 6.10; see also fig. 2.5). The anger of the kings is evident as they lean forward and remonstrate with him. Becket and the two monarchs are next depicted leaving on horseback, after these negotiations break down. It is this image, more than any other in the Leaves, that reveals how St Thomas was perceived in the thirteenth century (fig. 6.11). Twisting his body around towards Henry and Louis, Becket raises a single defiant finger which points towards the word 'beatus' (blessed) above his head. There can be little doubt of his righteous indignation. To the right-hand side, the archbishop is greeted by the common people, 'vulgus' as they are labelled, and, according to the text, it is for them he fights. This was a novel direction for his cult to take, especially since Becket's opposition to Henry had primarily been about defending ecclesiastical liberty. Here, he is shown fighting against the monarch for both Church and the wider public, who are his enthusiastic supporters.[32] Paris, writing at much the same time as the author of the Leaves, also considered Becket to be on the side of the people of England. In the *Chronica majora* he recounted the tale of a London priest who received a vision in which he saw a man dressed in archiepiscopal robes approach the new walls of the Tower of London, which had been recently erected in 1241 by Henry III.[33] The figure in the vision struck the stones with his staff, causing the walls to crumble to the ground. Clearly

6.8 (opposite top)
Henry II orders Becket's family into exile (left) and Becket reclines in bed (right), the Becket Leaves, *c*.1230–40. Vellum. 30.3 × 22.3 cm (folio). Private collection, f. 1r

6.9 (left)
Pope Alexander embraces Becket, the Becket Leaves, *c*.1230–40. Vellum. 30.3 × 22.3 cm (folio). Private collection, f. 1v

6.10 (opposite bottom)
Becket excommunicates his enemies (left) and Becket in conference with Henry II and Louis VII at Montmirail (right), the Becket Leaves, *c*.1230–40. Vellum. 30.3 × 22.3 cm (folio). Private collection, f. 2r

6.11 (left)
Becket leaves Henry and Louis on horseback, the Becket Leaves, *c*.1230–40. Vellum. 30.3 × 22.3 cm (folio). Private collection, f. 2v

6.12 (right)
Coronation of Henry the Young King (left) and Henry II presents a cup to the Young King at the coronation banquet, the Becket Leaves, *c.*1230–40. Vellum. 30.3 × 22.3 cm (folio). Private collection, f. 3r

6.13 (below right)
Becket receives news of the coronation (left) and sends a letter to Pope Alexander about it (right), the Becket Leaves, *c.*1230–40. Vellum. 30.3 × 22.3 cm (folio). Private collection, f. 3v

6.14 (opposite top)
Becket prepares to depart for England and is warned not to return by Milo, the agent of the Count of Boulogne, the Becket Leaves, *c.*1230–40. Vellum. 30.3 × 22.3 cm (folio). Private collection, f. 4r

6.15 (opposite bottom)
Becket lands at Sandwich, the Becket Leaves, *c.*1230–40. Vellum. 30.3 × 22.3 cm (folio). Private collection, f. 4v

terrified, the priest asked who the man was and a nearby clerk replied: 'it is St Thomas the martyr, a Londoner by birth, who considered these walls to be an insult and prejudice to Londoners and therefore irreparably destroyed them'.[34]

Following on from Henry and Becket's inability to repair their relationship at Montmirail, the next scene in the Leaves is the divisive coronation of Henry the Young King on 14 June 1170 (fig. 6.12; see also fig. 2.9). It was this single act that set the dispute alight and was presided over by Becket's arch enemy Roger de Pont l'Évêque, Archbishop of York, who is labelled in red ink to make him easy to identify. This image is coupled with a depiction of Henry II serving a cup to his son, the newly crowned Young King, at a celebratory banquet. After the coronation, Becket and Alexander III receive news of the event from messengers carrying letters bearing green-coloured seals (fig. 6.13). Denuded of his right to perform the coronation, Becket is spurred to action, and over the final two scenes he makes his way to England. In the first of these, as Becket prepares to depart, he is warned of the dangers that await him in England (fig. 6.14). In the second, he lands at Sandwich, Kent, on 1 December 1170, and is received by a crowd of people (fig. 6.15; see also fig. 2.10). However, not all are his supporters and the presence of two of the king's knights demonstrates that Becket's return was met with powerful opposition. Even without the final surviving pages of the Leaves it is not hard to predict how the story would have ended. Henry, so villainously portrayed, would no doubt have been implicated in the eventual murder of his archbishop. Without the earliest pages it is not clear how the author and illuminator of the Leaves chose to frame Becket's origins. Other accounts, however, reveal the inventiveness and creativity his biographers brought to bear on the legend of St Thomas.

Becket's parents and the story of the 'Saracen' princess

One curious silence in the documentary record was inventively filled by those who sought to tackle the backstory of Becket's parents, their meeting, marriage, and the conception and birth of Thomas. Although Gilbert and Matilda Becket were probably born in Normandy, possibly Rouen, in the late eleventh century, their history, like their son's, underwent a dramatic overhaul. The earliest story of their legendary meeting arose within a hundred years of the murder and can be found as an addition to Edward Grim's Latin version of the saint's life.[35] This became the definitive version, which was translated into the vernacular and, as with all aspects of Becket's cult, developed and

mutated over time. To create the legend, its inventors drew on a common stock of stories from medieval romances, troubadour songs and popular tales.[36] This provided Becket's origins with an air of familiarity for a public who were well versed in the romance genre. The meeting between Becket's parents was recast as a fantastical tale set in the Middle East. Matilda was reimagined as a 'Syrian' princess and Gilbert as a pious Londoner on Crusade who was captured in the Holy Land. Various elaborations exist – in one version it is not a 'Saracen' but a Jewish man who imprisons Gilbert, and in another Matilda is renamed as 'Alisaundre'.[37] However, the Saracen legend was immensely popular and seems to have become generally accepted as the legitimate history of Matilda and Gilbert's meeting.[38]

Although the legend appears in a variety of textual sources, only two visual depictions of the story are known. The first is contained within one of the most sumptuously illustrated manuscripts of the Middle Ages, called the Queen Mary Psalter, made in London around 1310–20, probably for a royal patron.[39] This deluxe book is a collection of lavishly decorated psalms intended to stir devotion in the mind of the beholder during prayer and worship. In contrast, the second series of images was created two hundred years later for a more public audience. These are stained-glass panels produced around 1525–37 for St Michael le Belfrey, a major civic parish church in York.[40] At some point, possibly in the 1580s, the glass was split up and part of the series was moved to York Minster's chapter house.[41] The images are some of the last of Becket to have been made before the English Reformation and demonstrate the vitality of Becket's cult well into the sixteenth century.[42] Evidently, the legend of the 'Saracen' princess was a key part of his ongoing popularity.

As the story goes, Gilbert took up the cross as part of a vow of penance and travelled to Jerusalem.[43] On arriving in the Holy Land he went to pray and was soon captured and imprisoned after leaving a church. After a year and a half his abductor recognised him as a man of talent and sought his advice on important matters, all the while keeping him imprisoned.[44] In a twist of fate the captor's beautiful daughter fell in love with his prisoner. Taking the opportunity of an illicit moment, she spoke with Gilbert and discovered him to be an Englishman from London. She went on to tell him that she desired to become both a Christian and his wife. Fearing that he was being deceived, Gilbert refused her and planned to escape. Along with his fellow captives, he broke free from his chains and fled to Christian-occupied territory. On hearing of Gilbert's escape, the daughter plotted her own flight and, relinquishing her wealth and inheritance, followed in his footsteps. Her journey to England was difficult, however, on account of her lack of English. A thirteenth-century version of the tale recorded that on arriving in England 'there the maiden was separated from her companions, with no other means of inquiring her way than by exclaiming, "London, London"'.[45] Without realising it, she passed by Gilbert's house but was tormented by a gang of boys in the street, until a servant who had been with Gilbert in the Holy Land recognised her and relayed the information of her presence to his stunned master. Not knowing what to do, Gilbert sought the advice of the Bishop of London, who was, coincidentally, speaking with five other bishops. Upon hearing the story, one of the bishops present declared that the woman's arrival was 'undoubtedly the work not of human but divine power, and that [she] would be the mother of a son whose sanctity and labours would elevate the Church, to the glory of Christ'.[46] All the bishops agreed that the couple should marry, but only once she had been baptised. The baptism took place the next day in St Paul's Cathedral under their supervision (fig. 6.16). Soon after, the two wed and Thomas was conceived. Gilbert, however, still harboured a desire to fight in the Holy Land and so left London only to return three years later to find Thomas now a small child (figs 6.17–6.18).

In 1518 or 1519 the Saracen legend took to the streets of London as part of a spectacular midsummer pageant sponsored by the Skinners' Company.[47] Records show that Thomas Bakehowse played Thomas Becket, Richard Mathewe his father, Gilbert, and Robert Hyndstock his mother, Matilda.[48] Carpenters were paid to construct and take apart Gilbert's prison, repair broken sets, hoist ladders and undertake general maintenance. There is even a record of 20d. paid to Hans for his role as a giant. Fantasy mixed with hagiography and the entire show was pulled through the streets on a horse-drawn carriage. It brought to life a legend close to the heart of many Londoners that was set four hundred years earlier in the very same streets. This was Becket's city and the pageant was a celebration of one of its greatest sons, paid for by one of its foremost civic institutions. His memory was part of the warp and weft of the cityscape. In the early days following the murder, Londoners accounted for the second largest number of visitors to his shrine after those from Kent.[49] In the city, the saint also worked miracles, such as that of Solomon, a one-hundred-year-old man who regained his sight and attributed the cure to St Thomas.[50] When the Mayor of London was inaugurated, a procession to St Paul's Cathedral began and ended at the site of Becket's birth and passed by what was considered to be the grave of his

6.16
Becket's mother is baptised by two bishops, detail in the Queen Mary Psalter, c.1310–20. Parchment codex. 27.5 × 17.5 cm (closed). British Library, London, Royal MS 2 B VII, f. 289r

parents in the churchyard.[51] In 1465 Václav Šašek, who was visiting England
from Bohemia, recalled a trip to the site where Becket was born, which was
by that time a chapel and part of Mercers Hall. In a written account of
his visit, he stated that he had seen what were supposed to be the tombs of
Becket's mother and sister.[52] Across the Thames, at Southwark, a hospital,
established in 1173, was dedicated to the saint. But he could be found on the
river too. London Bridge, arguably the most important architectural structure
in the city at the time, was built shortly after his martyrdom. The chapel at
the centre was funded through donations in Becket's memory and dedicated
to him.[53] Relics of the saint were present in many of London's parish
churches, and the entire city was under his special patronage. In 1219 a new
seal matrix was commissioned for London and shows St Thomas enthroned
on a giant rainbow above a panorama of the walled city (fig. 6.19).[54] To either

side of the saint is a group of figures representing the people of London. Its text declares: 'Cease not, Thomas, to protect me who brought you forth.'[55] In the minds of its citizens, London had given birth to Becket and now it was St Thomas who, in turn, protected them.

St Thomas and the rebels

Becket's status as London's patron underlined the independence of its inhabitants, serving as an additional warning that English rulers should exercise caution when dealing with them. This was true of others too. For centuries the memory of his defiance of Henry II simmered on the surface of English politics. His status as a figure of opposition to those in secular authority played out beyond the Church, and political adversaries of medieval kings were often likened to St Thomas. One of these was Simon de Montfort (*c.*1208–1265), who led a bloody rebellion against his brother-in-law Henry III in the 1260s.[56] Ultimately unsuccessful, he died on the battlefield at Evesham on 4 August 1265. For de Montfort's supporters his passing intertwined with the legacy of Becket's own, as expressed in a contemporary song: 'But by his death the Earl Montfort gained the victory,—like the martyr of Canterbury he finished his life;—the good Thomas would not suffer holy Church to perish,—the Earl fought in a similar cause, and died without flinching.—now is slain.'[57] Becket's memory was a historical cause to rally around, and in de Montfort's case, by adducing the similarities to St Thomas's own martyrdom, his supporters were able to charge a fledgling popular cult with the power of a more established model. It did not last, and although many miracles were attributed to de Montfort, he was never officially canonised.[58] Nearly sixty years later, in the case of another rebel, St Thomas once again came to the fore.

In March 1322, Thomas of Lancaster (*c.*1278–1322) was captured and executed for leading a rebellion against his cousin, Edward II.[59] Edward's favouritism towards several close advisers, particularly Piers Gaveston (1284–1312), had led to dissent from those who felt that the king's judgement was being unduly swayed. Factions formed and Thomas rose to lead the rebels. In the course of the dispute Thomas captured and executed Gaveston. This failed to quash ongoing problems at court, and after years of hostility royal forces seized Thomas and brought him to Edward at Pontefract Castle. Following what was effectively a mock trial, he was beheaded on a nearby hill and buried in the Priory of St John the Evangelist, Pontefract. Thomas's

6.19
Seal of the barons of London, *c.*1504. Wax. The National Archives, Kew, E329/428. The matrix from which this later impression was made was produced in 1219. The inscription around the edge reads '+ ME QVE TE PEPERI NE CESSES THOMA TVERI' (Cease not, Thomas, to protect me who brought you forth).

6.20
The martyrdoms of Thomas Becket (left) and Thomas of Lancaster (right), c.1330. Wall painting. Church of St Peter ad Vincula, South Newington, Oxfordshire

6.21 (opposite top)
Pilgrim badge showing the bust of Thomas of Lancaster inside an architectural frame, c.1330. Lead alloy. 9.2 × 5.7 cm. British Museum, London, 1859,1005.1. Donated by Rev C. G. Vernon Harcourt

6.22 (opposite bottom)
Pilgrim badge showing the beheading of Simon of Sudbury, c.1381. Lead alloy. 5.9 × 2.9 cm. British Museum, London, OA.4652

supporters looked to St Thomas to provide a model for his burgeoning political cult. For them, he had fought and died to oppose royal tyranny.[60] In the moments before his death he had even prayed to St Thomas.[61] Soon pilgrims made their way to Pontefract and stories began to circulate of miracles taking place at the site of his murder. Several were attributed to his blood, a clear connection to the central role of the same substance in Becket's cult.[62] One drop of this miraculous fluid restored the sight of a blind priest and Thomas of Lancaster's own tomb was said to have secreted blood.[63]

Representations of the execution can be found in a number of medieval manuscripts, often near to an image of Becket's martyrdom.[64] A wall painting of the two, shown side by side, is in the Church of St Peter ad Vincula, South Newington, Oxfordshire (fig. 6.20). The artist took care to portray the extremely violent nature of their deaths, emphasising the power of the blood that flowed from their wounds.[65] A number of lead-alloy badges, likely sold at Pontefract, portray Thomas of Lancaster's beheading and probably derive from similar images of Becket's death (fig. 6.21).[66] Thomas was also celebrated in London, where pilgrims visited his effigy in St Paul's Cathedral and could buy lead-alloy badges of the murder scene, as well as large, detailed plaques depicting a narrative of his life and death.[67] Edward II attempted to ban devotion of this sort, but, like Becket's cult, Thomas's grew stronger in the face of early royal opposition.[68] This quickly changed and, five years later, the new king, Edward III – who, unlike his father, was favourably disposed to Thomas's claims – petitioned the Pope to canonise him, but was unsuccessful.[69] Despite never receiving a sanctioned sainthood, his cult, unlike de Montfort's, continued to be popular until the English Reformation. He also found broad support among the English elite, who noted the connection between his death and that of Becket.[70] Humphrey de Bohun (1309–1361), who had known him personally, made provision in his will for 'a good and loyal man to go to Canterbury and there offer for us forty shillings of silver. And another such man to go to Pontefract and offer there at the tomb of Thomas formerly count of Lancaster forty shillings.'[71]

The continued vitality of Becket's legend can be traced through the visual and textual threads that link the memory of his murder with those of rebels such as Simon de Montfort and Thomas of Lancaster. Other English political 'saints' – none were ever officially canonised – including Simon Sudbury, Archbishop of Canterbury (c.1316–1381), Richard Scrope, Archbishop of York (c.1350–1405) and even King Henry VI (1421–1471), are in some way part of the same continuum.[72] Unlike Becket, Sudbury was not an opponent of the king, but was beheaded by rebels outside the Tower of London during the 1381 Peasants' Revolt. Public anger towards Sudbury stemmed from the perception of his role in levying an unpopular poll tax.[73] He had powerful supporters who encouraged his cult, and lead-alloy badges, probably depicting his murder, have surfaced in London, suggesting they were made for sale near the site of the event (fig. 6.22).[74] John Gower (c.1325–1408), writing in the wake of the events of 1381, composed an epic poem called *Vox clamantis* (*The Voice of One Crying Out*). In it he stresses the similarities between Becket and Sudbury, but acknowledges the vastly different circumstances of their deaths: 'Each of the righteous men suffered undeservedly'.[75] Sudbury was buried at Canterbury and his tomb, located at the foot of the steps leading to Becket's shrine, was fitted with niches allowing pilgrims to kneel down and pray near his body.[76] The proximity of Sudbury's tomb to the shrine explicitly makes the connection between the two, but despite receiving political support Sudbury's cult never took off.[77] Nonetheless, the ease with which images associated with Thomas of Lancaster, or Simon Sudbury, may be confused with those of Becket's own death demonstrates how closely aligned their cults were considered to be. Despite inspiring countless imitators, St Thomas and his shrine at Canterbury proved to be a force that no other English saint was able to match, both in terms of its sustained longevity and its grip on the popular imagination.

'From every shires ende'

By the time Geoffrey Chaucer (*c.*1340–1400) composed the General Prologue to *The Canterbury Tales*, Becket's status as a major European saint was beyond question. Over two hundred years had passed since his murder, including four jubilee celebrations, the most recent taking place in 1370. His renown had eclipsed that of St Edmund the Martyr, St Edward the Confessor and St Cuthbert, and all across Europe he was the saint most associated with England. Although the vast majority of visitors to Canterbury were English pilgrims, it was a convenient port of call for many European travellers on their way to London. As foreign visitors continued to come to England in search of St Thomas, his cult in turn made itself felt abroad.[2] This internationalism was a core part of his enduring legacy: German merchants who did business with their English colleagues commissioned altarpieces of the saint's life for their city churches (fig. 7.1). These can be found in important mercantile centres on the Baltic coast such as Hamburg, Tettens and Wismar (see fig. 3.9).[3] They were no doubt aware of St Thomas's role as a patron of international commerce and trade via his connection with the English Merchant Adventurers, who operated in the Low Countries and even had an image of Becket engraved on their seal. It shows St Thomas standing in the middle of a ship set on a calm sea (fig. 7.2).[4] For over three

Thanne longen folk to goon on pilgrimages,
And palmeres for to seken straunge strondes,
To ferne halwes, kowthe in sondry londes;
An specially from every shires ende
Of Engelond to Caunterbury they wende,
The hooly blisful martir for to seke
The hem hath holpen whan that they were seeke.[1]

Geoffrey Chaucer, *The Canterbury Tales*, c.1388–1400

7.1
Master Francke, *The Martyrdom of Thomas Becket*, from the Thomas-Altar, c.1426. Tempera and oil on panel. 91.8 × 81.5 cm. Hamburger Kunsthalle, HK-492

7.2
Seal matrix of the English
Merchant Adventurers
showing St Thomas of
Canterbury in a ship,
late 15th century. Copper
alloy. Diam. 4.4 cm.
British Museum, London,
1880,0624.1. The Latin
legend on this seal reads:
'SIGILLU : ANGLICOR IN
FLANDRIA : BRABANCIA :
HOLLANDRIA: ZEELADIA :
M'CAT' (Seal of English
merchants in Flanders,
Brabant, Holland and
Zealand).

hundred and fifty years the shrine of St Thomas was at the heart of a
dynamic cult that drew in pilgrims from across Europe. What they saw when
they arrived at Canterbury impressed them beyond belief.

Chaucer, Becket and medieval pilgrimage

In *The Canterbury Tales* Chaucer brings to life a group of fictional pilgrims,
situating them at the outset of their springtime trip to Becket's shrine.
It begins with a prologue, set in Southwark, at the Tabard Inn, where
the characters spend the night before making their way to Canterbury.
Chaucer conveys their excitement as they dine merrily together. The
Tabard's innkeeper, Harry Bailly, who himself joins the pilgrimage, exclaims
enthusiastically: 'Ye goon to Caunterbury – God yow speede,/ The blissful
martir quite yow youre meede [give you your reward]!'[5] However, the poem
is not a detailed account of their journey or of the sites they encounter, but
a diverse series of tales told as part of a contest, by each in turn to pass the
time. Chaucer did not finish his work, and so the pilgrims never actually
reach the cathedral. After leaving Southwark the travellers go east, towards
Dartford and Strood, passing through Harbledown before arriving at the city
walls of Canterbury.[6] Like London, the city of Canterbury inevitably became
entwined with Becket's cult and adopted the image of his martyrdom for its
seal (fig. 7.3). As Chaucer's text remained incomplete, other medieval authors
wrote continuations. In one manuscript the tales are arranged as a two-way
journey, with an episode inserted in the middle, detailing the pilgrims arriving
at Canterbury.[7] This episode, known as the 'Canterbury Interlude', or the
Prologue to the *Tale of Beryn*, takes the pilgrims into the cathedral and around
Becket's shrine. There they marvel at the stained-glass windows, which prove
difficult to interpret for some of the more boisterous members of the group:

> The Knyghte went with his compers toward the holy shryne
> To do that they were com fore, and after for to dyne.
> The Pardoner and the Miller and other lewde sotes
> Sought hemselff in the chirch, right as lewd gotes [goats],
> Pyred fast [looked intently] and poured [peered] highe oppon the glase.[8]

At the time of Becket's death Christian pilgrimage, which had
been taking place since the early Middle Ages, was a well-established

phenomenon.[9] Many of the major pilgrimage routes were clearly defined, and spanned Europe and the Near East. Physical access to a holy relic or site of special religious significance was the goal of every pilgrim. This included body parts, burial sites, wells and caves, rocks, dust, blood, milk, miraculous hosts and even contact relics like clothing or footprints.[10] Becket's clothing was highly prized and a number of European church treasuries still display textiles claimed to have been worn by him, including Sens Cathedral, where he was in exile, Fermo Cathedral in the Marche region of Italy and the Basilica of Santa Maria Maggiore in Rome.[11]

Ancient sites, especially those associated with Christ, the Virgin Mary or the apostles, had an elevated status. In Jerusalem a pilgrim could visit Christ's tomb; in Rome the body of St Peter; in Compostela the body of St James; and in Amiens the skull of St John the Baptist. Like Becket's relics, the body parts of other saints were often held in sumptuous caskets crafted out of precious materials by highly skilled smiths.[12] Reasons for going on pilgrimage varied: the journey was an act of religious devotion, but might also be undertaken in fulfilment of a vow; to seek a cure for illness; simply to experience long-distance travel; or to do penance for a sin. In some cases the journey was taken on behalf of another, often posthumously, as a kind of pilgrimage by proxy.[13] For instance, in 1415 Thomas, Earl of Arundel (1381–1415), provided in his will for 'William Ryman, or another in my name, [to] go with all possible haste after my passage from this light on foot from London in pilgrimage to St Thomas of Canterbury.'[14] Another major draw for pilgrims was the chance to see otherworldly works of art, such as stained-glass windows, wall paintings or fabulous reliquaries, in which churches invested heavily.[15] The journey was, at times, an act of physical exertion with long stretches of walking but, depending on the destination and the pilgrim's wealth, some sections might be undertaken on horseback or by boat.[16] By the 1390s there was a two-stage pilgrim horse relay from Southwark to Canterbury, costing four shillings for a return journey.[17] Travel could be dangerous and pilgrims needed to be careful. In 1322 Walter Botereaux and his companions were physically assaulted and robbed on their way to Canterbury.[18] It is perhaps for this reason that a number of Chaucer's characters are armed: the Reeve 'baar a rusty blade',[19] and, as for the Miller, 'a swerd and bokeler [small shield] bar he by his syde'.[20] Trouble along the way could even lead to a pilgrim being jailed: in 1285 William de Faccumbe was pardoned for the death of Peter de Cumpton, whom he killed by 'misadventure' en route to Becket's shrine.[21]

7.3
City seal of Canterbury, 1492. Wax. Canterbury Cathedral Archives and Library, CCA-DCc/ChAnt/C/1154. The matrix from which this later impression was made was produced in the 13th century.

Pilgrimage united diverse groups of people from different backgrounds and countries of origin. Becket's appeal was widespread and he was popular from Sweden to Scotland and well beyond.[22] In the late twelfth century, around twenty-five years after Becket had been made a saint, Hrafn Sveinbjarn travelled from Iceland and offered two walrus tusks at Becket's tomb.[23] Over two hundred years later in 1415, Wytfrid, son of Juari, also made the journey from Iceland, and turned up in Canterbury with silver and sixty barrels of cod to give to Becket's shrine, claiming to be a descendant of St Thomas.[24] Pilgrimage was also a central part of the performative aspect of medieval kingship, in which displays of charity and piety were essential in communicating a benevolent majesty.[25] From Henry II to Henry VIII (1174–1538) each King of England visited St Thomas's shrine. Most made the trip more than once, and some, like Edward III (1312–1377), made the journey annually throughout their reign.[26] Royal devotees from abroad included King John II of France (1319–1364) and Holy Roman Emperors Sigismund (1368–1437) and Charles V (1500–1558), their visits a sign of the high esteem in which St Thomas was held internationally.[27]

Some pilgrims took to the life as a professional activity, relying on charity and the goodwill of others to get by. Their clothing and behaviour made them easy to identify. Wearing black hats with upturned brims and rosary beads around their necks, and carrying walking sticks, a group of figures from a painting called *The Seven Works of Mercy* are quintessential models of what a good pilgrim should be (fig. 7.4).[28] Pinned to their caps are lead-alloy badges, each one from a specific place, serving as a visual marker of where they have been. The scallop shells and crossed keys tell us that they have visited Compostela and Rome. Chaucer's Pardoner, who had just returned from Rome himself, is distinguished by a vernicle badge showing St Veronica's veil, which he 'sowed upon his cappe'.[29]

Chaucer's pilgrims

Chaucer provides a lively description of the various social positions, origins, dress and manners of his pilgrims. They are from a relatively broad cross section of society, although only three of the group are women. Among the pilgrims are a Knight, a Yeoman, a Prioress, a Merchant, a Shipman and a Ploughman. While Chaucer's pilgrims are fictional and intended to be comedic characters, they represent the kinds of people who went on

7.4
Master of Alkmaar, *The Seven Works of Mercy* (detail), 1504. Oil on panel. 103.5 × 56.8 cm. Rijksmuseum, Amsterdam, SK-A-2815

7.5

The Wife of Bath in Geoffrey Chaucer's *Collected Works Including the Canterbury Tales*, c.1400–25. Vellum. 18 × 15.8 cm. Cambridge University Library, MS Gg.4.27, f. 222r. Several portraits of Chaucer's pilgrims are included in this manuscript. Many of them, like the Wife of Bath, carry a whip and are shown riding a horse. This image appears between the end of her prologue and the start of the tale. The volume, containing many of Chaucer's works besides the *Canterbury Tales*, is one of the earliest attempts to collect his poetry into a single anthology. It was possibly made in East Anglia but its first owners are unknown. Before 1600 it somehow came into the possession of the lawyer and antiquarian Joseph Holland (d. 1605).

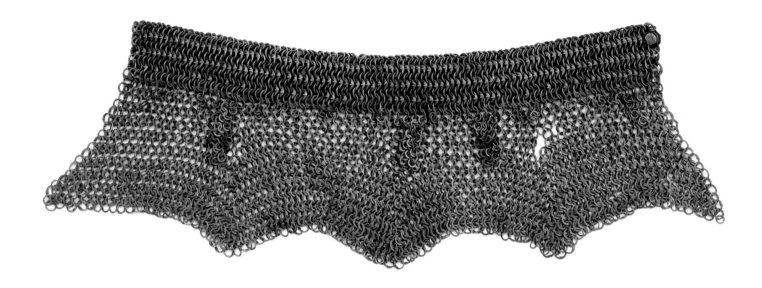

pilgrimage during the later Middle Ages.[30] The wealthier members of the group were more likely to have the resources to go on pilgrimages abroad, whereas local and national journeys were accessible to a wider range of people. In the 1430s, a few decades after Chaucer wrote *The Canterbury Tales*, Margery Kempe (*c.*1373–after 1438), a middle-class business owner from King's Lynn, Norfolk, recorded her numerous trips throughout Europe and the Near East.[31] She visited the Holy Land, Rome, Assisi, Santiago de Compostela, Gdańsk and many other places, including Canterbury.[32] Like Kempe, Chaucer's character Alison, the Wife of Bath, travelled widely: 'At Rome she hadde been, and at Boloigne,/ In Galice at Seint-Jame, and at Coloigne' (fig. 7.5).[33] Chaucer lived in various parts of London, as well as Kent, but often travelled abroad and probably encountered many pilgrims like Margery.[34] His description of each individual character adds to the overall picture of an internationally connected group and conveys their material world. His well-travelled Knight ('At Alisaundre [Alexandria] he was whan it was wonne') is dressed in clothing stained by battle: 'Of fustian he wered a gypon/ Al bismotered with his habergeon [he wore a fustian tunic/ all stained by rust from his coat of mail]' (fig. 7.6).[35] Clad in imported furs, the Merchant, who traded overseas, might well have carried coins from the Burgundian Netherlands and a scale to weigh and prove the true value of his currency: 'Wel koude he in eschaunge sheeldes selle' (a 'sheeld' was a medieval unit of exchange).[36] Chaucer's Shipman, on the other hand, is an experienced sailor who 'knew alle the havenes, as they were/ Fro Gootland to the cape of

7.6
Mail collar, *c.*1350. Iron and copper alloy. 26 × 67 cm. British Museum, London, 1856,0701.2244. Discovered near Moorgate Street, London.

Fynystere/ And every cryke in Britaigne and in Spayne'.[37] As an accomplished navigator he probably used scientific instruments, like astrolabes or quadrants, for calculating the position of the stars relative to the horizon: 'But of his craft to rekene [skill to reckon] wel his tydes,/ His stremes, and his daungers hym bisides,/ His herberwe [harbours], and his moone, his lodemenage [navigation skills],/ Ther nas noon swich from Hulle to Cartage' (fig. 7.7).[38]

Beyond these broad international connections, Chaucer further provides us with a sense of the pilgrims' individual personalities through the objects they wear or carry. His Prioress had 'A peire of bedes, gauded al with grene,/ And theron heng a brooch of gold ful sheene,/ On which ther was first write a crowned A,/ And after *Amor vincit omnia* [Love conquers all]'.[39] Various pieces of medieval jewellery carry the motto 'Love conquers all' and were probably given as affectionate tokens of love, but here, in the hands of a prioress, the brooch raises questions about her past (fig. 7.8).[40] Similarly, Chaucer provides his Yeoman with 'A Cristofre on his brest of silver shene'.[41] Such a silver-gilt brooch of St Christopher, although a little later in date, was found at Kingston upon Thames, a few miles upriver from where the pilgrims began their journey at the Tabard Inn (fig. 7.9). It is fitting that Chaucer's Yeoman wore a brooch of this saint as he was the patron of safe travel and provided protection to those on the move. There is, however, more to it. Perhaps the Yeoman, and indeed the Prioress too, planned to donate their precious objects in thanksgiving to Becket's shrine. In the 'Canterbury Interlude', when the pilgrims arrived at the cathedral they went 'To pas and to wend [go], to make hir offringes/ Righte as hir devocioune was, of sylver broch and rynges'.[42] At Hereford Cathedral in 1307, '116 gold and silver rings and brooches' were left at the shrine of St Thomas de Cantilupe.[43] Likewise, donations to Becket's shrine included numerous coins, rings, brooches and even individual jewels, many of which were applied to the casket itself.[44]

Pilgrims and Canterbury Cathedral

Once inside the cathedral, pilgrims were able to visit four principal sites associated with Becket: his shrine in the Trinity Chapel; the skull relic in the Corona Chapel; the altar of the Martyrdom, and his former tomb in the crypt (see fig. 4.2 for a floor plan of the cathedral).[45] There was no set route and pilgrims could, within reason and depending on the activities of the clergy, make their own way round depending on their status – VIP guests

7.7
Astrolabe, 1326. Copper alloy. Diam. 13.2 cm. British Museum, London, 1909,0617.1. This instrument is the earliest datable English astrolabe.

7.8
Annular brooch, 14th century. Gold. Diam. 1.5cm. British Museum, London, AF.2687. Bequeathed by Sir Augustus Wollaston Franks. It is inscribed with 'AMOR VINCIT OMNIA' (Love conquers all).

were usually given a personal guide. By the fourteenth century it seems that the majority of visitors first made their way to the shrine itself and then proceeded to other destinations within the church. They probably entered through the south porch, moved up the aisle of the nave, and then passed through the south aisle of the choir and into the shrine area.[46] Most pilgrims were not, however, left entirely to their own devices, and access to certain areas in the church was carefully controlled. After all, Canterbury Cathedral was primarily a working monastery and the monks' focus was on performing the Divine Office. A document from 1428, called the 'Customary of the Shrine of St Thomas', describes its administration in detail.[47] In the Trinity Chapel there were four full-time custodians comprising two monks, one called the 'spiritual' and the other the 'temporal', and two clerks.[48] Visitors were allowed into the space earlier in summer months than in winter, 5am as opposed to 6am, in order to make best use of the changing light. The dance of morning sun throughout the building, diffused by multicoloured stained glass and illuminating the polished columns at the east end, must have been an immense sight for the pilgrims to behold. At this time the doors were opened and a bell was rung three times inviting people in. One of the cathedral bells, given in 1316 by Prior Henry Eastry, weighed 8,000 pounds and was called Bell Thomas in honour of Becket.[49]

Each morning, after the 'spiritual' shrine-keeper had performed confession alone, he celebrated a special Mass, assisted by the 'temporal', at the altar of St Thomas's shrine, which pilgrims were expected to attend.[50] Numerous candles were lit, both the shrine and the altar were blessed, and the space was filled with perfume and smoke from a swinging censer held aloft by a dutiful clerk. An impression of this event is given by a Florentine merchant, who recorded his visit to Canterbury in 1444: 'in fact we arrived just when Mass was being said at the altar of St Thomas which, with the candles and those jewels and so great a quantity of gold it seemed as if Paradise was opening up'.[51] Around midday the gates around the shrine were locked, but before this it was thoroughly searched, with one keeper instructed to remain at the site at all times to prevent theft. Certain days of the week were of importance, particularly Tuesdays, which were special to Becket's cult: his birth, death, translation, and a number of other important events all took place on that day.[52] In addition to facilitating access to the shrine, the custodians had to manage the behaviour of the pilgrims. In the 'Canterbury Interlude' a shrine-keeper, described as a 'goodly monke', advises the pilgrims in their devotion:

7.9
Brooch of St Christopher,
15th century. Silver-gilt.
H. 7.8 cm. British Museum,
London, 1900,0719.1.

7.10

John Carter, *The Martyrdom of Thomas Becket*, 1786. Hand-coloured engraving. 40 × 23.2 cm. National Portrait Gallery, London, NPG D23960. The original painting, from which Carter made his copy, still survives at Canterbury Cathedral, but it is now in a damaged state. It was made to hang behind the tomb of Henry IV and Joan of Navarre, opposite another painting of the Assumption of the Virgin Mary.

Then passed they forth boystly [boisterously], goglyng with hir hedes,

Kneled adown tofore the shryne, and hertlich hir bedes [rosaries]

They preyed to Seynt Thomas, in such wise [ways] as they couth
[knew how].

And sith [then] the holy relikes ech man with his mowth

Kissed, as a goodly monke the names told and taught.[53]

Becket's shrine thus played a significant role in the day-to-day running of Canterbury Cathedral and was factored into its yearly plans. Given the number of pilgrims and the value of donations taken, this is entirely understandable; it was the main draw for visitors. Over time other objects and locations inside the cathedral became linked with St Thomas, such as his hair shirt, a sculpture of the Virgin Mary with which Becket was said to have conversed, and a well from which pilgrims could drink, whose waters turned first into milk and then into blood.[54] In 1465 Gabriel Tetzel of Nuremberg (1426–1479), a companion of Leo of Rozmital (c.1425–1486), a Bohemian traveller who undertook a long journey through Europe, stopped in Canterbury and recorded his impression of some of these sites:

Beneath the shrine is the spot where the beloved St Thomas was beheaded, and above the shrine hangs a coarse hair shirt which he wore, and to the left, as one approaches, there is a spring from which St Thomas drank daily. During St Thomas's lifetime it changed five times into milk and blood. My lord Lev and all his servants drank of it. Afterwards one goes into a small crypt-like chapel where St Thomas was martyred. They show the sword with which his head was struck off. … From the chapel one goes to a stone chair with the picture of our Lady which often conversed with St Thomas.[55]

The spring described by Tetzel was depicted in a painting from the early fifteenth century, made to hang at the head of Henry IV and Joan of Navarre's tomb. The original painting is now severely damaged but an antiquarian copy, produced in the late eighteenth century by John Carter, helps to suggest what has been lost (fig. 7.10). Carter unintentionally darkened the image of the spring, which appears on the step between St Thomas and one of the knights, where Becket's blood drips down; his error transformed what was once the swirling mass of clear spring water to a pool of red.[56]

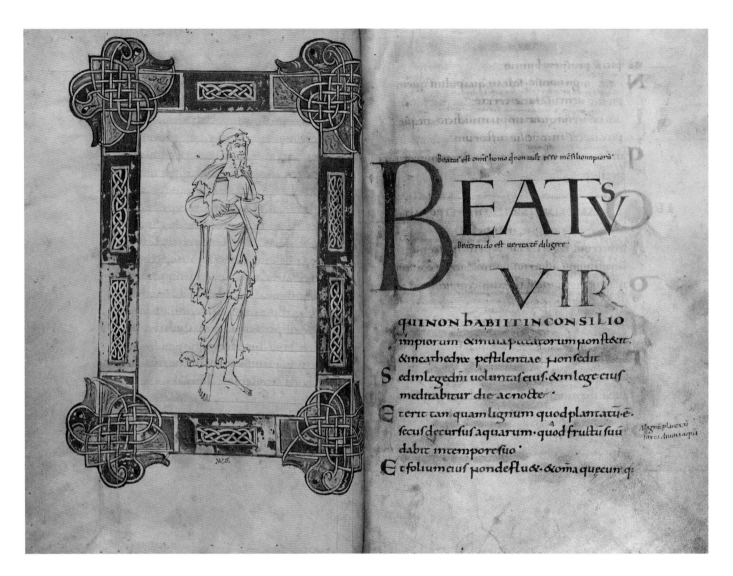

7.11
Psalter, late 10th–early
11th century. Vellum. 21 ×
14.5 cm. Parker Library,
Corpus Christi College,
Cambridge, MS 411,
ff. 1v–2r. On the left is
a line drawing of an
unknown man at the
centre of a decorative
border. To the right the
book is open at the
beginning of the Psalms.

7.12
Detail of a 16th-century
inscription from the
psalter. Parker Library,
Corpus Christi College,
Cambridge, MS 411, f. 140v.
This inscription records the
binding of the psalter in the
Middle Ages. It further claims
that this book was previously
owned by two archbishops
of Canterbury, one of whom
was Thomas Becket.

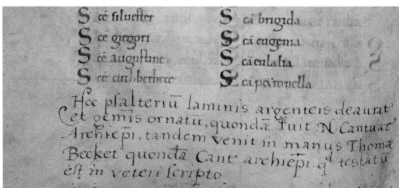

High-status guests such as Tetzel and Rozmital were granted access to the most important sites and were taken round by a guide.[57] The same was true of the visit of Desiderius Erasmus of Rotterdam (1467–1536), who had a letter of introduction from the Archbishop of Canterbury. Erasmus, a peripatetic priest, polymath and humanist of extraordinary scholarly breadth, who advocated simple piety based on the Bible, framed his visit to the cathedral as an exaggerated satire of a pilgrimage. He gives an evocative description of the interior of the cathedral, written the decade before the destructive consequences of the English Reformation changed it for ever. According to Erasmus, near to the tomb in the crypt were 'the hair shirts, the girdles, and bandages, with which that prelate subdued his flesh; striking horror with their very appearance, and reproaching us for our indulgences and our luxuries.'[58] He was also shown various relics, including the sword-point, which he was invited to kiss: 'the sacred rust of this iron, in love of the martyr, we religiously kissed'.[59]

From the broken sword-point to St Thomas's hair shirt, there were a number of objects said to have been owned or used by him, or connected to him, which carried a relic-like status. At the altar of the Martyrdom was a gold ring that was believed to have belonged to the saint.[60] Set with a sapphire, it was offered to pilgrims, most likely to kiss, and was said to help those suffering from problems with their eyes.[61] A manuscript, probably made at Canterbury Cathedral in the early eleventh century, now at Corpus Christi College, Cambridge, contains a sixteenth-century inscription in Latin stating that it was owned by Thomas Becket (figs 7.11–7.12).[62] The text further states that the book was originally contained within a silver-gilt binding, covered with precious gems, all of which have since been lost. Recently, the significance of the inscription, previously thought to be an antiquarian folly, has been re-evaluated. An identical passage was found in a fourteenth-century inventory, made by the sacristan of the cathedral, suggesting that by this time, at least, the manuscript was associated with Thomas Becket and his cult.

Donations to Becket

On arriving at the cathedral it was customary to make a gift to St Thomas in thanksgiving, especially if the pilgrimage had been undertaken in fulfilment of a vow. The cathedral treasurers' accounts provide evidence for the takings at the principal shrines throughout the church.[63] What remains is patchy and incomplete, but they give an overview of the economic impact of Becket's cult. Between 1198 and 1213 Becket's tomb took £309 but this was nothing compared to the £702 received at the main shrine in 1220.[64] Repairs and new work are also described: £115 was spent in 1313 to purchase gold and precious stones for the reliquary bust of St Thomas, displayed in the Corona Chapel.[65]

Donations were at their greatest during Becket's jubilee years, with £500 taken at the shrine in 1320 and £466 in 1370.[66] In those years, papal indulgences for the remission of sin were granted for visiting pilgrims, which no doubt encouraged many travellers from across Europe.[67] The treasurers' accounts end around 1380, but other documentary sources, including the priors' account rolls, fill in the gaps. In 1420, the fifth jubilee, £360 was collected at the shrine. This was apparently an immense year in terms of the number of pilgrims who visited, estimated to be over 100,000.[68] The number was probably an exaggeration, but was still a sign of the many who came to Canterbury that year. Over the course of the fifteenth century there appears to be a drop in overall donations, an indicator of changing accounting practices, and not necessarily evidence of Becket's cult in decline.[69] Still, only £10 was recorded in 1453 at the shrine, a measly amount compared to the sums taken in the previous centuries. At this time there was a national turn towards local saints, such as Richard Caister of St Stephen's, Norwich, or John Schorne of North Marston, Buckinghamshire, and as a result most major shrines saw fewer pilgrims.[70] Nonetheless, the records still demonstrate several significant donations from devotees of St Thomas. One was from the cathedral's plumber, a man called John Brun, who in 1434 donated 'one pair of beads to the value of £10 of purest gold'.[71]

The extraordinary volume of material donations to Becket's shrine explains why it made such an impression on those who visited, including Tetzel, who stated: 'The coffin wherein St Thomas lies is all of gold and is long and broad, large enough for a middling-sized person to lie in it. It is so richly adorned with pearls and precious stones that one would think there is no richer shrine in all Christendom.'[72] Precious metals were part of the material landscape of medieval pilgrimage: valuable coins, for instance, were sometimes folded in half in the promise of a future journey to a saint's shrine, and were probably later donated in thanks.[73] In 1465 Lady Margaret Aske left instructions in her will that a pilgrim should go to the shrine of 'the blessed Thomas archbishop of Canterbury and there offer on my behalf one *salut* of gold'.[74] In 1300 King Edward I (1239–1307) offered a gold florin to St Thomas on behalf of his queen, Margaret of France (c.1279–1318), to protect her during pregnancy.[75]

Among the more dazzling gifts were those from royalty; Edward also donated silver statues of St George, St Edmund and a pilgrim, worth £347 combined.[76] Henry V (1386–1422) gave a golden head of St Thomas and a pair of gold candlesticks.[77] Henry VII (1457–1509) requested that a silver-gilt image of himself with the inscription 'Sancte Thomae, intercede pro me' (St Thomas, intercede for me) be set as close to the shrine as possible.[78] Gifts like these had special significance and the stories of their donation were retold by the monks to countless pilgrims. Erasmus records that 'the Prior with a white rod pointed out each jewel, telling its name in French, its value, and the name of its donor; for the principal of them were offerings sent by sovereign princes'.[79] One of the most famous of these tales is connected to the 1179 visit of Louis VII of France,[80] which Tetzel was told by a custodian at the shrine:

> Once upon a time a King of France made a vow on the field of battle. He defeated his enemies and came to the Cathedral and to [the shrine of] the holy St Thomas. He knelt at the shrine and prayed and had a ring on his hand, in which was a very precious stone. The Bishop of the cathedral at Canterbury begged the King to give the ring with the stone to the shrine. The King replied that the ring was too dear to him, since he believed firmly that whatever he undertook would not miscarry so long as he had the ring on his hand. But in order that the shrine might be better adorned he would give it 100,000 florins. … But no sooner had the King spoken those words, and had refused to give the ring to the Bishop, than the stone sprang forthwith from the ring and embedded itself in the shrine as if it had been placed there by a goldsmith. … No one knows what the stone is. It has a clear glistening brilliance and burns with such a bright light that no one can bear to examine it closely, so as to distinguish its colour.[81]

The story of Louis's donation of the Regale is most likely a later creation but it was a powerful one and was certainly widely believed in the Middle Ages.[82] It demonstrates how objects associated with Becket's shrine were mythologised, much like his legend (the 'Saracen' story), and contributed to the continued dynamism of his cult. At the heart of the matter was the deep rooted connection between Canterbury Cathedral and St Thomas. Becket's murder and the sites connected to him were a key part of the cathedral's identity. From 1234 a scene of the saint's death was included as the primary image, engraved on its institutional seal (fig. 7.13). As Tetzel's description

7.13
Cast of the reverse of the third seal of Canterbury Cathedral, c.1234. Plaster. Society of Antiquaries, London. Becket's martyrdom can be seen taking place inside the central doorway of the church depicted. Above, his soul is guided upwards by angels, towards the Trinity holding a crown of martyrdom. The Latin legend reads: '+EST HVIC VITA MORI PRO QVA DVM VIXIT AMORI/MORS ERAT ET MEMORIE PER MORTEM VIVIT HONORI' (Death is life to this one, which, when he lived for love,/ Meant death; through death he lives to honour and memorial).

shows, the Trinity Chapel had come to function as a site of self-reflective mythologising on the part of the priory.[83] It was a place for the public to interact with the cathedral's history, facilitated through objects, chief among them Becket's shrine itself. In other institutions such myth-making was achieved through great wooden tablets, called tabulae, comprising parchment pasted onto large boards.[84] These were displayed publicly and served as a guide to the institution's history. None remain for Canterbury, but it is likely they once existed and would have resembled the surviving set of tablets from Glastonbury Abbey.

Wax and light

Apart from coins, gems and jewellery, pilgrims to Becket's shrine also left more ephemeral offerings. Wax candles were among the most frequently recorded donations.[85] Henry II's annual gift of £40, begun in 1174, was probably used for candles to light Becket's tomb.[86] The Customary is peppered with references to the burning of candles, and on occasions the entire Trinity Chapel must have been flooded with flickering light.[87] On the cathedral's principal feast days twelve candles were kept continuously lit on a beam above St Thomas's shrine.[88] Medieval authors used light as a metaphor to describe the saint: Becket was routinely called the 'Lamp of England' by both Benedict of Peterborough and William of Canterbury.[89] Those who chose to donate a candle did so as a material reminder of their presence at the shrine, or of their particular devotion. These often came in the form of a coiled wax candle, called a trindle, that burned for a long period of time. However, images in wax known as *ex-votos* were probably the most popular item donated, as they were at shrines across the rest of England.[90] In 1307, at Hereford Cathedral, '129 images of men or their limbs in silver, 1,424 in wax' were left by pilgrims at the shrine of St Thomas Cantilupe.[91] An indication of what this might have looked like can be seen in a stained-glass panel at York Minster showing a pilgrim giving a wax leg to the shrine of St William of York (fig. 7.14). Fragile wax figures such as this rarely survive, although a small group dating to the fifteenth or early sixteenth century were found at Exeter Cathedral in 1943 and include models of a praying woman, various body parts and a horse's head (fig 7.15).[92] It was common for *ex-votos* of animals to be presented too, and in 1286 Edward I gave a wax image of his sick falcon to St Thomas's shrine.[93]

Royal tombs

The area surrounding Becket's shrine changed markedly over time, not least through the introduction of royal and archiepiscopal tombs, which altered how pilgrims would have perceived and interacted with the space. Before the fourteenth century, a monument to Archbishop Hubert Walter was the only one of its kind permitted in the Trinity Chapel.[94] Around the time of the Black Death of 1349, pilgrims visited Canterbury in unprecedented numbers, giving a financial boost to the cathedral and, in the decades that followed, new tombs were allowed near the shrine.[95] William Courtenay (1341/2–1396) was the first archbishop since Walter to be buried there, probably at the request of Richard II, but two royal tombs were also added: Edward of Woodstock, now known as the Black Prince (1330–1376), and

7.14
Stained-glass panel showing a pilgrim offering a wax votive of a leg at the shrine of St William of York, c.1414. St William window, York Minster, window N7 22b

7.15
Votive in the shape of a woman praying, 15th or early 16th century. Wax. H. 20 cm (approx.). Exeter Cathedral Library and Archives

7.16
The tomb of the Black Prince,
c.1376. Trinity Chapel, Canterbury
Cathedral

the combined monument to Henry IV, King of England (1367–1413), and his queen Joan of Navarre (c.1368–1437) (figs 7.16–7.17). Since the reign of Henry III, Westminster Abbey, like St-Denis for the kings of France, was the desired resting place for senior members of the English royal family.[96] When the Black Prince chose to be buried at Canterbury Cathedral, no English royal had ever been interred there. He was no lesser member of the family, however. Widely seen as a chivalric hero, his fame derived from dramatic victories won in the Hundred Years' War, most notably at Poitiers, where he had captured the French king John II. He was the eldest son of Edward III, brother of John of Gaunt, and father of Richard II. The Black Prince had been devoted to Canterbury for his entire life, and although he had requested burial in the crypt, his gilded metal effigy was placed next to Becket's shrine, probably to encourage visitors to come and see the tomb of a national hero, and to boost overall donations.[97]

Henry IV, on the other hand, was the first English king since Edward II (1284–1327) to be buried away from Westminster Abbey. After usurping the throne from his cousin Richard II (1367–1400) he had a troubled reign. Henry's choice of Canterbury was linked both to St Thomas and to Richard's father, the Black Prince, via a prophecy concerning holy coronation oil given to Becket by the Virgin Mary.[98] This story was probably invented by Archbishop Thomas Arundel (1353–1414), who was a fierce supporter of Henry. Thomas of Walsingham recorded the prophecy in a chronicle, wherein he described Henry's coronation as the will of God:

> This, so men thought, could not have happened without a divine
> miracle … he was anointed with that heavenly oil, which the blessed
> Mary, mother of God, entrusted to the blessed Thomas [Becket],
> martyr and archbishop of Canterbury, while he was in exile,
> prophesying to him that the kings of England who were anointed with
> this oil would be champions of the church and men of benevolence.[99]

According to Thomas of Walsingham, this chrism (anointing oil) was held in a golden-eagle-shaped ampulla and was given to the Black Prince by a 'holy man' in order 'that he might be anointed as king with it'.[100] As the Black Prince died before he had a chance to use it, the oil was said to have lain in the Tower of London until Richard II discovered it and sought a second coronation.[101] Archbishop Arundel refused and eventually took possession of the ampulla, keeping hold of the oil until Henry's coronation 'who was

the first of the kings of England to be anointed with so precious a liquid'.[102] Henry's choice to be buried at Canterbury, next to Becket's shrine and directly opposite the tomb of the Black Prince with its magnificent effigy, is a visual fulfilment of this prophecy and demonstrated for all to see that he, and by extension his Lancastrian heirs, was legitimate in the eyes of the Church.[103] It carried the message that they, unlike Henry II, were committed to maintaining the perfect balance in the relationship between Church and State.

7.17
The tomb of Henry IV and Joan of Navarre, before 1437. Trinity Chapel, Canterbury Cathedral

Collecting souvenirs at Canterbury

At the end of a pilgrimage to Canterbury each and every pilgrim bought a souvenir to take home with them. A sense of how this trade worked is provided by the 'Canterbury Interlude', which states: 'Then, as manere and

7.18
Casket-shaped ampulla
showing the martyrdom
of Becket, 13th or 14th
century. Lead-tin alloy.
5.4 × 4.1 × 2.3 cm. British
Museum, London, 2001,0702.3

custom is, signes [badges] there they boughte,/ For men of contre shuld know whom they had soughte./ Ech man set his sylver in such thing as they liked.'[104] Becket's image was probably best known and most widely distributed in the form of these cheap souvenirs.[105] The volume and range are remarkable and surpass those of any other European pilgrimage destination.[106] Broadly, two types of souvenir were available to Canterbury pilgrims: ampullae (usually dated to the late twelfth or thirteenth century), vessels filled with St Thomas's Water and worn around the neck; and badges, intended to be pinned to clothing or a hat.[107] Over time, and as the cult shifted away from the consumption of St Thomas's Water, badges outstripped ampullae in terms of popularity. Again, the 'Canterbury Interlude' describes how pilgrims wore such badges: 'They set hir signes oppon hir hedes, and som oppon hir capp.'[108] Both ampullae and badges were frequently called 'signum' or 'sigillum' (sign or seal), and Benedict of Peterborough, in his miracle collection, explains why: 'We know it was divine will that the ampullae of Canterbury's healer be carried through the whole world and that all the world should recognise his sign in his pilgrims and in his cured ones.'[109] When Gerald of Wales visited Canterbury Cathedral in the late twelfth century he returned home with an ampulla around his neck.[110] On the journey he passed through Southwark where he easily recognised other Canterbury pilgrims who were wearing ampullae too.[111]

Canterbury ampullae came in different shapes and sizes but each had to be large enough to contain a ladleful of St Thomas's Water. Several were casket-shaped and incorporated the story of Becket's murder through embossed imagery. Most, however, took the form of pilgrim's flasks, either a rounded costrel or bag, in reference to the containers pilgrims used to hold water while travelling. Like the badges, they were made by pouring a molten mixture of lead and tin into stone moulds, a process by which hundreds could be produced within a short space of time (fig. 7.18). Some ampullae were elaborately cast, with Becket holding a crozier and flanked by two of his murderers (fig. 7.19). The Canterbury badges display a similar level of complexity to the ampullae. There are narrative badges showing Becket on a boat, or on a horse returning from exile, badges of bells with text reading 'St Thomas', badges of St Thomas inside a star, and even badges of the murder weapon with tiny detachable swords (figs 7.20–7.24). Several badges are miniature versions of Becket's reliquaries, including the shrine itself and the bust kept in the Corona Chapel (see figs 4.5 and 4.10).

In buying a souvenir the pilgrims captured and transmitted some of the special power of a holy site back into their own communities. Souvenirs

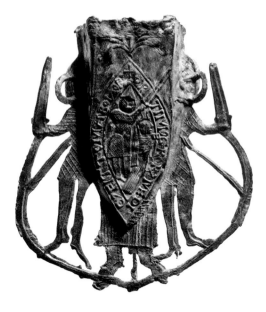

were not simply 'tourist tat' and they were seen by some as relics in their own right.[112] They often feature in miracle stories and have the power to heal and protect.[113] In Rochester in the late twelfth century a fire was prevented when a pilgrim placed a Canterbury ampulla on a stick and waved it towards the flames.[114] This was partly because the object had taken on something of Becket's holy presence. Another miracle story demonstrates the power of these 'signs'. When a London metalworker named Augustine tried to melt down old ampullae to make new ones, the example from Canterbury rose to the surface of the liquefied metal and would not melt: 'investigating the causes of the phenomenon, he realised that something of the body of the holy martyr had infused the container, which conferred strength upon it and repelled the assaults of combustion'.[115] The desire among pilgrims for a souvenir from Canterbury pushed some of them to steal, a situation that usually ended badly. One visitor from Ireland is said to have developed a tumour after he stole an ampulla, but was cured after confessing his crime.[116] In the 'Canterbury Interlude' the Miller pocketed a few badges when no one was looking: 'And in the meenwhile, the Miller had i-piked [stuffed]/ His bosom ful of signes of Caunterbury broches,/ Huch [which] the Pardoner and he pryvely [secretly] in hir pouches/ They put hem afterward.'[117]

As Chaucer well demonstrates, pilgrims were easy targets for satire. Erasmus went so far as to mock their appearance, lampooning the wearing

7.21
Pilgrim badge of Thomas
Becket, late 14th–early 15th
century. Lead alloy.
9 × 3 cm. British Museum,
London, 2001,0702.5

7.22
Pilgrim badge of Becket on
horseback returning from
exile, 14th century. Lead alloy.
9.3 × 7.7 cm. British Museum,
London, 1984,0505.1

of badges: 'But what means this? You are covered with scallop shells, stuck
all over with figures of lead and tin, decorated with straw necklaces, and a
bracelet of serpent's eggs.'[118] In the *Canterbury Tales* it is the badge-wearing
Pardoner who seeks to deceive those he encounters, travelling through the
countryside extracting money from the poor with a glass of pigs' bones
('holy relics') and a cross set with stones: 'But with thise relikes, whan that

he fond/ A povre person dwellynge upon lond/ Upon a day he gat hym moore moneye/ Than that the person gat in monthes tweye.'[119] But this criticism sometimes went beyond satire: at the very same time Chaucer was writing the *Tales*, a group of religious reformers called Lollards were vocal in their opinions of St Thomas.[120] They were opposed to church rituals not directly sanctioned by the Bible, such as praying to saints for intervention, venerating images and the act of pilgrimage.[121] Their views were held as heresy by the Church and led to imprisonment or even death. In 1407 a Lollard priest called William Thorpe recorded an account of his conversation with Archbishop Arundel during a stint in prison.[122] When his views on pilgrimage were questioned, Thorpe answered that these journeys were made for selfish reasons, and he condemned the lewd and loud behaviour of pilgrims, including the 'jangling of their Canterbury bells'.[123] Critics of pilgrimage believed that pilgrims treated their journey as a carnival, a time freed from normal responsibilities, rather than as a chance for penitence and self-reflection. In the sixteenth century voices like these grew louder, and, in an unexpected change of fate, gained the support of Henry VIII, who, once devoted to St Thomas, turned his royal favour away from him.

7.23
Pilgrim badge in the shape of a Canterbury bell, 14th or 15th century. Lead alloy. 4 × 3.7 cm. British Museum, London, 2001,0702.4

7.24
Pilgrim badge of a sword, 14th or 15th century. Lead alloy. 12.4 × 3.5 cm. British Museum, London, 2001,0702.7

+ Edwand +

Becket and the Tudors

On 5 September 1538 Henry VIII arrived in Canterbury.[2] His stay was brief, lasting just three days, but on this visit he had no intention of worshipping at Becket's shrine. While he was there, and possibly even in his presence, workmen began dismantling the ornate structure holding the body of St Thomas, which had been the destination for pilgrims from across Europe for over three hundred years. Working as quickly as they could, the men stripped away its precious metal casing and prised off its jewels. Becket's bones, still holy relics for so many, were removed, mostly never to be seen again.[3] At the time, a rumour spread that they had been burnt and the ashes scattered. The shock of this blow, delivered in the first years of the English Reformation, might well have been the last chapter in Becket's story, but more was yet to come. By the end of the year he was publicly declared an enemy of the Crown. This proclamation announced that Becket was no saint but a man who had the audacity to question the authority of an English king. Across the country, on royal orders, images of Becket were pulled down and broken into pieces, paintings were whitewashed and his name was erased from books. In certain places these measures completely eradicated vestiges of Becket, as can be seen in the cloister at Canterbury Cathedral, where a sculpture of his martyrdom was chiselled away almost beyond recognition (fig. 8.1).

... from henceforth the said Thomas Becket shall not be esteemed, named, reputed, nor called a saint, but Bishop Becket, and that his images and pictures through the whole realm shall be put down.[1]

Royal Proclamation of Henry VIII, 16 November 1538

Detail of fig. 8.5

Becket and the Tudor court

The destruction of Becket's shrine happened at a time of momentous change in the political and religious structures of Europe. A radical movement to reform the Catholic Church, known as the Reformation, swept across northern Europe and had a profound and long-lasting impact well beyond Henry VIII's reign. English medieval kings had generally supported the papacy in eradicating what they perceived to be heresy. Initially Henry was no different: during the first decades of his reign he was a staunch ally of the Pope and Catholic orthodoxy.[4] In 1521 the priest and scholar Martin Luther (1483–1546), from Saxony (now

8.1 (top)
Damaged vault boss from a cloister in Canterbury Cathedral, originally showing Becket's martyrdom

8.2 (above and right)
Surgical instrument case, c.1520–30. Wooden core, silver, gilding, enamel, and leather. H. 18 cm (without chain). The Worshipful Company of Barbers, London, S1152. A detail of Becket's martyrdom on the case's reverse is shown on the right.

8.3 (opposite)
The Howard Grace Cup, 1525–6 (mounts). Ivory, silver, gilding, pearls and gemstones. H. 27.3 cm. Victoria and Albert Museum, London, M.2680:1, 2–1931

part of Germany), was excommunicated by Pope Leo X (1475–1521). Luther was a radical figure whose scholarly publications and public stance against the papacy are widely seen as the major catalyst for the Reformation. That same year the king's name was attached to a diatribe against Luther titled *Assertio Septem Sacramentorum adversus Martinum Lutherum* (*Defence of the Seven Sacraments against Martin Luther*).[5] Leo, who was the dedicatee, was delighted with this work.[6] In recognition he issued a papal bull granting Henry the title 'fidei defensor' (Defender of the Faith), which he proudly used on his seal.[7]

There is little to suggest that Henry bore a lifelong grudge against Becket: the evidence points to the contrary. His father, Henry VII, the first Tudor king, had been a devotee of the saint, having paid for the Lady Chapel in Westminster Abbey, which contains two sculptures of St Thomas. In Canterbury, the silver figure that Henry VII had requested in his will to be placed in the Trinity Chapel was a reminder of their dynastic history of devotion. Henry VIII must have seen this statue when he paid homage at Becket's shrine, which he did at least five times; the most splendid occasion was his visit in May 1520, marking the sixth jubilee celebration of the saint's translation.[8] Accompanied by Queen Katherine of Aragon (1485–1536) and a vast retinue, he stopped at Canterbury on his route to France.[9] There, he and Katherine met her nephew, the Holy Roman Emperor Charles V, who was travelling via England on his way to Germany. During their stay the royal group visited Becket's relics on several occasions, paying homage to the saint and making offerings at the high altar.[10]

A record of Henry's devotion to St Thomas can be found in a high-status commission for which he was probably personally responsible. Decorated with an enamelled heraldic shield of the royal arms, it is a prestigious and ornate silver instrument case made around 1520–30 for a surgeon (fig. 8.2).[11] On the reverse is an unusual depiction of Becket's murder. Uncharacteristically, the archbishop is shown from behind, facing towards the altar, with knights approaching him from both sides. Two of them stab him in the back with pikes, and to the left a third raises a sword for the final blow. On the right a figure crouches behind the altar to avoid the fracas. The instrument case was probably made as a presentation item, rather than for practical use, but it would once have held surgical instruments and been worn suspended by its chain from the owner's belt. One of Henry's most trusted surgeons was Thomas Vicary (*c*.1490–1561), and this may have been a gift to him.[12]

Apart from the instrument case, another rare object related to Becket, and connected to Henry's court, has survived (fig. 8.3). In 1513 Sir Edward

Howard (*c*.1476–1513) bequeathed a plain turned ivory vessel to Queen Katherine, which was described in his will as 'St Thomas' cup'.[13] Around 1525–6 Katherine had it encased in silver-gilt mounts but left the middle undecorated so that the ivory could still be seen and handled. The new silver additions bore her emblem, the pomegranate, and were decorated with pearls and gems.[14] A mitre and the initials 'TB', potentially a reference to Becket, were also added to the mounts. Items associated with St Thomas, like Katherine's cup, were relatively common and a number existed in church treasuries.[15] In 1515 Thomas Boleyn (*c*.1477–1539), the father of Henry's future second wife, Anne (*c*.1500–1536), inherited an ivory horn that had been in the family's possession since the twelfth century, and from which, according to tradition, Becket had once drunk.[16] Objects like these brought people close to the saint and they reveal the strong links that existed between the king, his court and St Thomas.

Erasmus and growing criticism

At some point between 1512 and 1514, around the time Katherine inherited the ivory cup, Desiderius Erasmus made his own journey to Canterbury to see the shrine of St Thomas (fig. 8.4).[17] Although he was a devout Roman Catholic, Erasmus was suspicious of the cult of saints and was unimpressed by what he found in the cathedral. For him, the opulence of the Trinity Chapel and Becket's shrine were both overwhelming and distasteful. Fellow humanist John Colet (1467–1519), Dean of St Paul's Cathedral, was his companion and in 1526 Erasmus satirised their visit in *Peregrinatio religionis ergo* (*A Pilgrimage for Religion's Sake*).[18] He reimagined himself and Colet as two pilgrims named Ogygius and Gratian: the former travels to several destinations, including Santiago de Compostela and Walsingham. When he journeys to Canterbury he is joined by the sceptical Gratian. Ogygius repeatedly dwells on the absurdity of venerating relics. To him, and by extension Erasmus too, the Canterbury monks were preoccupied more with the material wealth of Becket's shrine than the relics within:

> The cheapest part was gold. Everything shone and dazzled with
> rare and surpassingly large jewels, some bigger than a goose egg.
> Some monks stood about reverently. When the cover was removed,
> we all adored.[19]

8.4
Albrecht Dürer, *Portrait of Desiderius Erasmus*, 1526. Engraving. 24.9 × 18.9 cm. British Museum, London, E,3.30. Bequeathed by Clayton Mordaunt Cracherode. Wearing scholarly robes and seated at a writing desk, Erasmus is shown alongside Latin and Greek inscriptions declaring 'His writings present a better picture of the man than this portrait.'

Erasmus's *Pilgrimage* was first published in Basel as part of a Latin volume of *Colloquies*, a selection of imagined conversations used as teaching aids.[20] However, in the years before Becket's shrine was destroyed, the satire was reissued by those seeking religious reform in England. Around 1536–7 it was translated into English and published as *The Pilgrimage of Pure Devotion*. Despite the fact that Erasmus had never intended his work to be used as a manifesto for reform, the translator declared that the author had desired to assist Henry VIII, in 'the reformacyon of all pernicious abuses & chiefly of detestable ydolatrye'.[21]

8.5

Panels from a chancel screen with defaced images of St Edward the Confessor (left) and St Thomas (right), 1530s. St Andrew's Church, North Burlingham, Norfolk. Chancel screens were common in medieval churches, typically located at the junction between nave and chancel. The majority were destroyed or damaged in the English Reformation, but a large number survive in Norfolk and Devon. The whole screen contains images of ten saints. All have been damaged, but Becket is by far the most severely treated.

At the time of this new translation, the majority of the English population would have been unaware of Erasmus's text, or the murmurings of suspicion surrounding relics and their veneration. St Thomas's cult thrived and his feast days were still celebrated with enthusiasm. Civic pageants were held in the city of Canterbury on 6 July 1505 and 1520 to mark the eve of his translation.[22] Numerous paintings, stained glass and other works of art, which told the story of Becket's life and martyrdom, continued to be commissioned for churches and chapels and there were more English parish churches dedicated to him than to any other saint.[23] In the 1530s a Norfolk family by the name of Bennet paid for the painting of a chancel screen in its parish church at Burlingham St Andrew.[24] St Thomas of Canterbury was among the saints depicted (fig. 8.5). All the images now left on this screen bear the scars of tools used to scratch away the paint, as seen on St Thomas and St Edward the Confessor beside him. The destruction of Becket's shrine, and the proposed eradication of his cult, came as a complete and entirely unexpected shock to such families as the Bennets, for whom he was a cherished saint.[25]

Breaking from Rome

Although he was still considered to be the Defender of the Faith, Henry was growing discontented with Rome. Chief among the king's worries was his lack of a legitimate male heir. He sought to rectify this through a papally sanctioned annulment of his marriage to Katherine in order that he might marry Anne Boleyn. Katherine refused to cooperate and sought powerful support from her nephew Charles V. The Pope equivocated by commissioning an investigation, which took a number of years and tested Henry's patience. Katherine was backed by several prominent figures such as Thomas More, Lord Chancellor (1478–1535), William Warham, Archbishop of Canterbury (c.1450–1532) and John Fisher, Bishop of Rochester (c.1469–1535). By 1532 the issue remained unresolved, but when Warham died in August of that year, his passing opened the way for the king to appoint an archbishop more aligned with his plan. Warham, like his predecessors, had been devoted to St Thomas.[26] In contrast his replacement, Thomas Cranmer (1489–1556), was keen to see Church reform of the type taking place on the Continent (fig. 8.6). Cranmer was part of a growing group that included Thomas Cromwell (c.1485–1540), a rising political star, who had made his name in the household of Cardinal Thomas Wolsey, Archbishop of York (1470/1–1530). Cromwell's

8.6
Gerlach Flicke, *Thomas Cranmer*, c.1545–6. Oil on panel. 98.4 × 76.2 cm. National Portrait Gallery, London, NPG 535. Cranmer is shown holding *The Epistles of St Paul* open. Placed on the table in front of him are a letter and two books, one of which is St Augustine's *De Fide et Operibus* (*On Faith and Works*).

extraordinary journey, from London-born commoner to archbishop's clerk, to close friend, adviser and ultimately enemy of the king, was much like Becket's own. By the time of Cranmer's appointment, Cromwell was in the king's service and his thoughts were preoccupied by the Canterbury pilgrimage. In 1533, in a list of tasks to follow up at court, Cromwell wrote a note querying how to deal with these pilgrims: 'What the kynges [king's] highness wool [would] have done with them that shall go to Canterburye to doo penance.'[27] The coinciding of Cromwell and Cranmer's desire for reform with Henry's wish for an annulment had dramatic consequences for Becket's cult.

Their position was shared by many but it remained dangerous, heretical even, to air such views publicly.

In the years preceding Henry's break with Rome, critics took aim at St Thomas and ramped up their attacks in spite of the danger involved. One such detractor was William Tyndale (*c*.1494–1536), an English scholar who sought Church reform. His work provoked the ire of many enemies in England, and by 1526 he was in exile, hiding from his detractors on the Continent. In 1530 he wrote a polemical account, *The Practice of Papistical Prelates*, in which he sought to expose what he perceived to be the unscrupulous behaviour of the Pope and senior clergy.[28] Tyndale homed in on Becket, characterising him as a hot-headed warmonger who was more interested in worldly matters than religious ones.[29] He declared that instead of being assaulted in Canterbury Cathedral, Becket had, in fact, fought the knights 'with a lusty courage of a man of war'.[30] Tyndale went so far as to compare Becket with Wolsey, describing the latter as 'a counterfeiting of St Thomas of Canterbury'.[31] He was not alone in his criticism of the saint and in late 1531 an anonymously published 'book against St Thomas of Canterbury' was publicly destroyed in London at St Paul's Cross.[32] The following year, James Bainham, a lawyer, was burnt at the stake as a heretic after questioning Becket's status as a saint.[33] His last words were recorded as, 'Thomas becket is no saint but dampned [dammed] in hell, for this I reade on him that he was a wicked man, a traitour to the crown and Realme of England.'[34] Although Bainham suffered for expressing such sentiments, within a number of years the situation dramatically shifted, and his opinions of St Thomas, which had resulted in such a violent death, came to receive full endorsement from the Crown.

With Cranmer on the archiepiscopal throne, Henry circumvented the papacy and called on him to grant the annulment of his marriage. Cranmer duly obliged, after which matters moved quickly. Henry and Anne were married in 1533, and soon after the English Church officially broke with Rome. In 1534 the Act of Supremacy declared the king Supreme Head of the Church of England, and the Act of Succession pronounced his marriage to be legally binding and his sole legitimate heir to be his new-born daughter Elizabeth. All were commanded to swear an oath in recognition that Henry and not the Pope was head of the English Church. The prior and sixty-nine monks from Canterbury Cathedral followed suit and publicly took the pledge.[35] Those who had supported Katherine now found themselves at odds with the king and therefore in danger. In 1534 Thomas More was imprisoned in the Tower of London for refusing the oath. He was tried, found guilty and sentenced to death. Here, his story and that of St Thomas's interweave.[36] Like Becket, More was killed for refusing to acknowledge royal supremacy over Church affairs, but he also had a personal affinity with the saint, who was both his namesake and a fellow Londoner.[37] His execution took place on 6 July 1535, the eve of Becket's translation. The significance of this coincidence was important to More, who wrote to his daughter the night before saying, 'I would be sorry, if it should be any longer than tomorrow, for it is St Thomas eve, and the utas [eighth day of the feast] of Saint Peter and therefore tomorrow long I to go to God.'[38] Just two weeks before More's death, another of Katherine's supporters, Cardinal John Fisher, was executed for treason. He too was soon compared to Becket. Around a month after his death, the Pope wrote to the King of France stating that the cardinal had died for an even greater cause than St Thomas's, 'the truth of the universal church'.[39] The memory of Fisher's and More's executions played a pivotal role in the English Catholic opposition to the Reformation.

More's death brought history full circle: it was widely perceived that nearly four hundred years on from Becket's murder, this was another Thomas

8.7

Double portrait of John Fisher and Thomas More, c.1550–1600. Engraving. 17.3 × 25.1 cm. British Museum, London, O,7.104. Bequeathed by Clayton Mordaunt Cracherode

IOANNES ROFFENSIS   THOMAS MORE

IOANNES FISCHER prior, Roffensis, imago,
  Antistes THOMA MORE, secundà tui est.
Anglia uos quondam communis patria iunxit,
  Indigna, heu, tantis, mundus ut ipse, uiris,
Sed magis ingenium probitas, doctrina que pellens,

Et uerae iunxit religionis amor.
  Ob quem carnificis uos perculit una securis.
Vná que nex bmis, unaque causa necis.
Quàm bene caelesti iunctorum sede duorum
  Iunxit et effigies una tabella duas!

8.8
Pendant, known as the
George or Barnborough
Jewel, c.1520–35. Gold,
enamel. Diam. 9.1 cm.
British Jesuit Province

8.9
Reliquary crucifix, early 16th
century. Gold, niello, pearls.
12 × 10.4 cm. Stonyhurst
College

standing up to the tyranny of another Henry. His last words on the scaffold had resonances of Becket's final utterance before he died. More told the assembled crowd that he was a loyal 'servant' to the king, but above all was a servant of God. His death, like Becket's, and along with Fisher's, was seen through the lens of political martyrdom and both Tudor figures were venerated as saints, although they were not officially canonised until 1935.[40] A devotional engraving made in Holland around 1550–1600 shows Fisher and More together: the inscription at the base declares their joint status as martyrs (fig. 8.7).[41] As was the convention, objects associated with them were gathered together over time by the faithful and preserved as relics. Among these is a cameo ring, believed to have been Fisher's, showing the bearded face of a scholar, perhaps Aristotle.[42] More's descendants also preserved several objects connected with him, such as two seal matrices, a crucifix-shaped reliquary and an enamelled pendant (fig. 8.8).[43] The latter is a virtuoso piece of goldsmith's work. It is decorated on one side with a scene of St George defeating the dragon. On the reverse is Christ as the Man of Sorrows.[44] Contained inside this jewel is a painted miniature of More himself. An inscription around the rim comes from Virgil's *Aeneid*, and states that God will bring an end to suffering, an allusion to the hardship of More's final days and the redemption of divine judgement. Parts of the pendant appear to have been repurposed from other objects – the side showing St George and the dragon probably came from a hat badge; the piece is likely to have been made as a commemorative item, possibly for one of More's daughters.[45] Another relic with a long-standing connection to More is a crucifix decorated with pearls, which may have belonged to his second wife, Lady Alice (*c*.1474–*c*.1551), who is depicted wearing it in sixteenth-century paintings (fig. 8.9).[46] On the reverse of the pendant is a Greek inscription identifying it as 'a reliquary of the Apostle Thomas'.[47] The relationship between More, the apostle Thomas and Thomas Becket was developed by writers who sought to compare their three lives for devotional contemplation.[48] In 1588 Thomas Stapleton, a Jesuit priest, published a triple biography of them, titled *Tres Thomae* (*Three Thomases*), which presents their lives and martyrdoms as models for imitation.[49] Becket and More were so closely aligned in the minds of Catholics that they are even depicted together on jewellery (fig. 8.10).[50]

By 1534 religious reform was on Henry's agenda and the status of monastic houses like Canterbury Cathedral was scrutinised and subject to royal control. In the same year as More's and Fisher's executions, Cromwell was appointed Vicegerent in Spirituals, placing him in charge of the king's religious policy. He investigated and suppressed monastic foundations, first through visitations undertaken by a network of commissioners, and secondly through Valor Ecclesiasticus ('the value of the Church'), which surveyed the wealth of all the monastic houses in England, Wales and parts of Ireland. Cromwell was a determined and passionate reformer and by targeting monasteries he identified a source of untapped wealth for the Crown. In 1536 he issued a document called the 'Ten Articles' in which he set out changes to English religious doctrine. Images of saints, including Becket, were allowed to remain in churches as an aid to prayer but were not to be worshipped. It was the first of many blows to the cult of saints.[51] That same year Cromwell ratified a set of injunctions abolishing certain feast days, including those that fell during harvest.[52] Becket's translation, annually celebrated on 7 July since 1220, was removed from the calendar.[53] This was the first official censure of St Thomas under Henry VIII, but it would not be the last.

Despite significant shifts in royal policy, public devotion to Becket's cult continued to flourish, and Henry remained connected to the saint. In early 1537 he and his third wife, Jane Seymour (1508/9–1537), travelled to Canterbury and gave thanks at St Thomas's shrine for her pregnancy.[54] Becket was not, however, short of critics. Around the time of Henry and Jane's Canterbury trip, John Bale (1495–1563), an ex-monk from Ipswich turned evangelical polemicist,

8.10
Double-sided portrait medal of Thomas More and St Thomas of Canterbury, 17th century. Silver. Diam. 3.7 cm. British Museum, London, M.6791. Donated by Edward Hawkins. The two Latin inscriptions translate as 'The image of Thomas More, English Martyr' and 'St Thomas, Archbishop of Canterbury, Martyr, 1171'. Note the incorrect year of death has been given here.

composed a play, now lost, called *The Knaveries of Thomas Becket* or *On the Treasons of Becket*.[55] Views like his, once considered heretical, were now becoming part of mainstream political and religious discourse. Bale, for instance, was patronised by Cromwell and toured the country with actors performing plays with a strong Protestant message.[56] In mid-August 1538 Cranmer authorised an investigation into a phial of Becket's blood to test its supposed miraculous nature.[57] He wrote to Cromwell, saying: 'I have in great suspect that St Thomas of Canterbury his blood, in Christ's church in Canterbury, is but a feigned thing and made of some red ochre or of such like matter.'[58] Cranmer's scepticism surrounding Becket's relics would have serious implications for the saint, suggesting that he and Cromwell had plans for dealing with his cult.

Dismantling the cult

One of the last recorded visits to Becket's shrine was on 31 August 1538, just days before its destruction. Madame de Montreuil, a French noblewoman, and Sir William Pension were given a tour of the cathedral by the prior.[59] Pension reported to Cromwell that the prior had 'Showed her the church and St Thomas' shrine, at which she marvelled. The prior showed her St Thomas' head but she would not kiss it.'[60] Montreuil's refusal to kiss Becket's skull was a portent of things to come. How far in advance the decision had been taken to suppress the cult remains unclear,[61] but throughout that summer images were taken down from other pilgrimage sites, like Walsingham Priory, whose famous Virgin and Child was brought to London in July.[62] Both Cranmer and Cromwell had been searching for a way to divert Canterbury's vast wealth. At the same time, they must have been concerned that as Henry was asserting unprecedented control over the Church, Becket's status as a figure of opposition to the Crown might provide a cause around which detractors could rally.[63]

An opportunity to act against the saint presented itself in 1538 as part of the royal summer progress through Kent, which passed through Canterbury. At some point between 5 and 7 September, Cromwell's men, led by Richard Pollard, began the considerable task of taking down the shrine. Given that Henry was in the city until 8 September, it is possible that he might even have witnessed some of the destruction at first hand.[64] One of those present during these events was the merchant John Husee (d. 1548), who conveyed his impression of the scene in a letter to Lady Lisle (1493/5–1566), the wife of his patron. Husee mockingly compared Cromwell's agent to a devout pilgrim: 'Mr. Pollerd [*sic*] has been so busy night and day "in prayer with offering unto S. T. [St Thomas's] shrine and head, with other dead relics, that he could have no idle worldly time".'[65] Before the king left Canterbury the royal retinue watched a performance by Bale and the players, possibly one satirising Becket.[66] The precious metal, gemstones and jewellery stripped from the shrine were packed up and transported back to London. How much this all amounted to is not exactly clear. Some sources suggest it was as much as twenty cartloads, while others say that enough was taken from the shrine to fill two heavy boxes, requiring several men to lift and carry them away.[67] The king profiting from St Thomas in this way was remarked upon sarcastically at the time by one Welsh soldier, who described the saint as 'a loyal treasurer to today's king'.[68] The shrine's rose-pink marble base was smashed into pieces and later reused as building material. The silver from the casing was probably melted down and the gems were reappropriated for jewellery. The famous Regale of France, supposedly given by Louis VII in 1179 and variously described by visitors, one calling it 'a carbuncle which shines at night and which is half the size of a hen's egg',[69] was set into a ring for Henry VIII.[70] What effect the dismantling of the shrine had on the monks of Canterbury is difficult to judge, but witnessing a process of destruction that left an empty space at the heart of their institution must surely have been a profoundly disturbing experience.[71]

News of St Thomas's shrine spread far and wide. On 22 October Cromwell received a letter from one of his agents in Padua, Italy, informing him that, 'they have made here a wondrous matter and report of the shrine and burning of the idols burnt at Canterbury'.[72] As for Becket's relics, a widely believed rumour spread that they too had been burnt. On hearing this, Pope Paul III (1468–1549) was outraged.[73] Their fate and what exactly transpired at Canterbury remain unclear. However, in 1539, the year after Becket's shrine was destroyed, Cromwell was involved in the preparation of a pamphlet, which remained unfinished and unpublished, wherein he claimed to have hidden away Becket's bones and only burnt a separate skull, which he argued was a false relic:

> His [Becket's] shrine and bones are therefore taken away and
> bestowed where they will cause no superstition … and there was in
> that church a great skull of another head, but much greater by the
> three quarter parts than that part which was lacking in the head
> closed within the shrine, whereby it appeared that the same was but

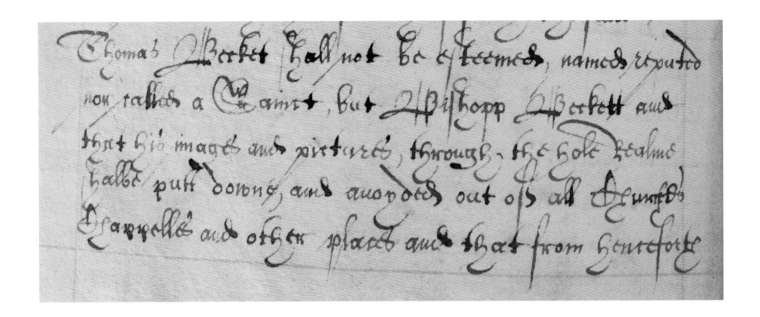

8.11
Royal proclamation outlawing Becket's image and name, 16 November 1538. British Library, London, Cotton MS Titus B I, ff. 520r–521v. The detail above reads '[the said] Thomas Becket shall not be esteemed, named, reputed, nor called a Saint+, but Bishopp Beckett, and that his images and pictures, through the hole realme, shalbe putt downe, and avoyded out of all Churches, Chappelles, and other places …'

a feigned fiction; if this head was burnt, was therefore St. Thomas['s] burnt? Assuredly it concludeth not.[74]

Whatever the case, the majority of the saint's bones were never seen again and their whereabouts remain a mystery.[75] On 16 November 1538 the attack on St Thomas continued (fig. 8.11). A royal proclamation was issued instructing that his name and image were to be completely eradicated across the country:

> … that from henceforth the said Thomas Becket shall not be esteemed, named, reputed nor called a saint, but Bishop Becket, and that his images and pictures through the whole realm shall be put down and avoided out of all churches, chapels, and other places, and that from henceforth the days used to be festival in his name shall not be observed, nor the service, office, antiphons, collects, and prayers in his name read, but razed and put out of all the books; and that all other festival days, already abrogate, shall be in no wise solemnized.[76]

Nationwide censorship on this scale provoked international outrage. One month later, on 17 December, the Pope retaliated by excommunicating Henry. He gave the destruction of Becket's shrine as just cause for this most extreme action on his part. In the bull pronouncing his decision, he refers to the burning of Becket's remains, framing it in legal terms: 'the King had caused the said St Thomas, for the greater scorn of religion, to be summoned to trial and condemned for contumacy and declared a traitor, he has commanded those bones to be exhumed and burned, and the ashes scattered to the wind'.[77]

Destruction and survival

Across the country images of Becket were defaced, destroyed or hidden to prevent them from being damaged. Those closest to Henry quickly set about removing offending likenesses of St Thomas from their personal belongings. Cranmer immediately ordered his seal matrix to be recut, and in place of Becket's martyrdom he opted for an image of the Crucifixion (fig. 8.12).[78] His decision to replace Becket on his archiepiscopal seal put an end to a centuries-old tradition starting with Hubert Walter in 1193.[79] Cranmer also made sure that items in his library were suitably amended. On the opening page of his

8.12

Thomas Cranmer's archiepiscopal seals in 1534 and 1540, reproduced in a 19th-century engraving. On the left is Cranmer's pre-Reformation seal and on the right is his post-Reformation seal, which he had altered to remove the central image of Becket. The text reads 'SIGILLV THOME CRANMER DEI GRAT CANTVARIEN ARCHIEP' (Seal of Thomas Cranmer, by the Grace of God, Archbishop of Canterbury).

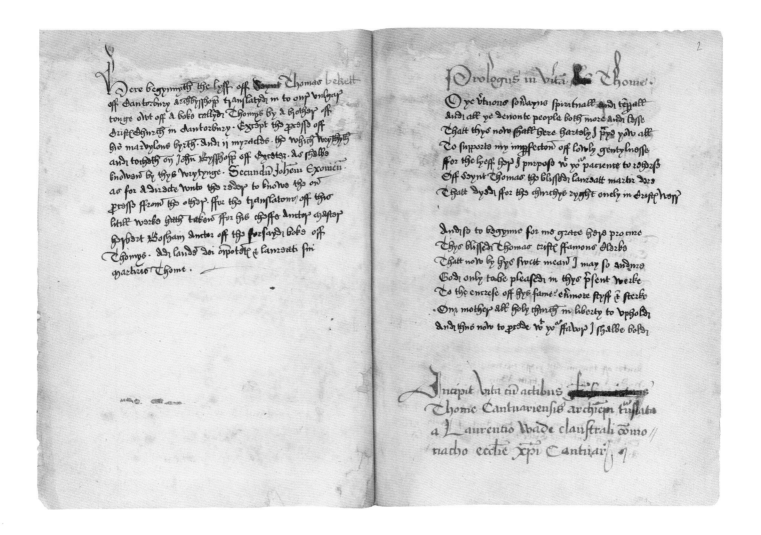

8.13

Thomas Cranmer's copy
of Laurence Wade's *Life of
Becket*, c.1500–25. Paper.
26.2 × 19.5 cm (closed).
Parker Library, Corpus
Christi College, Cambridge.
MS 298, ff. 1v–2r

personal copy of Laurence Wade's *Life of Becket*, Cranmer had once signed his name (fig. 8.13).[80] It is tempting to think that he was the one who now crossed out the words 'saint' and 'martyr' each time they appeared in the text.[81] Others, keen to adopt official policy, followed suit, with the Corporation of London erasing Becket from its seal.[82] In 1539 the lawyer Edward Hall (1497–1547) was ordered to take down a stained-glass window from the chapel of Gray's Inn, London, which had an image of Becket 'gloriously painted' on it.[83] This was replaced with a panel depicting Christ praying.[84] Institutions with long-standing connections to Becket faced particular censure. In October 1538 the Hospital of St Thomas of Acre, built on the site of his childhood

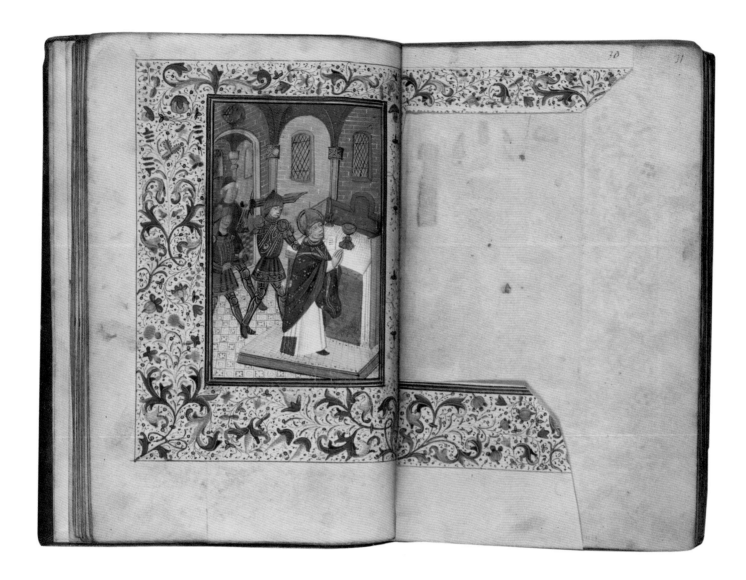

home, was dissolved and its lay patrons, the Worshipful Company of Mercers, removed every appearance of Becket.[85] The chapel of St Thomas on London Bridge was rededicated to St Thomas the Apostle and all forbidden images were destroyed or erased.[86] There were, however, instances of resistance and non-compliance. Richard Whiting, Abbot of Glastonbury (1461–1539), was executed in November 1539 after an investigation found that he owned various incriminating materials, including a printed life of St Thomas.[87] In a time of political turbulence, it is likely some discoveries may have been deliberate attempts to discredit opponents of the Crown.[88]

8.14
Becket's martyrdom (left) and a removed page of text (right) from a book of hours, 1450–75. Parchment. 21.5 × 15 cm (closed). British Library, London, MS Harley 2985, ff. 29v–30r

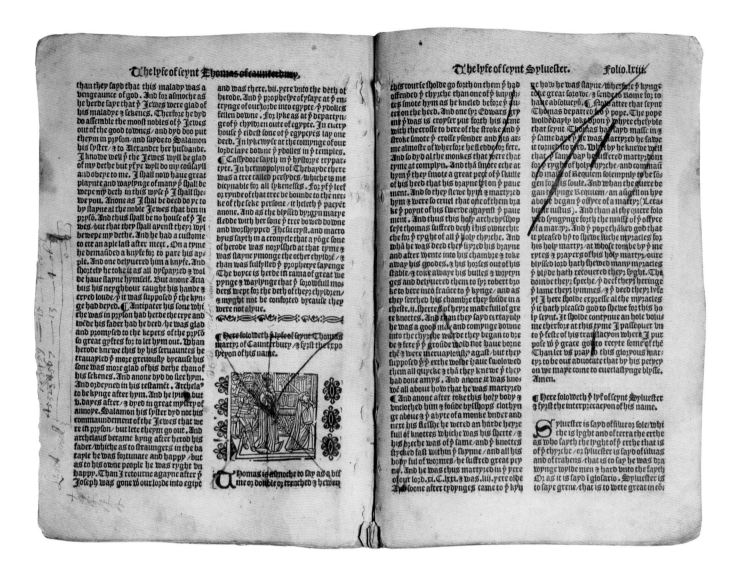

8.15

Becket's story and image defaced, in Jacobus de Voragine's *Golden Legend*, printed by Wynken de Worde, 1521. Paper. 28.5 × 20 cm (closed). Stonyhurst College, XIV.H.3, ff. 62v–63r

From the time of his canonisation all the way up to the Reformation, Becket's name and image was entered into thousands of manuscripts made for both institutional and private use. These now all needed to be removed. However, people had different interpretations of the proclamation's order to 'put out' the saint. Some drew lines through their manuscripts, smudged ink into the pages or scored the images with a knife. In many cases St Thomas's name has simply been rubbed away but remains identifiable. In one book of hours, a prayer book for personal use, an invocation to Becket was removed, but his image was retained (fig. 8.14).[89] The text to the right was meticulously

cut out but on the left the martyrdom remains relatively undamaged. At the front of the manuscript both of his feast days have been neatly erased from the calendar.[90] In a printed edition of the *Golden Legend* by Jacobus de Voragine the text of Becket's biography has been crossed through. A small woodcut of the murder is struck out, and the saint's name in the title 'The lyfe of seynt Thomas of caunterbury' has been faintly inked over; yet, the text and image are still perfectly legible (fig. 8.15). More effective was the use of dark ink smeared across the page. The text of St Thomas's liturgy from a fifteenth-century missal has been obscured by thick red ink (fig. 8.16).

8.16
Missal with the Mass for St Thomas obliterated with red ink, mid-15th century. 26 × 35 cm. Cambridge University Library, MS Add. 6688, ff. 28v–29r. This manuscript was previously owned by the church of St John the Baptist, Bromsgrove.

8.17
Becket meeting the Pope,
c.1400–25. Alabaster. St
Mary's Church, Nottingham

8.18 (opposite)
The martyrdom of Becket,
before 1376. Alabaster. 53.3 ×
61 cm. Private collection

Paintings of St Thomas in parish churches were whitewashed or defaced but sculptures needed to be broken.[91] At Ashford in Kent a statue of Becket was modified to save it from destruction.[92] By replacing his crozier with a wool comb, the parishioners transformed him into St Blaise.[93] A number of images, in various states of preservation, have been discovered in churches under floors or bricked up into walls or niches.[94] In St Mary's Church, Nottingham, an alabaster panel of Becket meeting the Pope in Sens was unearthed from under the choir stalls during renovation work in the nineteenth century (fig. 8.17). Similarly, in 1905 a group of stone figures, probably representing the four knights who killed Becket, were found set into the north wall of All Saints, Tilsworth.[95] Some sculptures survived in private ownership, never coming to the attention of the authorities. A larger than usual alabaster of the saint was protected from destruction by the same family who had originally commissioned it (fig. 8.18). Beneath the central scene of his martyrdom are three heraldic shields. The shield to the far left represents the Ireland family and the one to the far right is that of the Foljambe family. A quartered shield, placed at the centre, relates to the marriage of Sir Godfrey Foljambe (d. 1376) and Avena Ireland (d. 1382), who were presumably the patrons of the sculpture.[96] It is unclear exactly where the alabaster was originally located, but, as Godfrey and Avena were patrons of Beauchief Abbey, near Sheffield, and All Saints' Church, Bakewell, it could possibly have come from either.[97] Beauchief, founded in the late twelfth century and dedicated to St Thomas, is the stronger candidate of the two. Instead of allowing the sculpture to be damaged, a descendant of Godfrey and Avena removed it from the church, protecting it from destruction.[98] Other alabasters fared less well. In 1547 a Welshman, Stephen ap Powell, was accused of erecting a five-panel alabaster altarpiece in New Radnor Church showing scenes from the archbishop's life and death.[99] Whether it was newly commissioned, or was simply made up of old images that he reinstated, ap Powell's desire to decorate his church with sculptures of St Thomas demonstrates ongoing resistance to the 1538 proclamation.

Becket and the Tudor dynasty

Following Henry's death in 1547, his three children, Edward VI (1537–1553), Mary I (1516–1558) and Elizabeth I (1533–1603), ruled in succession. A portrait of the family by William Rogers (fl. 1584–1604) shows this dynasty

with Henry enthroned at its centre, and flanked by his children (fig. 8.19).[100] Edward kneels before his father, who hands him a sword. To Henry's right is his daughter Mary, who remained a devoted Catholic, standing alongside her husband, Philip II, King of Spain (1527–1598). Behind them, rushing into the scene fully armed, is a personification of War. In contrast, Elizabeth, Henry's other daughter, is shown to her father's left, holding hands with an allegorical figure of Peace, next to one of Plenty. The image speaks to a family united by blood but divided by religion. In turn, each child either developed or sought to retract the policies of their father. Edward led a Protestant government. He ushered in more stringent religious reforms and issued further rulings against the veneration of saints and the use of religious images. One of Edward's first major parliamentary acts was directed towards their censure.[101] During Mary's reign England briefly turned back to Rome, but she ruled for just five years and the return of Catholicism did not last. Under Elizabeth the country once again became Protestant, with the queen as Supreme Head of the Church. Becket's fate was now sealed and there was no national re-emergence of his cult. However, English Catholics kept his memory alive, in secret at home and in public on the Continent.

In Edward's reign, Becket's status as a figure of opposition to royal tyranny continued to be felt. In 1549 a rebellious protest against the private enclosure of agricultural land emerged in Norfolk, led by Robert Kett (*c*.1492–1549), a local yeoman. It began in the town of Wymondham as people gathered to watch a play of Becket's martyrdom, marking the feast of his translation.[102] A public performance of this sort was a subversive act in itself and those present were surely aware of how controversial the play was. Within a month the rebels were suppressed and Kett executed. Edward died four years later, aged just fifteen and without an heir. After a failed attempt to transfer power to his cousin, the Protestant Lady Jane Grey (1537–1554), Edward's Catholic elder sister, Mary, became queen. She immediately began to reverse the changes brought about by her father and brother. Becket's feast days were revived across the country but his shrine at Canterbury was not restored, perhaps because of the absence of his relics.[103] However, Mary did have the Regale of France, which had decorated Becket's shrine, removed from her father's ring and set into a collar. Only at Westminster Abbey was St Edward the Confessor's shrine rebuilt, but this was the initiative of the monks rather than on royal orders.[104] Back at Canterbury, steps were taken to reinstate Becket as a major civic saint. In July 1554, for the first time in sixteen years, St Thomas's pageant was performed in the city.[105] Payments

Now Prudent Edward dyinge in tender youth,
Queen Mary then the Royall Scepter swayd.
With foraine blood she mateht and put down truth,
Which Englands glory suddainly decayd:
Who brought in warr & discord by that deed.
Which did in comon wealth great sorow breed.

Behoulde the figure of A Royall Kinge.
One whom sweet victory euer did attende:
From euery parte wher he his power did bringe.
He homewarde brought y Conquest in y end.
And when y fates his vitall thred had spunne:
He gaue his glory to A Vertuous Sunne.

But Sorow care & ciuill broyles lykewise.
This Sacred Queene ELIZABETH exylde
Fallhood did fall before her Gratious eyes.
And perticution turnd to mercy mylde.
Plenty and peace throughout hir dayes are seene.
And all the world admyr's this mayden Queene.

To the Right Reuerend father in God John by the *Prouidence of God Archb of Canterb primat of Engl,* *& Metropol seath ~ Grauen by Rogers*

8.19
William Rogers after
Lucas de Heere, *Henry VIII
Enthroned with Successors*,
c.1595–1600. Engraving.
36 × 49.1 cm. British Museum,
London, 1842,0806.373

are recorded in the cathedral treasurer's accounts for 1555/6 for 'writing
St Thomas Legends' and for adding 'St Thomas storye' to manuscripts.[106]
Gradually the work of the preceding years was being revised but, with the
pendulum now swinging the opposite way, there were Protestants who openly
resisted these changes. In 1554 Christopher Hunningwood was imprisoned in
the Tower of London charged with beheading a statue of St Thomas.[107] That
same year another sculpture of Becket, newly made and set above the door
to the chapel of the Worshipful Company of Mercers, was also attacked.[108]
At first just the neck and crozier were damaged, but, over a month later, the

The description of Doctour Cranmer, howe he was plucked downe from the stage, by Friers and Papistes, for the true Confession of his faith.

And then Cranmer being pulled downe from the stage, was led to the fire, accompanied with those friers, vexing, troubling, and threatning him most cruelly. What madnesse, say they, hath brought thee againe into this error, by which thou wilt draw innumerable soules with thee into hel? To who he answered nothing, but directed all his talke to the people, saying that to one troubling him in the way, he spake and exhorted him to get him home to his studie, and applie his booke diligently, saying if he did diligently call vpon God, by reading more hee should gette knowledge.

But the other Spanish barker, raging and foming, was almost out of his wits, alwaies hauing this in his mouthe: Non fecisti? diddest thou it not?

But when hee came to the place where the holy Bishops and martyrs of God, Hugh Latimer and Ridley were burnt before him for the confession of the trueth, kneeling downe hee praised

The burning of the Archbishop of Canturbury Doctor Thomas Cranmer, in the Towneditch at Oxford, with his hand first thrust into the fire, wherewith he subscribed before.

8.20
Thomas Cranmer seized and burnt at the stake, in John Foxe, *Actes and Monuments of these Latter and Perillous Days, Touching Matters of the Church* (popularly known as his *Book of Martyrs*), late 16th century. Woodcut. 34 × 23 cm. British Museum, London, 1868,0822.6342. Bequeathed by Felix Slade

arms of the figure were broken too.[109] A reward of one hundred gold crowns was offered for any news of the culprit, but they were never found.[110]

Under Mary, Cranmer was deposed and eventually put on trial for heresy. He was burnt at the stake in Oxford on 21 March 1556.[111] On the day of his death he reaffirmed his commitment to Protestantism, stating 'as for the Pope, I refuse him as Christ's enemy'.[112] Like More and Fisher, Cranmer was seen as a martyr, but in his case by the Protestant Church. He is remembered as such in John Foxe's (1516–1587) widely read martyrology, popularly known as *Foxe's Book of Martyrs*. Foxe presents the reader with images of Cranmer's violent death, stating that 'he had to rejoice, that dying in such a cause, he was to be numbered amongst Christ's martyrs, much more worthy the name of St Thomas of Canterbury, than he whom the pope falsely before did canonize' (fig. 8.20).[113] Mary's new archbishop was Cardinal Reginald Pole (1500–1558), a staunch Catholic who had been in exile on the Continent for over twenty years. There, he had been head of the English Hospice in Rome, dedicated to St Thomas and the Holy Trinity. Pole was well aware of Becket's powerful legacy. During his exile he played a part in whipping up fury at Henry's treatment of St Thomas's relics, spreading the original rumour that the king had burnt the saint's bones.[114] In 1539 he authored an *Apology* to Charles V, in which he described this desecration.[115] Pole, too, reinstated Becket's martyrdom on the archiepiscopal seal.[116] The reunification of the English Church with Rome was celebrated in a medal issued by the Pope (fig. 8.21).

8.21
Double-sided medal with Pope Julius III raising suppliant England (left) and bust of Pope Julius (right), 1544. Copper alloy. Diam. 4.4 cm. British Museum, London, M.6825. On the left, the scene shows England, taking the form of a kneeling woman, holding the Pope's hand. They are flanked by Mary I, her husband Philip of Spain, Charles V of Spain and Cardinal Pole. The Latin text declares 'ANGLIA RESVRGES. VT NVNO NOVISSIMO DIE' (England, thou shalt rise again, as now, at the last day).

But this union did not last long and, by coincidence, both Mary and Pole died on 17 November 1558. In death, Pole remained connected to St Thomas. His will requested that he be buried in the Corona Chapel at Canterbury, the former location of Becket's reliquary bust.[117]

'Prime glory of the English realm': protecting St Thomas

Elizabeth renewed the reforms of her father and brother. The cult of saints again came under attack, and images reinstated during Mary's reign were removed, including the beleaguered statue of Becket outside the Worshipful Company of Mercers.[118] It was taken down and replaced with the Company's crest, a bust of a maiden.[119] English Catholics had enjoyed five years of freedom from persecution but now found themselves forced to practise their faith in secret. Many fled to Europe. There, new institutions were established, called seminaries and run by Jesuits, who trained the sons of Catholic families to be priests and prepared them for a mission to reconvert England. Foundations were set up in France, Spain and Italy and had the backing of Mary's husband, Philip II. These new priests, many of whom on returning were brutally put to death for treason, kept the memory of the old English martyrs like Becket alive, and looked to them as models of opposition to royal tyranny. The home of the English Mission was in Rome at the Venerable English College. Previously the English Hospice, it was transformed into a seminary in 1576.[120]

From the outset Becket's martyrdom was central to the identity of the English College. In 1580 the rector received a gift of relics of the saint from the Basilica of Santa Maria Maggiore.[121] Every priest in training knew they had to be prepared to die for the cause of reconversion. In Becket they found a champion and guide.[122] As such he was both a focus for devotion and a cause around which to rally. A painting by Durante Alberti (1538–1613) known as *The Martyrs' Picture* was commissioned by the college and completed in 1581 (fig. 8.22). It crystallises the ethos and perception of martyrdom within the institution.[123] At its centre is the Holy Trinity in the form of God the Father, Christ and a dove as the Holy Spirit. God's rich vermilion cloak is held open by angels to reveal the scene of his son hanging limply in his arms, flanked by two further angels, who mourn. Blood from Christ's wounds, in his hands and side, pours out onto a globe. Each place touched by the salvific substance bursts into flames. Underneath, an angel carries a scroll with the words: 'Ignem veni mittere in terram' (I have come to bring fire to the earth).[124]

8.22
Durante Alberti, *Holy Trinity with Saints Thomas and Edmund of East Anglia* (known as *The Martyrs' Picture*), 1581. Oil on canvas. Venerable English College, Rome

Cum Anglis toto terrarum orbē unicum templum Catholicum reliĉtum fit, idq̄, Rômæ
Smē Trinitati Sacrum, cuius in Summa ara hæc tabula conspicitur; mérito in illo
suorum tum priscæ, tum huius ætatis martyrum certamina exprimi curarunt: ut
alios ad laudes, precesq̄, seuerò etiam ad parem animi conſtantiam, maiorum et
sociorum exemplis, excitarent.   2

8.23
After Durante Alberti,
The Martyrs' Picture, in
G. B. Cavalieri, *Ecclesiae
Anglicanae trophaea*
(*The Trophies of the
English Church*), pl. 2, 1584.
Engraving. 24 × 17.8 cm.
British Museum, London,
1973,0512.3.2

Looking up towards this scene are St Thomas of Canterbury on the left and
St Edmund of East Anglia on the right. An angel behind each figure holds
up symbols of their martyrdom. Both Thomas and Edmund interact with
the physical space outside the frame, turning towards the locations of their
respective altars within the church and to the priests of the college below.
Becket holds out his open hands towards the viewer. He is positioned in an
act of presentation, offering up those trained at the college to the Trinity as
future martyrs.

A. S. Thomas Archiepꝰ Cantuariensis ab Henrico II. Anglię rege iniquè
   damnatus ad Pont. Max. appellat, fugamꝗ init.

B. Coram Alexandro III. ſumo Pontifice Senone in Gallia causā ſuā agit.

C. A regijs ſatellitibus pro ecclesiaſtica libertate occiditur anno 1171.

D. Eius ſanguis at cerebrum in templi angulo proiecta, fontem aquæ
   producunt; qui ſemel in lac, quater in cruorem uersus eſt.

25

8.24
The life and martyrdom of Thomas Becket, in G. B. Cavalieri, *Ecclesiae Anglicanae trophaea* (*The Trophies of the English Church*), pl. 25, 1584. Engraving. 24 × 17.8 cm. British Museum, London, 1973,0512.3.25. In the upper left of the image, marked A, Becket meets King Henry II and is exiled. In the upper right, marked B, Becket kneels before Pope Alexander III. At the centre, marked C, the archbishop is murdered by the knights. D marks the legendary spring which turned into Becket's blood.

In the months following the completion of *The Martyrs' Picture* several students and associates of the college were captured in England and executed, including Edmund Campion (1540–1581), Ralph Sherwin (1550–1581) and Alexander Briant (1556–1581), who were hanged, drawn and quartered.[125] All three were quickly proclaimed as Catholic martyrs. Their relics were collected, and these circulated both in England and abroad.[126] Within the English College their deaths were remembered as part of a significant thirty-three scene fresco cycle, painted by Niccolò Circignani

8.25

The martyrdoms of
Edmund Campion,
Alexander Briant and
Ralph Sherwin, in
G. B. Cavalieri, *Ecclesiae
Anglicanae trophaea* (*The
Trophies of the English
Church*), pl. 33, 1584.
Engraving. 24 × 17.8 cm.
British Museum, London,
1973,0512.3.33. Across
the scenes marked A
to C the men are killed,
dismembered, their body
parts are boiled, and
then they are hung from
the gates and walls of
the tower.

A. Edmundus Campianus societatis Iesu sub patibulo concionatur, statimq́
cum Alexandro Brianto Rhemensis, et Rodulpho Sheruino huius Collegij
alumno suspenditur.

B. Illis adhuc tepentibus cor et uiscera extrahuntur, et in ignem proijciuntur.

C. Eorundem membra feruenti aqua elixantur, tum a urbis turres et portas
appenduntur, regnante Elizabetha Anno M.D.LXXXI. die prima Decēbris
Horum constanti morte aliquot hominum millia ad Romanam Ecclesiam
conuersa sunt.

33

(*c*.1517–*c*.1598), located on the walls of the chapel's nave. The cycle was later destroyed, but was recorded in printed form, published as a book of etchings in 1584 entitled *Ecclesiae Anglicanae trophaea* (*The Trophies of the English Church*). *The Martyrs' Picture* is the first plate in this series (fig. 8.23). It is followed by a chronological history of English Christianity and martyrdom, beginning with St Peter converting the English. Becket's martyrdom (fig. 8.24) appears between the murder of two foreign missionaries to England and that of St William of Norwich, who is shown crucified. The executions of John Fisher and Thomas More, which follow, link these older, pre-Reformation martyrs with the new, including Campion, Sherwin and Briant (fig. 8.25). Seen together, the image cycle of the college presents Roman Catholicism in England as an unbroken history, and the contemporary English martyrs as heirs to Becket's crown. By the end of the century, the next generation of Catholics were continuing faithfully to keep their hearts and minds on St Thomas. A play, written to be performed on the feast of Becket's martyrdom, was put on by schoolboys on 29 December 1599 at the Jesuit English College in Saint-Omer, France. As part of the play, those present were reminded that they were called to follow Becket's example in all things, which, in light of the dire state of England, might mean being prepared to sacrifice themselves in martyrdom.[127] Beyond serving as a call to arms, the play reveals the pivotal role that the English Catholic community abroad played in keeping Becket's memory alive. Over the course of the sixteenth century, Becket's cult had been through a phase of radical transformation. By means of royal decree he was downgraded from holy martyr to traitor. And yet, for those who resisted these changes, he remained a figure to be emulated. A model of opposition to tyranny.

Legacy

In the 1590s John Fortescue (1561–1659) and his wife Helen, both devoted Roman Catholics, fled England for the Continent to avoid persecution. Hidden among their belongings were a small fragment of St Thomas's skull and part of his breast bone. These precious items had been entrusted to them by the Bishop of Lincoln, Thomas Watson (1513–1584).[1] At this time the veneration, or even mere possession, of relics in England was illegal, and the Fortescues' actions were therefore treasonous in the eyes of the law: if caught, they faced imprisonment and possibly even death. Once in France, and out of immediate danger, they headed for the recently founded English Jesuit college at Saint-Omer, located about twenty-five miles inland from the coast at Calais in the Spanish-controlled Netherlands. After their arrival they deposited the skull fragment and breast bone with the college. It served as a safe house for relics of the old saints like Becket, but also those of the new martyrs like Campion and Sherwin. To preserve was to remember and to remember was to refute the idea that the long history of Roman Catholicism in England could be wiped out entirely.

Around seventy years later, in 1666, the future rector of the college, Thomas Cary, commissioned a silver sculpture of St Thomas of Canterbury from Liège's premier silversmith Henri de Flémalle (fig. 9.1). The figure shows Becket with a sword wedged deeply into his head but his right hand raised defiantly in blessing. Two small holes located at his breast allow a separate reliquary of gilded silver to be fixed into place (fig. 9.2). This small oval box was made to appear like a morse, that is, a clasp to hold together an ecclesiastical garment. An inscription around its rim in Latin declares its contents to be a piece of St Thomas's cranium: 'EX CRANIO ST. THOMAE CANTVARIENSIS' (From the skull of St Thomas of Canterbury). The relic, wrapped in red velvet and secured with golden thread, is visible through the glass casing. Whether or not this was the same fragment brought out of England at great personal risk by the Fortescues is unknown. It may be another skull fragment of Becket's, which the Jesuit priest John Gerard was shown during a secret mission to England in 1593. He recorded that the relic was held in a small silver head and was 'thought to be the piece that was chipped off when he [Becket] was so wickedly slain'.[2] Whatever the case, the relic's preservation by the college, and its

9.1 (opposite)
Henri de Flémalle, *Reliquary Statue of Thomas Becket*, 1666.
Silver. 36.3 × 15.8 × 19.4 cm.
British Jesuit Province

9.2 (left)
Skull relic and reliquary of Thomas Becket, 12th century (relic attrib.), *c.*1666 (reliquary).
Silver, gold, glass, copper alloy, velvet and silk. 6.1 × 7.6 × 2.2 cm.
British Jesuit Province

subsequent placement in a costly new reliquary, demonstrated the continued human connection between St Thomas and the faithful. Possibly carried in procession as part of church services, it was also a material reminder of the ongoing resistance to royal authority, connecting the moment of Becket's medieval martyrdom with the fragile survival of his cult throughout the time of early modern persecution.

Where, then, does the Becket story end? Between the seventeenth and eighteenth centuries, in England at least, his popular appeal waned. There was no longer a shrine in Canterbury to visit and his image had been stripped from all church interiors. English Catholics still venerated St Thomas but this took place behind closed doors. Antiquarians and historians studied his life and legacy, looking for material evidence of the once flourishing cult, and investigating the circumstances of his dispute with Henry II. But their output was generally academic and inaccessible to the majority of the public. However, in the nineteenth century Becket was resurrected as an historical figure for the stage.[3] Alfred Tennyson's 1884 play *Becket* was enormously popular and toured internationally. Henry Irving (1838–1905), one of the leading actors of his day, took on the title role, which he continued to perform for the remainder of his life. In 1964 the friendship and fallout between Henry and Thomas took a flamboyant turn in director Peter Glenville's *Becket*, with Peter O'Toole playing the king and Richard Burton the archbishop. And yet, St Thomas also resurfaced as a figure for contemplation at moments of real tyranny. T. S. Eliot's tense and dramatic play *Murder in the Cathedral* (1935) is an exploration of the months leading up to the archbishop's violent death. It was written and first performed when the spectre of Fascism loomed large over Europe. Such a connection would not have been lost on audiences at the time. At one point in the play the archbishop even asks, 'Does it seem strange to you that the angels should have announced Peace, when ceaselessly the world has been stricken with War and the fear of War?'[4] Our perception of Becket is still marked by the destructive consequences of the English Reformation. At Canterbury Cathedral today the site of his shrine is marked by a single candle; a constant light in a lost space. Light, so often used to invoke the memory of the dead at sites of special significance, is particularly apt for Becket. Edward Grim framed the saint's legacy with the metaphor of a candle:

> And now the candle has been placed upon a candlestick, so that they who enter may see the light. Now in him we see fulfilled what the Saviour promised to the elect, 'He who conquers, I will make him a pillar of fire in my temple'. And now, thanks to heavenly providence we have a pillar. Let us fix our gaze on the light.[5]

The solitary candle at Canterbury thus offers us a moment to reflect on the remarkable story of a murder and the making of a saint.

Notes

BL – British Library, London
TNA – The National Archives, Kew

Introduction

1. Michael Staunton, ed. and trans., *The Lives of Thomas Becket*, Manchester: Manchester University Press, 2001, p. 200, n. 39.

Chapter 1

1. Taken from Edward Grim's account, edited and translated in Michael Staunton, *The Lives of Thomas Becket*, Manchester: Manchester University Press, 2001, p. 40.

2. Becket himself made this claim, although there is no clear evidence that his family were of Norman or knightly descent. For an overview of Becket and London, see John Jenkins, 'St Thomas Becket and Medieval London', *History*, vol. 105 (2020), pp. 652–72.

3. Translated by H. E. Butler in Frank M. Stenton, *Norman London*, London: G. Bell and Sons, 1934, p. 29.

4. See John Clark's general survey (*Saxon and Norman London*, London: Museum of London, 1999) and Christopher Thomas, *The Archaeology of Medieval London*, Stroud: Sutton, 2002.

5. William FitzStephen estimated that in addition to St Paul's Cathedral there were thirteen monastic houses and 126 parish churches in and around the city. For monastic houses, see FitzStephen, translated by Butler, in Stenton, *Norman London*, pp. 26–7; for parish churches, see Clark, *Saxon and Norman London*, p. 32 and Thomas, *The Archaeology of Medieval London*, p. 40.

6. See map of London, *c.*1200, in Clark, *Saxon and Norman London*, pp. 40–1 and Marjorie B. Honeybourne, 'Map of London under Henry II', in Stenton, *Norman London*, pp. 68–9. Francis Sheppard, *London: A History*, Oxford: Oxford University Press, 1998, p. 84; John Schofield, *London, 1100–1600: The Archaeology of a Capital City*, Sheffield: Equinox Publishing, 2011.

7. Joe and Caroline Hillaby, *The Palgrave Dictionary of Medieval Anglo-Jewish History*, London: Palgrave Macmillan, 2013, pp. 1–4. A twelfth-century lamp found in the early 1800s is similar in form to the sabbath lamp and may have been used by a member of the city's Jewish community; it is in the Museum of London, inv. no. 1374. See George Zarnecki et al., *English Romanesque Art 1066–1200*, London: Arts Council of Great Britain, 1984, no. 258, pp. 253.

8. Staunton, *The Lives*, p. 40.

9. Ibid., p. 41.

10. Anne Duggan, *Thomas Becket*, London: Arnold, 2004, p. 8.

11. Neil Stratford argues that this object was engraved in England, but also points out that it is not known where bowls of this type were made and that there were probably multiple centres of production, including Germany, in Zarnecki et al., *English Romanesque Art 1066–1200*, no. 259, pp. 253–4.

12. The association was stressed in the sixteenth century in Thomas Stapleton, *Tres Thomae*, Douai: Ex officina Ioannis Bogardi, 1588.

13. The Icelandic Saga describes how Becket studied in the schools of Paris, see Staunton, *The Lives*, pp. 13 and 42, as does William FitzStephen, see *Materials for the History of Thomas Becket* (hereafter *MTB*), ed. James Craigie Robertson and J. Brigstocke Sheppard, vol. III, London: Longman & Co., 1877, p. 14. Very little is known about this period of Becket's life; in addition to these two mentions, Everlin, abbot of St Lawrence in Liège, stated he had met Becket in Paris when he was younger, see Frank Barlow, *Thomas Becket*, Berkeley: University of California Press, 1986, p. 20.

14. Thomas, *The Archaeology of Medieval London*, p. 5. Jenkins, 'St Thomas Becket and Medieval London', pp. 659–60.

15. Barlow, *Thomas Becket*, pp. 14–15; Duggan, *Thomas Becket*, p. 8. The history of this site is discussed in further detail in Chapter 5.

16. Thomas, *The Archaeology of Medieval London*, p. 24.

17. A. G. Vince and M. A. Jenner, 'The Saxon and Early Medieval Pottery of London', in *Aspects of Saxo-Norman London*, vol. II: *Finds and Environmental Evidence*, ed. A. G. Vince, London and Middlesex Archaeological Society Special Paper 12, 1991, pp. 19–119. See also J. Pearce, A. G. Vince and M. A. Jenner, *A Dated Type Series of London Medieval Pottery*, vol. II: *London-type Ware*, London and Middlesex Archaeological Society Special Paper 6, 1985.

18. Derek J. Keene and Vanessa Harding, 'St Mary Colechurch 105/0: Parish Church of St Mary Colechurch', in *Historical Gazetteer of London before the Great Fire Cheapside; Parishes of All Hallows Honey Lane, St Martin Pomary, St Mary Le Bow, St Mary Colechurch and St Pancras Soper Lane*, London: British History Online, 1987, pp. 405–15, available at www.british-history.ac.uk/no-series/london-gazetteer-pre-fire/pp405-415 (accessed 21 August 2020).

19. More information can be found at 'All Hallows Honey Lane', The Worshipful Company of Parish Clerks website, www.londonparishclerks.com/Parishes-Churches/Individual-Parish-Info/All-Hallows-Honey-Lane (accessed 9 April 2020). See also Derek J. Keene and Vanessa Harding, 'All Hallows Honey Lane 11/0', in *Historical Gazetteer of London before the Great Fire Cheapside; Parishes of All Hallows Honey Lane, St Martin Pomary; St Mary Le Bow, St Mary Colechurch and St Pancras Soper Lane*, London: British History Online, 1987, pp. 3–9, available at www.british-history.ac.uk/no-series/london-gazetteer-pre-fire/pp3-9 (accessed 9 April 2020). Our thanks to Dr Richard Plant and John McNeill for sharing their thoughts on this sculpture.

20. Sheppard, *London: A History*, p. 79. After the Norman Conquest, it became traditional for kings to confirm that the citizens of London enjoyed the existing customs they had had under the previous king and to grant special privileges at a cost.

21. Duggan, *Thomas Becket*, p. 8; Clark, *Saxon and Norman London*, p. 44; Susan Reynolds, 'The Rulers of London in the Twelfth Century', *History*, vol. 57 (1972), pp. 337–57, at p. 354.

22. Sheppard, *London: A History*, p. 82.

23. William FitzStephen, translated by H. E. Butler in Stenton, *Norman London*, p. 31. For reference to surviving bone skates see Clark, *Saxon and Norman London*, p. 48.

24. Duggan, *Thomas Becket*, p. 9.

25. Ibid., p. 11.

26. Erwin Panofsky, *Gothic Architecture and Scholasticism*, London: Meridian Books, 1957.

27. John Willinsky, *The Intellectual Properties of Learning: A Prehistory from Saint Jerome to John Locke*, Chicago: University of Chicago Press, 2018, p. 23. See also C. Stephen Jaeger, *The Envy of Angels: Cathedral Schools and Social Ideals in Medieval Europe, 950–1200*, Philadelphia: University of Pennsylvania Press, 2000.

28. M. L. Rampolla, 'Melun, Robert de (*c.*1100–1167), theologian and bishop of Hereford', *Oxford Dictionary of National Biography*, 23 September 2004, www.oxforddnb.com/view/10.1093/ref:odnb/9780198614128.001.0001/odnb-9780198614128-e-23727 (accessed 9 April 2020). Later, in 1163, Robert would be consecrated as Bishop of Hereford by Becket, as Archbishop of Canterbury.

29. Laura Cleaver, *Education in Twelfth-Century Art and Architecture: Images of Learning in Europe, circa 1100–1220*, Woodbridge: The Boydell Press, 2016, p. 9.

30. Zarnecki et al., *English Romanesque Art 1066–1200*, no. 287, pp. 270–1. See also Laura Cleaver, 'The Liberal Arts in Sculpture and Metalwork in Twelfth-Century France and Ideals of Education', *Immediations*, vol. 1 (2007), pp. 56–75.

31. Several images of Grammar demonstrate the important relationship between punishment and learning, see Cleaver, 'The Liberal Arts in Sculpture and Metalwork', pp. 56–75.

32. John of Salisbury, *The Metalogicon of John of Salisbury: A Twelfth-Century Defense of the Verbal and Logical Arts of the Trivium*, trans. Daniel D. McGarry, Berkeley: University of California Press, 1955, p. 72.

33. Hugh of St Victor, *The Didascalicon of Hugh of St Victor, A Medieval Guide to the Arts*, trans. Jerome Taylor, London and New York: Columbia University Press, 1961, p. 97.

34. John of Salisbury, *The Metalogicon*, p. 103.

35. Duggan, *Thomas Becket*, p. 11; Frank Barlow, *Thomas Becket and his Clerks*, Oxford: Friends of Canterbury Cathedral, 1987, p. 8; John Guy, *Thomas Becket: Warrior, Priest, Rebel, Victim*, London: Viking, 2012, pp. 38–9.

36. Everett U. Crosby, *The King's Bishops: The Politics of Patronage in England and Normandy, 1066–1216*, New York: Palgrave Macmillan, 2013, p. 64; *MTB*, vol. IV, 1879, pp. 9. For an English translation of William FitzStephen's account, see David C. Douglas and George W. Greenaway, *English Historical Documents*, vol. II: *1042–1189*, London: Routledge, 1981, no. 119, p. 816.

37. Eiríkr Magnússon, ed., *Thómas Saga erkibyskups: A Life of Archbishop Thomas Becket, in Icelandic, with English Translation, Notes and Glossary, vol. 1*, London: Longman & Co., 1875, p. 37.

38. Avrom Saltman, *Theobald, Archbishop of Canterbury*, London: Athlone Press, 1956, p. 165.

39. Frank Barlow, 'Theobald (c.1090–1161), archbishop of Canterbury', *Oxford Dictionary of National Biography*, 7 January 2010, www.oxforddnb.com/view/10.1093/ref:odnb/9780198614128.001.0001/odnb-9780198614128-e-27168 (accessed 9 April 2020).

40. Saltman, *Theobald, Archbishop of Canterbury*, pp. 181–534.

41. Margaret Gibson, 'Normans and Angevins, 1070–1220', in *A History of Canterbury Cathedral*, ed. Patrick Collinson, Nigel Ramsay and Margaret Sparks, Oxford: Oxford University Press, 1995, pp. 38–68, at p. 48.

42. Peter Fergusson, *Canterbury Cathedral Priory in the Age of Becket*, New Haven and London: Yale University Press, 2011, pp. 11–24.

43. Saltman, *Theobald, Archbishop of Canterbury*, no. 31, pp. 259–60, translated in Peter Fergusson, 'Prior Wibert's Fountain Houses: Service and Symbolism at Christ Church Canterbury', in *The Four Modes of Seeing: Approaches to Medieval Imagery in Honor of Madeline Harrison Caviness*, ed. Evelyn Staudinger Lane, Elizabeth Carson Pastan and Ellen M. Shortell, London: Routledge, 2009, pp. 83–98, at p. 98.

44. Walter de Gray Birch, *Catalogue of Seals from the Department of Manuscripts in the British Museum, Vol. 1*, London: British Museum, 1887, nos 1173–4, p. 158.

45. Ibid.; T. A. Heslop, 'What is a Secret Seal? Ancient Gems and Individuality in Twelfth-Century England', forthcoming article. We are grateful to Sandy Heslop for sharing this in advance of publication.

46. Martin Henig, 'The Re-Use and Copying of Ancient Intaglios Set in Medieval Personal Seals, Mainly Found in England: An Aspect of the Renaissance of the 12th Century', in *Good Impressions: Image and Authority in Medieval Seals*, ed. John Cherry et al., London: British Museum Press, 2008, pp. 25–34.

47. The original script reads '+ SIGILLVM ECCLE XPI CANTVARIE: PRIME SEDIS BRITANNIE'.

48. Lloyd de Beer, 'The Temple of Justice and the Key of David: Anachronism and Authority in the Chichester Seal Matrix', *British Art Studies*, issue 6 (June 2017), available at http://britishartstudies.ac.uk/issues/issue-index/issue-6/chichester-seal (accessed 8 April 2020).

49. Ursula Nilgen, 'Intellectuality and Splendour: Thomas Becket as a Patron of the Arts', in *Art and Patronage in the English Romanesque*, ed. Sarah Macready and F. H. Thompson, London: Society of Antiquaries of London, 1986, pp. 145–58.

50. Our sincere thanks to Martin Henig for his help in identifying this gem and suggesting a date. He identified it as Apollo when for many years it had been thought to represent Mercury. When it was published in Joseph Burtt, 'Confirmation by Thomas, Archbishop of Canterbury, of the Church of Bexley, Kent, to the Canons of the Holy Trinity, London', *Archaeological Journal*, vol. 26 (1869), pp. 84–9, the drawing was elaborated to show the standing figure with a caduceus. Investigation of the actual seal at TNA revealed there is no caduceus present and the figure is instead holding a laurel spray and so can be identified as Apollo Daphnephoros.

51. Burtt, 'Confirmation by Thomas, Archbishop of Canterbury', pp. 84–9.

52. William of Canterbury's *Life of Becket*, in *MTB*, vol. I, 1875, p. 4; Guy, *Thomas Becket*, pp. 49–50; Jean Dunbabin, 'Canterbury, John of [John Bellesmains] (c.1120–1204?), Archbishop of Lyons', *Oxford Dictionary of National Biography*, 23 September 2004, www.oxforddnb.com/view/10.1093/ref:odnb/9780198614128.001.0001/odnb-9780198614128-e-2062 (accessed 21 August 2020).

53. Roger of Pontigny, quoted in Staunton, *The Lives*, p. 46.

54. Garnier de Pont-Sainte-Maxence, *A Life of Thomas Becket in Verse*, ed. and trans. Ian Short, Turnhout: Brepols, 2014, p. 29.

55. Frank Barlow, 'Pont l'Évêque, Roger de (c.1115–1181), Archbishop of York', *Oxford Dictionary of National Biography*, 23 September 2004, www.oxforddnb.com/view/10.1093/ref:odnb/9780198614128.001.0001/odnb-9780198614128-e-23961, (accessed 21 August 2020).

56. Expressed by William FitzStephen, in *MTB*, vol. III, 1877, p. 16.

57. John of Salisbury, in *MTB*, vol. II, 1876, p. 304, and William FitzStephen, in *MTB*, vol. III, 1877, p. 17.

58. John of Salisbury, in *MTB*, vol. II, 1876, p. 304.

59. Ibid. Discussed in Barlow, *Thomas Becket*, p. 37.

60. Hugh M. Thomas, *The Secular Clergy in England, 1066–1216*, Oxford: Oxford University Press, 2014.

61. Ursula Nilgen, 'Thomas Becket en Normandie', in *Les saints dans la Normandie médiévale*, ed. Pierre Bouet and François Neveux, Caen: Presses Universitaires de Caen, 2000, pp. 189–204; Thomas, *The Secular Clergy in England*, pp. 9–13.

62. Zarnecki et al., *English Romanesque Art 1066–1200*, no. 164, pp. 195–8. Deborah Kahn, *Canterbury Cathedral and its Romanesque Sculpture*, London: Harvey Miller, 1991, pp. 139–71. Jeffrey West, 'The Romanesque Screen at Canterbury Cathedral Reconsidered', in *Medieval Art, Architecture and Archaeology at Canterbury*, ed. Alixe Bovey, Leeds: Maney Publishing, 2013, pp. 167–79; Carolyn Malone, *Twelfth-Century Sculptural Finds at Canterbury Cathedral and the Cult of Thomas Becket*, Oxford: Oxbow Books, 2019.

63. Tim Tatton-Brown, 'The Two Mid-Twelfth-Century Cloister Arcades at Canterbury Cathedral Priory', *Journal of the British Archaeological Association*, vol. 159 (2006), pp. 91–104.

64. See note 62 above.

65. Tatton-Brown, 'The Two Mid-Twelfth-Century Cloister Arcades'.

66. Francis Woodman, 'The Waterworks Drawings of the Eadwine Psalter', in *The Eadwine Psalter: Text, Image, and Monastic Culture in Twelfth-Century Canterbury*, ed. Margaret Gibson et al., London: The Modern Humanities Research Association, 1992, pp. 168–77.

67. T. A. Heslop, 'Eadwine and his Portrait', in *The Eadwine Psalter: Text, Image, and Monastic Culture in Twelfth-Century Canterbury*, ed. Margaret Gibson et al., London: The Modern Humanities Research Association, 1992, pp. 178–85.

68. Heslop has argued that Eadwine produced a pontifical for Becket, now in the BL, Cotton MS Tiberius B VIII/1, see Heslop, 'Eadwine and his Portrait', p. 184, n. 33.

69. Christopher de Hamel, *Glossed Books of the Bible and the Origins of the Paris Book Trade*, Woodbridge: D. S. Brewer, 1984, pp. 38–47.

70. Ibid.

71. BL, Royal MS 20 A II, f. 6v. Scot McKendrick, John Lowden, and Kathleen Doyle, *Royal Manuscripts: The Genius of Illumination*, London: British Library, 2011, no. 116, pp. 342–3.

72. Marjorie Chibnall, *The Empress Matilda: Queen Consort, Queen Mother and Lady of the English*, London: Blackwell, 1991, p. 55; Catherine Hanley, *Matilda: Empress, Queen, Warrior*, New Haven and London: Yale University Press, 2019; Warren, *Henry II*, p. 11.

73. These included their request to have control of castles promised to Geoffrey as part of Matilda's dowry.

74. Chibnall, *The Empress Matilda*, pp. 61–5.

75. Ibid., p. 65. Warren, *Henry II*, pp. 14–16.

76. David Crouch, *The Reign of King Stephen, 1135–1154*, Harlow: Pearson Education Limited, 2000, p. 38.

77. Ibid., p. 330.

78. Chibnall, *The Empress Matilda*, p. 79–83.

79. Ibid., pp. 79–80. Crouch, *The Reign of King Stephen*, p. 97.

80. Stephen was kept prisoner first in Gloucester and then Bristol.

81. Walter de Gray Birch, 'A Fasciculus of the Charters of Mathildis, Empress of the Romans, and an Account of her Great Seal', *Journal of the British Archaeological Association*, vol. 31 (1875), pp. 376–98.

82. Ibid., p. 380.

83. Fiona Tolhurst, *Geoffrey of Monmouth and the Translation of Female Kingship*, New York: Palgrave Macmillan, 2013, pp. 41–2.

84. R. P. Mack, 'Stephen and the Anarchy 1135–1154', *British Numismatic Journal*, vol. 35 (1966), pp. 38–115; Marion Archibald, 'Coins', in Zarnecki et al., *English Romanesque Art, 1066–1200*, pp. 320–41; Mark Blackburn, 'Coinage and the Currency', in *The Anarchy of King Stephen's Reign*, ed. Edmund King, Oxford: Clarendon Press, 1994, pp. 145–205; Crouch, *The Reign of King Stephen*, pp. 329–31.

85. Most of his early life was spent in Anjou but as a boy Henry visited England on several occasions. For a summary of the trips he made to England prior to becoming king, see Henry William Carless Davis, *Regesta regum Anglo-Normannorum, 1066–1154*, vol. III, Oxford: Clarendon Press, 1913, pp. xlvi–xlviii.

86. 'The Genealogy of the Kings of the English,' in *Aelred of Rievaulx: The Historical Works*, ed. Marsha L. Dutton, trans. Jane Patricia Freeland, Kalamazoo: Cistercian Publications, 2005, pp. 39–122.

87. Saltman, *Theobald, Archbishop of Canterbury*, p. 27.

88. Ibid., p. 38.

89. John T. Appleby, ed. and trans., *The Chronicle of Richard of Devizes of the Time of King Richard the First*, London: Thomas Nelson & Sons Ltd, 1963, p. 25.

90. Richard Barber, *Henry Plantagenet: A Biography*, London: Barrie and Rockliff with Pall Mall Press, 1964, p. 55. These vast dominions required extensive travel and Aurell notes that during his thirty-four-year reign Henry traversed the English Channel twenty-eight times and crossed the Irish Sea twice. See Martin Aurell, *The Plantagenet Empire 1154–1224*, trans. David Crouch, Harlow: Pearson, 2007, p. 27.

91. Taken from Anonymous I (Roger of Pontigny), in Staunton, *The Lives*, p. 49.

92. William FitzStephen, translated in Staunton, *The Lives*, p. 48.

93. Douglas and Greenaway, *English Historical Documents*, no. 16, p. 405. For a general discussion of Henry's character see Warren, *Henry II*, pp. 207–11.

94. Barber, *Henry Plantagenet: A Biography*, p. 83.

95. Letter from Becket to Henry II in late May/early June 1166, in *The Correspondence of Thomas Becket, Archbishop of Canterbury, 1162–1170*, vol. I, ed. Anne Duggan, Oxford: Clarendon Press, 2000, no. 74, pp. 292–9.

96. Canterbury Cathedral Library: CCA-CC-A/A/1.

97. Translation of the charter taken from Canterbury Archive database: https://archives.canterbury-cathedral.org/CalmView/Record.aspx?src=CalmView.Catalog&id=CCA-CC%2fA%2fA%2f1&pos=1 (accessed 31 December 2020).

98. Nicholas Vincent, 'The Court of Henry II', in *Henry II: New Interpretations*, ed. Christopher Harper-Bill and Nicholas Vincent, Woodbridge: The Boydell Press, 2007, pp. 278–334, at p. 283.

99. Duggan, *Thomas Becket*, p. 17.

100. Barlow, *Thomas Becket*, p. 42.

101. See, for example, William FitzStephen's account of Becket wearing a cape with long sleeves and playing chess in 1161, translated in Staunton, *The Lives*, p. 58.

102. Ibid., p. 55.

103. Ibid., p. 56.

104. Pont-Sainte-Maxence, *A Life of Thomas Becket in Verse*, p. 31.

105. Staunton, *The Lives*, p. 67.

106. Chibnall, *Empress Matilda*, pp. 166–8.

107. Foliot made this claim in his letter 'Multiplicem nobis', which is translated in Christopher Hill, 'Gilbert Foliot and the Two Swords: Law and Political Theory in Twelfth-century England', PhD thesis, University of Texas at Austin, 2008, p. 151.

108. Barlow, *Thomas Becket*, p. 73.

109. Michael Staunton, 'Thomas Becket's Conversion', in *Anglo-Norman Studies XXI: Proceedings of the Battle Conference 1998*, ed. Christopher Harper-Bill, Woodbridge: The Boydell Press, 1999, pp. 193–212, esp. p. 200. For figs 1.28–1.29, see Zarnecki et al., *English Romanesque Art 1066–1200*, no. 268a, p. 257 and no. 491, p. 357. For fig. 1.30, see Anne Ward et al., *The Ring: From Antiquity to the Twentieth Century*, London: Thames & Hudson, 1981, no. 61, p. 118.

110. Edward Carpenter, *Cantuar: The Archbishops in their Office*, 3rd edn, London: Mowbray, 1997, p. 47, translated from *MTB*, vol. IV, 1879, p. 19.

111. Carpenter, *Cantuar*, p. 43.

112. Translated in Staunton, 'Thomas Becket's Conversion', p. 206.

Chapter 2

1. Becket's reply to Henry when told of the king's plans to promote him to archbishop, as relayed in Herbert of Bosham's account, quoted and translated in Michael Staunton, *The Lives of Thomas Becket*, Manchester: Manchester University Press, 2001, p. 60.

2. C. Stephen Jaeger, *The Envy of Angels: Cathedral Schools and Social Ideals in Medieval Europe, 950–1200*, Philadelphia: University of Pennsylvania Press, 2000. For a summary of the Becket dispute see Martin Aurell, *The Plantagenet Empire 1154–1224*, trans. David Crouch, Harlow: Pearson, 2007, pp. 219–62.

3. Alan Harding, *Medieval Law and the Foundation of the State*, Oxford: Oxford University Press, 2002, p. 193.

4. Ibid.

5. Ibid., p. 81.

6. Anne Duggan, *The Correspondence of Thomas Becket, Archbishop of Canterbury, 1162–1170*, 2 vols, Oxford: Clarendon Press, 2000. For a full list of Becket's references to the Decretum, see vol. II, pp. 1432–6.

7. Christopher de Hamel, *Glossed Books of the Bible and the Origins of the Paris Book Trade*, Woodbridge: D. S. Brewer, 1984, pp. 45, 49.

8. István Pieter Bejczy, *The Cardinal Virtues in the Middle Ages: A Study in Moral Thought from the Fourth to the Fourteenth Century*, Leiden: Brill, 2011, p. 73.

9. William S. Monroe, 'The Guennol Triptych and the Twelfth-Century Revival of Jurisprudence', in *The Cloisters: Studies in Honor of the Fiftieth Anniversary*, ed. Elizabeth C. Parker, New York: Metropolitan Museum of Art, 1992, pp. 166–77; Johannes Fried, 'Time and Eternity in the Eschatology of the Guennol Triptych', *Viator*, vol. 29 (1998), pp. 363–76.

10. Richard M. Fraher, 'The Becket Dispute and Two Decretist Traditions: The Bolognese Masters Revisited and Some New Anglo-Norman Texts', *Journal of Medieval History*, vol. 4 (1978), pp. 347–68; Anne Duggan, *Thomas Becket*, London: Arnold, 2004, pp. 30–2; Wilfred L. Warren, *Henry II*, new edn, New Haven and London: Yale University Press, 2000, pp. 456–7.

11. The chronicler is Ralph Diceto, discussed in Duggan, *Thomas Becket*, p. 34.

12. For an overview of the situation, see Hugh M. Thomas, *The Secular Clergy in England, 1066–1216*, Oxford: Oxford University Press, 2014, pp. 209–26.

13. For a discussion of the legal dispute between king and archbishop, see Harold J. Berman, *Law and Revolution: The Formation of the Western Legal Tradition*, Cambridge: Harvard University Press, 1983, pp. 225–70.

14. Quoted and translated in Warren, *Henry II*, p. 462.

15. Anne Duggan, 'Clerical Exemption in Canon Law from Gratian to the Decretals', *Medieval Worlds*, vol. 6 (2017), pp. 78–100.

16. Translated and quoted in Thomas, *The Secular Clergy in England*, p. 210.

17. Peter G. Walsh and M. J. Kennedy, trans. and eds, *William of Newburgh: The History of English Affairs. Book 2*, Liverpool: Liverpool University Press, 2007, p. 71.

18. Reported by Herbert of Bosham, in *MTB*, vol. III, 1877, p. 207.

19. Quentin Taylor, 'John of Salisbury, the Policraticus and Political Thought', *Humanitas*, vol. 19 (2006), pp. 133–57, at p. 138.

20. See Cary Nederman's introduction to John of Salisbury, *Policraticus*, ed. and trans. Cary J. Nederman, Cambridge: Cambridge University Press, 2000, pp. xv–xxvi.

21. Larry Scanlon, *Narrative, Authority and Power: The Medieval Exemplum and the Chaucerian Tradition*, Cambridge: Cambridge University Press, 2007, p. 88.

22. Montague R. James, *The Sources of Archbishop Parker's Collection of MSS at Corpus Christi College, Cambridge, with a Reprint of the Catalogue of Thomas Markaunt's Library*, vol. 32, Cambridge: Cambridge Antiquarian Society, 1899, p. 22; De Hamel, *Glossed Books of the Bible*, Woodbridge: D. S. Brewer, 1984, p. 39.

23. Nederman, in John of Salisbury, *Policraticus*, p. vi.

24. Lloyd de Beer, 'The Temple of Justice and the Key of David: Anachronism and Authority in the Chichester Seal Matrix', *British Art Studies*, issue 6 (June 2017), available at http://britishartstudies. ac.uk/issues/issue-index/issue-6/chichester-seal (accessed 8 April 2020).

25. Karen Bollermann and Cary Nederman, 'John of Salisbury', *The Stanford Encyclopedia of Philosophy*, ed. Edward N. Zalta, 21 September 2016, available at https://plato.stanford.edu/archives/fall2016/ entries/john-salisbury (accessed 15 April 2020).

26. Translated and quoted in Kate Langdon Forhan, 'Salisburian Stakes: The Uses of "Tyranny" in John of Salisbury's "Policraticus"', *History of Political Thought*, vol. 11 (1990), pp. 397–407, at p. 401.

27. John of Salisbury, *The Statesman's Book: Policraticus*, trans. John Dickinson, New York: Knopf, 1927, pp. 396–7.

28. Bernhard W. Scholz, 'The Canonization of Edward the Confessor', *Speculum*, vol. 36 (1961), pp. 51–60; Janet Nelson, 'Royal Saints and Early Medieval Kingship', *Studies in Church History*, vol. 10 (1973), pp. 39–44; Elizabeth M. Hallam, 'Royal Burial and the Cult of Kingship in France and England, 1060–1330', *Journal of Medieval History*, vol. 8 (1982), pp. 359–80.

29. Duggan, *Thomas Becket*, p. 39.

30. From *Summa causa inter regnum et Thomam*, translated in Staunton, *The Lives*, p. 80.

31. Janet Backhouse and Christopher de Hamel, eds, *The Becket Leaves*, London: British Library, 1988.

32. Translated in Backhouse and de Hamel, *The Becket Leaves*, p. 31.

33. Garnier de Pont-Sainte-Maxence, *A Life of Thomas Becket in Verse*, ed. and trans. Ian Short, Turnhout: Brepols, 2014, p. 45.

34. From *Summa causa inter regnum et Thomam*, translated in Staunton, *The Lives*, pp. 82–3.

35. Roger of Pontigny, translated in Staunton, *The Lives*, p. 87.

36. Ibid., p. 90.

37. Herbert of Bosham, translated in Staunton, *The Lives*, p. 97.

38. Duggan, *Thomas Becket*, pp. 62–83; Anne Duggan, 'Roman, Canon and Common Law in Twelfth-Century England: The Council of Northampton (1164) Re-Examined', *Historical Research*, vol. 83 (2010), pp. 379–408.

39. Taken from Herbert of Bosham's account, translated in Staunton, *The Lives*, p. 121.

40. Roger of Pontigny, translated in Staunton, *The Lives*, p. 118.

41. For information on the relationship between Henry II and Louis VII, see Jean Dunbabin, 'Henry II and Louis VII', in *Henry II: New Interpretations*, ed. Christopher Harper-Bill and Nicholas Vincent, Woodbridge: The Boydell Press, 2007, pp. 47–62.

42. Jean Traux, *Archbishops Ralph d'Escures, William of Corbeil and Theobald of Bec: Heirs of Anselm and Ancestors of Becket*, London: Routledge, 2017, pp. 12–17, 126, 130, 187.

43. William FitzStephen, translated in Staunton, *The Lives*, p. 135.

44. Kay Slocum, *Liturgies in Honour of Thomas Becket*, Toronto: University of Toronto Press, 2003, pp. 46–8.

45. Herbert of Bosham, translated in Staunton, *The Lives*, p. 145.

46. Ibid., p. 159.

47. Alan of Tewkesbury, translated in Staunton, *The Lives*, p. 163.

48. Matthew Strickland, *Henry the Young King, 1155–1183*, New Haven and London: Yale University Press, 2016, p. 104.

49. Ibid., pp. 104–5.

50. Herbert of Bosham, translated in Staunton, *The Lives*, p. 192.

51. Translated in Frank Barlow, *Thomas Becket*, Berkeley: University of California Press, 1986, p. 235.

52. Garnier de Pont-Sainte-Maxence, translated in Staunton, *The Lives*, p. 189.

53. Nicholas Vincent, 'The Murderers of Thomas Becket', in *Bischofsmord im Mittelalter*, ed. Natalie Fryde and Dirk Reitz, Göttingen: Vandenhoeck & Ruprecht, 2003, pp. 211–72.

54. Thomas K. Compton, 'The Murderers of Thomas Becket', *The Historian*, vol. 35 (1973), pp. 238–55, p. 242; Vincent, 'The Murderers of Thomas Becket'.

55. Staunton, *The Lives*, p. 187.

56. Ibid., p. 198.

57. Ibid. This is also reported in Benedict of Peterborough's account, see *MTB*, vol. II, 1876, p. 10.

58. Barlow, *Thomas Becket*, p. 244.

59. Ibid., p. 243.

60. Edward Grim's account, translated in Staunton, *The Lives*, p. 201.

61. Ibid., p. 202.

62. Ibid.

63. Ibid., p. 205.

64. William of Canterbury, quoted in Latin in *MTB*, vol. I, 1875, p. 132.

65. Garnier de Pont-Sainte-Maxence, *A Life of Thomas Becket in Verse*, p. 165.

66. Rachel Koopmans, *Wonderful to Relate: Miracle Stories and Miracle Collecting in High Medieval England*, Philadelphia: University of Pennsylvania Press, 2011, p. 141.

67. Ibid.

68. Mary Aelred Sinclair, *An Annotated Translation of the Life of St. Thomas Becket by William Fitzstephen: Part Two*, Chicago: Loyola University Chicago, 1944, pp. 102–3.

69. Barlow, *Thomas Becket*, p. 250. On Becket's textile relics see Rachel Koopmans, 'Gifts of Thomas Becket's Clothing Made by the Monks of Canterbury Cathedral', *Journal of the British Archaeological Association*, vol. 173 (2020), pp. 39–60.

70. BL, Harley MS 5102, f. 17.

71. Translated in Warren, *Henry II*, p. 520.

72. Quoted in Strickland, who describes his account in *Henry the Young King*, p. 108.

73. Barlow, *Thomas Becket*, p. 251.

74. Warren, *Henry II*, p. 112; for further, equally verbose, letters written by Theobald of Blois and William, Archbishop of Sens, see p. 113.

75. Warren, *Henry II*, p. 113.

76. See Mary Cheney, 'The Compromise of Avranches of 1172 and the Spread of Canon Law in England', *English Historical Review*, vol. 56 (1941), pp. 177–97.

77. Nicholas Vincent, 'The Pilgrimages of the Angevin Kings of England, 1154–1272', in *Pilgrimage: The English Experience from Becket to Bunyan*, ed. Colin Morris and Peter Roberts, Cambridge: Cambridge University Press, 2002, pp. 12–45, at p. 23.

78. Warren, *Henry II*, pp. 519–20.

79. Barlow, *Thomas Becket*, p. 258.

80. Vincent, 'The Murderers of Thomas Becket'.

81. Ibid., p. 258.

82. Vincent, 'The Murderers of Thomas Becket', pp. 211–72.

83. This charter is held in the archives of Canterbury Cathedral, CCA-DCc-ChAnt/D/20. R. M. Franklin, 'Tracy, William de (d. in or before 1174), one of the murderers of Thomas Becket', *Oxford Dictionary of National Biography*, 23 September 2004, doi.org/10.1093/ref:odnb/27652 (accessed 15 April 2020).

84. R. M. Franklin, 'Fitzurse, Reginald (d. 1173×5), one of the murderers of Thomas Becket', *Oxford Dictionary of National Biography*, 23 September 2004, doi.org/10. 1093/ref:odnb/9647 (accessed 15 April 2020).

85. Warren, *Henry II*, pp. 530–1.

86. Ibid., pp. 531–4.

87. John of Salisbury, in Benedicta Ward, *Miracles and the Medieval Mind: Theory, Record and Event 1000–1215*, London: Scolar Press, 1982, p. 100.

88. Ronald E. Pepin, 'John of Salisbury as a Writer', in *A Companion to John of Salisbury*, ed. Christoph Grellard and Frédérique Lachaud, Leiden: Brill, 2014, pp. 145–79, at pp. 168–71; Barlow, *Thomas Becket*, p. 4.

89. Michael Staunton, *Thomas Becket and his Biographers*, Woodbridge: The Boydell Press, 2000, p. 20.

90. John Francis O'Connor, 'An Annotated Translation of the Letters of John of Salisbury', Master's thesis, Loyola University Chicago, 1947, no. 307/304, pp. 88–9.

91. Staunton, *Thomas Becket and his Biographers*, p. 22.

92. Barlow, *Thomas Becket*, p. 267. See also John R. Butler, *The Quest for Becket's Bones: The Mystery of the Relics of St Thomas Becket*, New Haven and London: Yale University Press, 1995, pp. 14–16.

93. Benedict of Peterborough, quoted in Arthur James Mason, *What Became of the Bones of St Thomas? A Contribution to his Fiftieth Jubilee*, Cambridge: The University Press, 1920, p. 67.

94. John Jenkins, 'Replication or Rivalry? The "Becketization" of Pilgrimage in English Cathedrals', *Religion*, vol. 49 (2019), pp. 24–47, at p. 28.

95. Martina Bagnoli et al., eds, *Treasures of Heaven: Saints, Relics, and Devotion in Medieval Europe*, London: British Museum Press, 2011, p. 186, cat. 97.

96. Lambeth Anonymous, translated in Staunton, *The Lives*, p. 210.

97. Richard W. Southern, *The Monks of Canterbury and the Murder of Archbishop Becket*, Canterbury: Friends of Canterbury Cathedral Trust and the Trustees of the William Urry Memorial Fund, 1985, pp. 10–12. Woodruff has observed that despite the substantial offerings received at sites in Canterbury Cathedral during the Middle Ages, the cost of hosting pilgrims, particularly royalty and nobility, was also high. See C. Eveleigh Woodruff, 'The Financial Aspect of the Cult of St Thomas of Canterbury', *Archaeologia Cantiana*, vol. 44 (1932), pp. 13–32.

98. Anne Duggan, 'Religious Networks in Action: The European Expansion of the Cult of St Thomas of Canterbury', in *International Religious Networks*, ed. Jeremy Gregory and Hugh McLeod, Woodbridge: Boydell and Brewer, 2012, pp. 20–43.

99. Julian Haseldine, 'Thomas Becket: Martyr, Saint – and Friend?', in *Belief and Culture in the Middle Ages*, ed. Richard Gameson and Henrietta Leyser, Oxford: Oxford University Press, 2001, pp. 305–17.

100. Simone Caudron, 'Thomas Becket et l'œuvre de Limoges', in *Valérie et Thomas Becket: de l'influence des princes Plantagenêt dans l'œuvre de Limoges*, ed. Véronique Notin, Limoges: Musée Municipal de l'Évêché/ Musée de l'Émail, 1999, pp. 56–68. See also Simone Caudron, 'Les châsses reliquaires de Thomas Becket émaillés à Limoges: leur géographie historique', *Bulletin de la Société Archéologique et Historique du Limousin*, vol. 121 (1993), pp. 55–82. Another useful source is Marie-Madeleine Gauthier et al., *Corpus des émaux méridionaux: Catalogue international de l'œuvre de Limoges*, vol. II, Paris: Éditions du Comité des Travaux Historiques et Scientifiques, 2011.

101. Karen Bollermann and Cary J. Nederman, 'A Special Collection: John of Salisbury's Relics of Saint Thomas Becket and Other Holy Martyrs', *Mediaevistik*, vol. 26 (2013), pp. 163–81.

102. Haki Antonsson, 'The Lives of St Thomas Becket and Early Scandinavian Literature', *Studi e Materiali di Storia delle Religioni*, vol. 81 (2015), pp. 394–413.

103. *Middelaldersk Guldsmedkunst I Norge*, Kristiania: Kunstindustrimuseum, 1922, no. 93, pp. 47–8; Thor Kielland, *Norsk gullsmedkunst i middelalderen*, Oslo: Steenske Forlag, 1927, p. 102; Leif Anker and Jiri Havran, *Kirker i Norge*, vol. IV: *Middelalder i tre: stavkirker*, Oslo: Arfo, 2005, pp. 234–40. Our thanks to Ingeborg Magerøy for her help with these references.

104. Anne Duggan, 'Becket's Cap and the Broken Sword: Jacques de Vitry's English Mitre in Context', The Cult of St Thomas Becket: Art, Relics and Liturgy in Britain and Europe (special issue), *Journal of the British Archaeological Association*, vol. 173 (2020), pp. 3–25.

105. Becket's life was rewritten into an Icelandic saga in the fourteenth century. See Eiríkr Magnússon, ed., *Thómas Saga erkibyskups: A Life of Archbishop Thomas Becket, in Icelandic, with English Translation, Notes and Glossary, vol. 1*, London: Longman & Co., 1875. For a full list of Icelandic and Old Norse legends of Becket and an extensive bibliography, see Kirsten Wolf, *The Legends of the Saints in Old Norse-Icelandic Prose*, Toronto: University of Toronto Press, 2013, pp. 354–66. Our thanks go to Erik Petersen of Det Kongelige Bibliotek, Denmark, for facilitating our research on the Thomaskinna, GKS1008.

106. For an overview, see Åslaug Ommundsen, 'The Cults of Saints in Norway before 1200', in *Saints and their Lives on the Periphery: Veneration of Saints in Scandinavia and Eastern Europe (c.1000–1200)*, ed. Haki Antonsson and Ildar H. Garipzanov, Turnhout: Brepols, 2010, pp. 67–93.

107. Paul Binski, *Becket's Crown: Art and Imagination in Gothic England, 1170–1300*, New Haven and London: Yale University Press, 2004, pp. 33–4.

108. Benedict of Peterborough, quoted in *MTB*, vol. I, 1875, pp. 544–5.

109. J. J. G. Alexander and Paul Binski, eds, *The Age of Chivalry: Art in Plantagenet England 1200–1400*, London: Weidenfeld and Nicolson, 1987, no. 44, p. 220.

Chapter 3

1. Anne Duggan, 'Diplomacy, Status and Conscience: Henry II's Penance for Murder', in *Thomas Becket: Friends, Networks, Texts and Cult*, Aldershot: Ashgate, 2007, pp. 265–90, at pp. 282–3. See also Anne Duggan, 'Becket is Dead! Long Live St Thomas', in *The Cult of St Thomas Becket in the Plantagenet World, c.1170–c.1220*, ed. Paul Webster and Marie-Pierre Gelin, Woodbridge: The Boydell Press, 2016, pp. 25–52, at pp. 30–1.

2. Geffrei Gaimar, *L'estoire des Engleis*, ed. and trans. Ian Short, Oxford: Oxford University Press, 2009, p. 329.

3. Ernst Kitzinger, 'World Map and Fortune's Wheel: A Medieval Mosaic Floor in Turin', *Proceedings of the American Philosophical Society*, vol. 117 (1973), pp. 344–73.

4. Gerald of Wales, *De principis instructione*, ed. and trans. Robert Bartlett, Oxford: Oxford University Press, 2018, p. 159. Björn Weiler, 'Kings and Sons: Princely Rebellions and the Structures of Revolt in Western Europe, c.1170–c.1280', *Historical Research*, vol. 82 (2009), pp. 17–40.

5. Gerald of Wales, *De principis instructione*, p. 455.

6. Duggan, 'Becket is Dead!', p. 40. The full letter is transcribed in Martin Bouquet et al., eds, *Recueil des historiens des Gaules et de la France*, new edn, vol. 16, Paris: Victor Palme, 1878, pp. 643–8.

7. Anne Duggan, 'The Coronation of the Young King in 1170', in *Thomas Becket: Friends, Networks, Texts and Cult*, Aldershot: Ashgate, 2007, pp. 165–78. For a synopsis of this period see Wilfred L. Warren, *Henry II*, new edn, New Haven and London: Yale University Press, 2000, pp. 108–36.

8. Duggan, 'Becket is Dead!', p. 40 (translation slightly altered by Nicholas Vincent).

9. A brief review of the situation is given in David Carpenter, *The Struggle for Mastery: Britain 1066–1284*, London: Penguin Books, 2004, pp. 223–7.

10. Robert Bartlett, *England Under the Norman and Angevin Kings, 1075–1225*, Oxford: Clarendon Press, 2000, p. 55.

11. Warren, *Henry II*, p. 109.

12. Colmán Ó Clabaigh and Michael Staunton, 'Thomas Becket and Ireland', in *Listen, O isles, unto me: Studies in Medieval Word and Image in Honour of Jennifer O'Reilly*, ed. Elizabeth Mullins and Diarmuid Scully, Cork: Cork University Press, 2011, pp. 87–100, at p. 88.

13. Ralph V. Turner, *Eleanor of Aquitaine: Queen of France, Queen of England*, New Haven and London: Yale University Press, 2011, p. 210. Alheydis Plassmann, 'The King and His Sons: Henry II's and Frederick Barbarossa's Succession Strategies Compared', in *Anglo-Norman Studies XXXVI: Proceedings of the Battle Conference 2013*, ed. David Bates, Woodbridge: The Boydell Press, 2014, pp. 149–166.

14. See chapter 8, 'A Queen's Discontent and her Sons' Thwarted Ambitions, 1173–1174', in Turner, *Eleanor of Aquitaine*, pp. 205–30. This event is recorded by Gervase of Canterbury.

15. See Matthew Strickland, *Henry the Young King, 1155–1183*, New Haven and London: Yale University Press, 2016, pp. 133, 138–9.

16. Quote by William of Newburgh, translated in Warren, *Henry II*, p. 118.

17. Roger J. Smith, 'Henry II's Heir: The Acta and Seal of Henry the Young King, 1170–83', *English Historical Review*, vol. 116 (2001), pp. 297–326; Strickland, *Henry the Young King*, p. 139. Strickland notes that no seals from this matrix are known to have survived because Henry II had all the documents sealed by Henry the Young King during the war subsequently destroyed.

18. See Warren, *Henry II*, p. 122.

19. Carpenter, *The Struggle for Mastery*, p. 224.

20. Warren, *Henry II*, p. 125.

21. The battle took place between the villages of Fornham St Genevieve and Fornham St Martin. For the discovery of the sword see 'Proceedings of the Association', *Journal of the British Archaeological Association*, vol. 32 (1876), pp. 501–2.

22. Strickland, *Henry the Young King*, p. 176. The discussion of the battle can be found on pp. 175–8.

23. Warren, *Henry II*, p. 130; see also Bartlett, *England Under the Norman and Angevin Kings*, for this battle.

24. Jordan Fantosme, translated in Strickland, *Henry the Young King*, p. 177.

25. See the discussion in 'Battle of Fornham (Med)', last amended 21 May 2020, Suffolk Heritage Explorer website, available at https://heritage.suffolk.gov.uk/hbsmr-web/record.aspx?UID=MSF6686-Fornham-Park-(Med) (accessed 12 December 2020).

26. Bartlett, *England Under the Norman and Angevin Kings*, p. 56.

27. Duggan, 'Diplomacy, Status and Conscience', pp. 282–3; see also Duggan, 'Becket is Dead!', pp. 30–1.

28. The best account of Henry's penances is Duggan, 'Diplomacy, Status and Conscience'. See also Frank Barlow, *Thomas Becket*, Berkeley: University of California Press, 1986, pp. 269–70; Thomas K. Keefe, 'Shrine Time: King Henry II's Visits to Thomas Becket's Tomb', *Haskins Society Journal*, vol. 11, 1998, pp. 115–22. For an overview of the place of Henry II's penance within a wider framework, see Nicholas Vincent, 'The Pilgrimages of the Angevin Kings of England, 1154–1272', in *Pilgrimage: The English Experience from Becket to Bunyan*, ed. Colin Morris and Peter Roberts, Cambridge: Cambridge University Press, 2002, pp. 12–45.

29. Duggan, 'Diplomacy, Status and Conscience', p. 265.

30. Duggan, 'Becket is Dead!', p. 37. Vincent, 'The Pilgrimages of the Angevin Kings of England'.

31. Garnier de Pont-Sainte-Maxence, *Garnier's Becket*, ed. and trans. Janet Shirley, London: Phillimore, 1975, p. 158.

32. Ibid., p. 159.

33. Duggan, 'Diplomacy, Status and Conscience', p. 279.

34. The references to the Great Rollright church are nineteenth century, see James Dallaway, *Observations on English Architecture*, London: J. Taylor, 1806, pp. 265–6; *Gentleman's Magazine* (April 1817), p. 310.

35. Garnier de Pont-Sainte-Maxence, *Garnier's Becket*, p. 60.

36. Duggan, 'Becket is Dead!', p. 37.

37. Duggan, 'Diplomacy, Status and Conscience', p. 279.

38. Jordan Fantosme, poem for Henry II's victory in 1174/5, quoted and translated in Webster and Gelin, *The Cult of St Thomas Becket in the Plantagenet World*, pp. 39, 100–1, 117.

39. Warren, *Henry II*, p. 138.

40. Richard Fawcett, *Arbroath Abbey*, Edinburgh: Historic Scotland, 2006, pp. 18–19.

41. Vincent, 'The Pilgrimages of the Angevin Kings of England', p. 28.

42. Aubrey Gwynn, 'The Early History of St. Thomas' Abbey, Dublin', *Journal of the Royal Society of Antiquaries of Ireland*, vol. 84 (1954), pp. 1–35; Clabaigh and Staunton, 'Thomas Becket and Ireland', pp. 87–101; Áine Foley, *The Abbey of St Thomas the Martyr, Dublin*, Dublin: Archaeology Section of the Planning and Property Development Department in conjunction with the South Central Office, Dublin City Council, 2017.

43. Barlow, *Thomas Becket*, pp. 269–70. Keefe, 'Shrine Time', pp. 115–22.

44. Warren, *Henry II*, p. 147. Robert Eyton, *Court, Household, and Itinerary of King Henry II*, London: Taylor and Company, 1878, p. 288.

45. Warren, *Henry II*, p. 147.

46. Nicholas Vincent, 'English Kingship: The View from Paris, 1066–1204', in *Anglo-Norman Studies XL: Proceedings of the Battle Conference 2017*, ed. Elisabeth van Houts, Woodbridge: The Boydell Press, 2018, pp. 1–24, at p. 13.

47. Raymonde Foreville, 'Charles d'Orléans et le "vin de saint Thomas"', *Cahiers d'Histoire et de Folklore*, no. 1 (1955), pp. 22–32; Nicholas Vincent, *Norman Charters from English Sources: Antiquaries, Archives and the Rediscovery of the Anglo-Norman Past*, Oxford: Oxford University Press, 2013, pp. 100–4, 203–4.

48. Sarah Blick, 'Pilgrimage to the Tomb and Shrine of St. Thomas Becket', in *Push Me, Pull You: Imaginative, Emotional, Physical, and Spatial Interaction in Late Medieval and Renaissance Art*, vol. II, ed. Sarah Blick and Laura Deborah Gelfand, Leiden: Brill, 2011, pp. 21–58, at p. 51. John Jenkins, 'Modelling the Cult of Thomas Becket at Canterbury Cathedral', *Journal of the British Archaeological Association*, vol. 173 (2020), pp. 100–23, at p. 105.

49. Colette Bowie, *The Daughters of Henry II and Eleanor of Aquitaine*, Turnhout: Brepols, 2014; Jitske Jasperse, 'Matilda, Leonor and Joanna: the Plantagenet sisters and the display of dynastic connections through material culture', *Journal of Medieval History*, vol. 43, 2017; Jitske Jasperse, *Medieval Women, Material Culture, and Power: Matilda Plantagenet and her Sisters*, York: Arc Humanities Press, 2020; José Manuel Cerda 'Leonor Plantagenet and the Cult of Thomas Becket in Castile' in *The Cult of St Thomas Becket in the Plantagenet World, c.1170–c.1220*, pp. 133–45.

50. Dirk Booms and Peter Higgs, *Sicily: Culture and Conquest*, London: British Museum Press, 2016, pp. 241, 243.

51. Carles Sánchez Márquez, 'An Anglo-Norman at Terrassa? Augustinian Canons and Thomas Becket at the End of the Twelfth Century', in *Romanesque Patrons and Processes: Design and Instrumentality in the Art and Architecture of Romanesque Europe*, ed. Jordi Camps, Manuel Castiñeiras, John McNeill and Richard Plant, London: Routledge, 2018, pp. 219–34. Gregoria Cavero Domínguez et al., *Tomás Becket y la península ibérica (1170–1230)*, León: Universidad de León, 2013.

52. Evelyn Jamison, 'Alliance of England and Sicily in the Second Half of the Twelfth Century', *Journal of the Warburg and Courtauld Institutes*, vol. 6 (1945), pp. 20–32.

53. *The Correspondence of Thomas Becket, Archbishop of Canterbury, 1162–1170*, vol. II, ed. Anne Duggan, Oxford: Clarendon Press, 2000, no. 221, pp. 966–71.

54. Duggan, 'Becket is Dead!', p. 45; see also Peter Anthony Newton, 'Some New Material for the Study of the Iconography of St Thomas Becket', in *Thomas Becket: Actes du Colloque International de Sédières, 19–24 août 1973*, ed. Raymonde Foreville, Paris: Beauchesne, 1975, pp. 260–2, and Jasperse, *Medieval Women, Material Culture, and Power*, pp. 28–33.

55. Bowie, *The Daughters of Henry II and Eleanor of Aquitaine*, p. 85.

56. Ibid., p. 89. Jasperse, *Medieval Women, Material Culture, and Power*, pp. 28–33.

57. See ibid., and *MTB*, vol. I, 1875, p. 452.

58. Kathleen Nolan, *Queens in Stone and Silver: The Creation of a Visual Imagery of Queenship in Capetian France*, London: Palgrave, 2009, p. 83. Jasperse, *Medieval Women, Material Culture, and Power*, pp. 55–62.

59. Devotion to St Thomas flourished across Italy and evidence of veneration of the saint can be found in many areas, see Costanza Cipollaro and Veronika Decker, 'Shaping a Saint's Identity: The Imagery of Thomas Becket in Medieval Italy', in *Medieval Art, Architecture and Archaeology at Canterbury*, ed. Alixe Bovey, Leeds: Maney Publishing, 2013, pp. 116–38; Ursula Nilgen, 'Presbyter of Fermo and the Cult of Thomas Becket in the Twelfth and Early Thirteenth Centuries', in *The Chasuble of Thomas Becket: A Biography*, ed. Avinoam Shalem, Munich: Hirmer, 2017, pp. 152–66. John Philip O'Neill, *Enamels of Limoges: 1100–1350*, New York: Metropolitan Museum of Art, 1996, no. 39, p. 164.

60. On his return to England in 1801, Hamilton presented the precious container to the Society of Antiquaries of London.

61. Colette Bowie, 'Matilda, Duchess of Saxony (1168–89) and the Cult of Thomas Becket: A Legacy of Appropriation', in Webster and Gelin, *The Cult of St Thomas Becket in the Plantagenet World*, pp. 113–32, at p. 120.

62. Ursula Nilgen, 'Thomas Becket und Braunschweig', in *Der Welfenschatz und sein Umkreis*, ed. Joachim Ehlers and Dietrich Kötzsche, Mainz: Philipp von Zabern, 1998, pp. 219–42, at pp. 223–7; Kay Slocum, *The Cult of Thomas Becket: History and Historiography through Eight Centuries*, New York: Routledge, 2019.

63. Bowie, 'Matilda, Duchess of Saxony', p. 122; William A. Chaney, *The Cult of Kingship in Anglo-Saxon England*, Manchester: Manchester University Press, 1970, pp. 78, 81–2; David Rollason, *Saints and Relics in Anglo-Saxon England*, Oxford: Basil Blackwell, 1989, pp. 137–63.

64. Dagmar Ó Riain-Raedel, 'Edith, Judith, Matilda: The Role of Royal Ladies in the Propagation of the Continental Cult', in *Oswald: Northumbrian King to European Saint*, ed. Clare Stancliffe, Stamford: Paul Watkins, 1996, pp. 210–29.

65. This is now in the collection of Cleveland Museum of Art, 1930.741.

66. The last three of these scenes were invented by the restorer Heinrich Brandes in the nineteenth century.

67. See especially Bowie, 'Matilda, Duchess of Saxony'.

68. Vincent, 'The Pilgrimages of the Angevin Kings of England, 1154–1272', p. 31, referencing Gerald of Wales, 'De principis instructione', in Gerald, *Giraldi*

Cambrensis Opera, ed. John S. Brewer, James F. Dimock and George F. Warner, 8 vols, Rolls Series 21, London: Longman & Co., 1861–91, vol. VIII, p. 309.

69. Warren, *Henry II*, pp. 594–630.

70. Turner, *Eleanor of Aquitaine*, p. 253.

71. Ibid., p. 254.

72. Ibid. See also Nolan, *Queens in Stone and Silver*, pp. 105–114.

73. It has been suggested that the final scene is Christ welcoming the martyr Becket into heaven. See Colin S. Drake, *The Romanesque Fonts of Northern Europe and Scandinavia*, Woodbridge: The Boydell Press, 2001.

74. 'The Murder of Thomas a Becket on a Swedish Font', *Reliquary and Illustrated Archaeologist*, new series, vol. 12 (1906), pp. 126–7; Folke Nordström, *Mediaeval Baptismal Fonts: An Iconographical Study*, Stockholm: Almqvist och Wiksell, 1984, p. 119; Drake, *The Romanesque Fonts of Northern Europe and Scandinavia*, pp. 145–7.

75. Cipollaro and Decker, 'Shaping a Saint's Identity'. Valentina Bernardi, 'Il complesso episcopale di Treviso tra XII e XIII secolo: gli edifici e le opere pittoriche e scultoree', unpublished MA thesis, Ca' Foscari University of Venice, 2012/13, pp. 82–196.

Chapter 4

1. Translated by Rachel Koopmans, the original Latin is 'magna enim et mirabilia erant valde quae circa martyris sui sepulcrum singulis operabatur diebus', quoted in *MTB*, vol. II, 1876, p. 61.

2. The following comes from Gervase of Canterbury's account of the fire: *Tractatus de combustione et reparatione Cantuariensis ecclesie*, trans. Robert Willis, in *The Architectural History of Canterbury Cathedral*, London: Longman & Co., 1845, pp. 32–62, at p. 32.

3. William of Malmesbury, *De gestis pontificum Angolorum libri quinque*, ed. N. Hamilton, Rolls Series 52, London: Longman & Co., 1870, p. 138.

4. Gervase of Canterbury, *Tractatus de combustione et reparatione Cantuariensis ecclesie*, trans. Willis, pp. 34–5. On Gervase's account more broadly, see also Carol Davidson Cragoe, 'Reading and Rereading Gervase of Canterbury', *Journal of British Archaeology*, vol. 154 (2001), pp. 40–53.

5. Margaret Gibson, 'Normans and Angevins, 1070–1220', in *A History of Canterbury Cathedral*, ed. Patrick Collinson, Nigel Ramsay and Margaret Sparks, Oxford: Oxford University Press, 1995, pp. 38–68, at pp. 63–5.

6. Peter Draper, *The Formation of English Gothic: Architecture and Identity, 1150–1250*, New Haven and London: Yale University Press, 2006, p. 15.

7. There is a large and complicated historiography for the rebuilding of the east end of Canterbury Cathedral. The oldest account is that of Gervase of Canterbury. Of the numerous antiquarian accounts

Willis's *Architectural History of Canterbury Cathedral*, first published in 1845, is invaluable. For the most recent publication see Peter Draper, 'Recent Interpretations of the Late-12th-Century Rebuilding of the East End of Canterbury Cathedral and its Historical Context', in *Medieval Art, Architecture and Archaeology at Canterbury*, ed. Alixe Bovey, Leeds: Maney Publishing, 2013, pp. 106–15. See also Francis Woodman, *The Architectural History of Canterbury Cathedral*, London: Routledge, 1981; Paul Binski, *Becket's Crown: Art and Imagination in Gothic England, 1170–1300*, New Haven and London: Yale University Press, 2004.

8. There is only one year of the building history where Gervase says that funds were lacking. See Willis, *The Architectural History*, p. 62. For an overall review of takings at shrines in Canterbury, see C. Eveleigh Woodruff, 'The Financial Aspect of the Cult of St Thomas of Canterbury', *Archaeologia Cantiana*, vol. 44 (1932), pp. 13–32.

9. See Willis's English translation, in *The Architectural History*, pp. 32–62.

10. Willis, *The Architectural History*, p. 35.

11. Ibid.

12. Ibid.

13. Ibid., pp. 35–6; Christopher Wilson, *The Gothic Cathedral*, London: Thames & Hudson, 1994, pp. 82–90.

14. For Gervase's account, see Willis, *The Architectural History*, pp. 34–5. The location of the saints' remains is known from Gervase but also from Eadmer of Canterbury's, *Lives and Miracles of Saints Oda, Dunstan and Oswald*, ed. and trans. Andrew J. Turner and Bernard J. Muir, Oxford: Oxford University Press, 2006, pp. 157–9.

15. Wilson, *The Gothic Cathedral*, pp. 82–90. The cathedrals at Canterbury and Sens share similar elevations in their eastern parts. See Peter Kidson, 'Gervase, Becket, and William of Sens', *Speculum*, vol. 68, no. 4 (1993), pp. 969–91, and a review of the evidence in Millard F. Hearn, 'Letters to the Editor: Peter Draper's Article "Interpretations of the Rebuilding of Canterbury Cathedral"', *Journal of the Society of Architectural Historians*, vol. 57 (1998), pp. 238–40. See also Kenneth W. Severens, 'William of Sens and the Double Columns at Sens and Canterbury', *Journal of the Warburg and Courtauld Institutes*, vol. 33 (1970), pp. 307–13. It has been suggested, without firm evidence, that Becket knew William during his exile and brought him over to England to work on his own architectural project, a church dedicated to St Stephen at Hackington, Kent. Whether or not this was the case will never be known. Little is known about Becket's role as a patron of the arts, see Ursula Nilgen, 'Intellectuality and Splendour: Thomas Becket as a Patron of the Arts', in *Art and Patronage in the English Romanesque*, ed. Sarah Macready and F. H. Thompson, London: Society of Antiquaries of London, 1986, pp. 145–58.

16. Willis, *The Architectural History*, pp. 50–1.

17. The question of which sections of the building each man was responsible for has been the subject of much debate. These matters are not readdressed in this book but for further reading, see Tim Tatton-Brown, 'Canterbury and the Architecture of Pilgrimage Shrines in England', in *Pilgrimage: The English Experience from Becket to Bunyan*, ed. Colin Morris and Peter Roberts, Cambridge: Cambridge University Press, 2002, pp. 90–107, at p. 96, and Peter Draper, 'Interpretations of the Rebuilding of Canterbury Cathedral, 1174–1186', *Journal of the Society of Architectural Historians*, vol. 56 (1997), pp. 184–203. See also note 7 above, which sets out the historiography of the east end.

18. Draper, 'Interpretations of the Rebuilding of Canterbury Cathedral, 1174–1186', p. 200.

19. Willis, *The Architectural History*, p. 52.

20. Ibid., p. 58.

21. For St-Denis, see Wilson, *The Gothic Cathedral*, pp. 31–43; Binski, *Becket's Crown*, pp. 9–23.

22. Binski, *Becket's Crown*, pp. 23–4.

23. Becket sought to link himself with St Stephen; he celebrated the Feast of St Stephen instead of St Edward the Confessor: see Jennifer O'Reilly, 'The Double Martyrdom of Thomas Becket: Hagiography or History?', *Studies in Medieval and Renaissance History*, vol. 7, ed. J. A. S. Evans and Richard Unger, New York: AMS Press, 1985, pp. 183–247, at p. 222–7; Laura Slater, *Art and Political Thought in Medieval England, c.1150–1350*, Woodbridge: The Boydell Press, 2018, pp. 54–9.

24. Anne Duggan, 'Canterbury: The Becket Effect', in *Canterbury: A Medieval City*, ed. Catherine Royer-Hemet, Newcastle: Cambridge Scholars Publishing, 2010, pp. 67–91, at p. 83. For more references to the discussion regarding the location of Becket's head relic in Canterbury, see her extended comments in n. 64.

25. From 1314 onwards the reliquary was embellished with gold, silver and precious gems. The Register of Prior Eastry of 1314 records that £115 12s. was spent on a new head reliquary that was decorated in this way. See John Jenkins, 'Replication or Rivalry? The "Becketization" of Pilgrimage in English Cathedrals', *Religion*, vol. 49 (2019), pp. 24–47, at pp. 36–7. See Millard F. Hearn, 'Canterbury Cathedral and the Cult of Becket, *Art Bulletin*, vol. 76 (1994), pp. 19–52, at p. 43.

26. This was first noted by Wilson in *The Gothic Cathedral*, p. 90, but was significantly expanded upon by Binski in *Becket's Crown*, pp. 3–12.

27. Jennifer O'Reilly, '"Candidus et rubicundus": An Image of Martyrdom in the *Lives* of Thomas Becket', *Analecta Bollandiana Bruxelles*, vol. 99 (1981), pp. 303–14, at pp. 303–4; Michael Staunton, *The Lives of Thomas Becket*, Manchester: Manchester University Press, 2001, p. 203.

28. O'Reilly, '"Candidus et rubicundus"', p. 307. In a sermon preached at Rome in 1220, Archbishop

Stephen Langton also likened Becket's martyrdom to the lily and the rose.

29. Binski, *Becket's Crown*, pp. 3–12.

30. Julian Luxford, 'The Relics of Thomas Becket in England', *Journal of the British Archaeological Association*, vol. 173 (2020), pp. 124–42, at p. 137. The translation is taken from Bede's *Ecclesiastical History of the English People*, ed. and trans. Bertram Colgrave and Roger A. B. Mynors, Oxford: Clarendon Press, 1969, pp. 510–11. See also Paul Binski, *Gothic Wonder: Art, Artifice and the Decorated Style, 1290–1350*, New Haven and London: Yale University Press, 2014, pp. 25–6.

31. Benedicta Ward, *Miracles and the Medieval Mind: Theory, Record and Event 1000–1215*, London: Scolar Press, 1982, p. 102.

32. Tim Tatton-Brown, 'The Trinity Chapel and Corona Floors', *Canterbury Cathedral Chronicle*, no. 75 (1981), pp. 50–5.

33. Ibid., pp. 52–4.

34. For an overview of luxury pavements in Italy and the Mediterranean see Fabio Barry, 'Walking on Water: Cosmic Floors in Antiquity and the Middle Ages', *Art Bulletin*, vol. 89 (2007), pp. 627–56.

35. Tatton-Brown, 'Canterbury and the Architecture of Pilgrimage Shrines', p. 91. Tatton-Brown refers to the argument originally made by Christopher Norton on 7 November 1998 at the Courtauld Institute at a conference on the Westminster Cosmati pavements. Thanks to Tim Tatton-Brown for discussing this pavement and sharing his thoughts. See also Christopher Norton, 'The Luxury Pavement in England before Westminster', in Westminster Abbey: The Cosmati Pavements, ed. Lindy Grant and Richard Mortimer, Aldershot: Ashgate, 2002, pp. 7–36, esp. pp. 11–13, 15.

36. For Becket relics in England see Luxford, 'The Relics of Thomas Becket in England'.

37. For an overview, see Nicholas E. Toke, 'The Opus Alexandrinum and Sculpted Stone Roundels in the Retro-Choir of Canterbury Cathedral', *Archaeologica Cantiana*, vol. 41 (1930), pp. 189–221; Elizabeth Eames, 'Notes on the Decorated Stone Roundels in the Corona and Trinity Chapel in Canterbury Cathedral', *Medieval Art and Architecture at Canterbury before 1220*, British Archaeological Association Conference Transactions 5, Leeds: British Archaeological Association, 1982, pp. 67–70; Binski, *Becket's Crown*, pp. 24–5; Tim Tatton-Brown, 'The Two Great Marble Pavements in the Sanctuary and Shrine Areas of Canterbury Cathedral and Westminster Abbey', in *Historic Floors: Their History and Conservation*, ed. Jane Fawcett, Oxford: Butterworth-Heinemann, 1998, pp. 53–62; E. C. Norton and M. C. Horton, 'A Parisian Workshop at Canterbury: A Late Thirteenth-Century Tile Pavement in the Corona Chapel, and the Origins of Tyler Hill', *Journal of the British Archaeological Association*, vol. 134 (1981), pp. 58–77.

38. For more on the abbey's pavements, see Richard Foster, *Patterns of Thought: The Hidden Meaning of the Great Pavement of Westminster Abbey*, London: Cape, 1992; Grant and Mortimer, eds, *Westminster Abbey: The Cosmati Pavements*; Warwick Rodwell, *The Cosmatesque Mosaics of Westminster Abbey*, Oxford: Oxbow Books, 2019; Paul Binski, *Westminster Abbey and the Plantagenets: Kingship and the Representation of Power, 1200–1400*, New Haven and London: Yale University Press, 1995, pp. 93–107. It has also been suggested that there was a Cosmatesque pavement at Wimbourne Minster in Dorset, see Lawrence Rees and Michael J. T. Lewis, 'A Fragment of Cosmatesque Mosaic from Wimborne Minster, Dorset', *Antiquaries Journal*, vol. 94 (2014), pp. 135–51.

39. Wilson, *The Gothic Cathedral*; Binski, *Becket's Crown*, pp. 53–77.

40. Wilson has also suggested that Canterbury had an impact across the Channel, at the cathedrals of Notre Dame in Paris and Lausanne.

41. *A Relation or Rather a True Account of the Island of England with Sundry Particulars of the Customs of these People and of the Royal Revenues under King Henry the Seventh, about the Year 1500*, trans. Charlotte Augusta Sneyd, London: Camden Society, 1847, pp. 30–1.

42. The destruction of the shrine is discussed in Chapter 7. For the most comprehensive discussion of what the shrine might have looked like, see Sarah Blick, 'Reconstructing the Shrine of St Thomas Becket, Canterbury Cathedral', in *Art and Architecture of Late Medieval Pilgrimage in Northern Europe and the British Isles*, vol. II, ed. Sarah Blick and Rita Tekippe, Leiden: Brill, 2005, pp. 405–41; Arthur James Mason, *What Became of the Bones of St Thomas? A Contribution to his Fiftieth Jubilee*, Cambridge: The University Press, 1920, pp. 123–70; Ben Nilson, *Cathedral Shrines of Medieval England*, Woodbridge: The Boydell Press, 1998, pp. 34–57; John Jenkins, 'Modelling the Cult of Thomas Becket at Canterbury Cathedral', *Journal of the British Archaeological Association*, vol. 173 (2020), pp. 100–23. For overviews, see Nicola Coldstream, 'English Decorated Shrine Bases', *Journal of the British Archaeological Association*, vol. 39 (1976), pp. 15–34; John Crook, *English Medieval Shrines*, Woodbridge: The Boydell Press, 2011, pp. 213–20.

43. Jenkins, 'Modelling the Cult', pp. 104–14. See also Desiderius Erasmus, *The Colloquies of Erasmus*, vol. II, ed. Rev. E. Johnson, trans. Nathan Bailey, London: Reeves and Turner, 1878, p. 31.

44. Blick, 'Reconstructing the Shrine', p. 409.

45. Crook, *English Medieval Shrines*, p. 214.

46. For a survey of the surviving fragments see William Urry, 'Some Notes on the Two Resting Places of St Thomas at Canterbury', in *Thomas Becket: Actes du Colloque International de Sédières, 19–24 août 1973*, ed. Raymonde Foreville, Paris: Beauchesne, 1975, pp. 195–208. Jenkins, 'Modelling the Cult', pp. 104–14.

47. It is possible that in time other fragments from the shrine will come to light.

48. Tatton-Brown, 'The Two Great Marble Pavements', p. 54.

49. Ibid., p. 54. See also Tatton-Brown, 'Canterbury and the Architecture of Pilgrimage Shrines', p. 96. More recently, Tatton-Brown has suggested that it probably came from Stavelot, pers. comm., January 2020. Our thanks to Tim for sharing his thoughts on the origin of the stone.

50. See also Desiderius Erasmus, *The Colloquies of Erasmus*, vol. II, ed. Rev. E. Johnson, trans. Nathan Bailey, London: Reeves and Turner, 1878, pp. 31–2.

51. Crook, *English Medieval Shrines*, p. 217.

52. Nicholas Vincent, 'Dereham, Elias of (d. 1245), ecclesiastical administrator', *Oxford Dictionary of National Biography*, 23 September 2004, www.oxforddnb.com/view/10.1093/ref:odnb/9780198614128.001.0001/odnb-9780198614128-e-37391 (accessed 20 April 2020).

53. Ibid.

54. Blick, 'Reconstructing the Shrine', p. 412. Crook, *English Medieval Shrines*, pp. 213–20.

55. Nilson, *Cathedral Shrines of Medieval England*, pp. 43–50. Crook, *English Medieval Shrines*, p. 251.

56. Luxford, 'The Relics of Thomas Becket in England', p. 136.

57. John Stow, *The Annales of England*, London: R. Newbery, 1592, p. 972. Crook, *English Medieval Shrines*, pp. 216–17.

58. Jenkins, 'Replication or Rivalry?', pp. 27–8.

59. Rachel Koopmans, *Wonderful to Relate: Miracle Stories and Miracle Collecting in High Medieval England*, Philadelphia: University of Pennsylvania Press, 2011, p. 142. Gesine Oppitz-Trotman, 'Penance, Mercy and Saintly Authority in the Miracles of St Thomas Becket', *Studies in Church History*, vol. 47 (2011), pp. 136–47.

60. See note 1 above.

61. Nicholas Vincent, 'William of Canterbury and Benedict of Peterborough: The Manuscripts, Date and Context of the Becket Miracle Collections', in *Hagiographie, idéologie et politique au Moyen Âge en Occident: Actes du Colloque International du Centre d'Études Supérieures de Civilisatione Médiévale de Poitiers 11–14 septembre 2008*, ed. Edina Bozóky, Turnhout: Brepols, 2012, pp. 347–88; see pp. 367–72 for the listing of the manuscripts.

62. William FitzStephen, quoted in Staunton, *The Lives*, p. 206. See also Alyce A. Jordan, 'The "Water of Thomas Becket": Water as Medium, Metaphor, and Relic', in *The Nature and Function of Water, Baths, Bathing and Hygiene from Antiquity through the Renaissance*, ed. Cynthia Kosso and Anne Scott, Leiden: Brill, 2009, pp. 479–500.

63. Garnier de Pont-Sainte-Maxence, *Garnier's Becket*, ed. and trans. Janet Shirley, London: Phillimore, 1975, p. 157.

64. Ward, *Miracles and the Medieval Mind*, p. 102.

65. The name is derived from the Latin 'amphora'.

66. Brian Spencer, *Pilgrim Souvenirs and Secular Badges: Medieval Finds from Excavations in London*, London: HMSO, 1998, pp. 38–72; Rachel Koopmans, '"Water Mixed with the Blood of Thomas": Contact Relic Manufacture Pictured in Canterbury Cathedral's

Stained Glass', *Journal of Medieval History*, vol. 42 (2016), pp. 535–58.

67. The original text is 'optimus egrorum medicus fit Thoma bonorum'.

68. Madeline Caviness, *The Early Stained Glass of Canterbury Cathedral, circa 1175–1220*, Princeton: Princeton University Press, 1977. Madeline Harrison Caviness, *The Windows of Christ Church Cathedral, Canterbury*, Corpus Vitrearum Medii Aevi, Great Britain 2, London: British Academy, 1981.

69. Ibid., p. 148; Koopmans, *Wonderful to Relate*, p. 201.

70. Alyce Jordan, 'Rhetoric and Reform: The St Thomas Becket Window of Sens Cathedral', in *The Four Modes of Seeing: Approaches to Medieval Imagery in Honor of Madeline Harrison Caviness*, ed. Evelyn Staudinger Lane, Elizabeth Carson Pastan and Ellen M. Shortell, Aldershot: Ashgate, 2009, pp. 547–64; Alyce Jordan, 'The St Thomas Becket Windows at Angers and Coutances: Devotion, Subversion and the Scottish Connection', in *The Cult of St Thomas Becket in the Plantagenet World, c.1170–c.1220*, ed. Paul Webster and Marie-Pierre Gelin, Woodbridge: The Boydell Press, 2016, pp. 171–207.

71. Jordan, 'Rhetoric and Reform', pp. 554–6.

72. Ibid., p. 564. For the Angers and Coutances windows, see Jordan, 'The St Thomas Becket Windows at Angers and Coutances'.

73. Koopmans, *Wonderful to Relate*, p. 114.

74. Koopmans emphasises that the images were accessible and designed to be seen by the average pilgrim, see ibid., p. 201. See also Koopmans, 'Kentish Pilgrims in Canterbury Cathedral's Miracle Windows', *Journal of the Warburg and Courtauld Institutes*, vol. 80 (2017), pp. 1–27, at p. 5.

75. Rachel Koopmans, 'Pilgrimage Scenes in Newly Identified Medieval Glass at Canterbury Cathedral', *Burlington Magazine*, vol. 161 (2019), pp. 708–15.

76. This is based on Rachel Koopmans's research and her forthcoming catalogue of the Canterbury miracle windows.

The fifth window of Canterbury's Thomas Becket cycle: new readings, by Rachel Koopmans

1. Canterbury Cathedral Archives, DCc/Fabric 48, unpaginated.

2. Ibid.

3. Arthur P. Stanley, *Historical Memorials of Canterbury*, 4th edn, London: John Murray, 1865, p. 267. The standard description of window nIII is found in Madeline Caviness's monumental volume *The Windows of Christ Church Cathedral, Canterbury*, Corpus Vitrearum Medii Aevi, Great Britain 2, London: British Academy, 1981, pp. 185–92. My interpretations of the narratives presented in nIII differ for panels 1–6, 9, 14 and 22. Note that these panels are numbered differently (counting from the bottom of the window up) in Caviness's volume.

4. Benedict of Peterborough, *Miracula S. Thomae Cantuariensis*, MTB, vol. II, 1876, book IV.24, pp. 201–2; the entire text of the *Miracula* is reproduced in *MTB*, vol. II, pp. 21–281. Translations from Benedict's Latin text throughout this section are by Rachel Koopmans.

5. Ibid., book III.69, p. 166.

6. Ibid.

7. Ibid., book III.77, pp. 170–1.

8. Ibid., book III.77, p. 170.

9. Ibid., book IV.2, pp. 173–82. The story was also told by William of Canterbury: *Miracula S. Thomae Cantuariensis*, MTB, vol. I, 1875, pp. 137–546, at book II.2–3, pp. 155–8.

10. Benedict of Peterborough, *Miracula S. Thomae Cantuariensis*, book IV.3, p. 183.

11. Ibid., book IV.2, p. 180.

12. Ibid., book III.60, pp. 159–60.

13. Ibid., book III.60, p. 159.

14. Ibid., book III.60, p. 160.

Chapter 5

1. Matthew Paris, quoted in Arthur James Mason, *What Became of the Bones of St Thomas? A Contribution to his Fiftieth Jubilee*, Cambridge: The University Press, 1920, p. 79.

2. For a full account of the translation ceremony and its political context see Richard Eales, 'The Political Setting of the Becket Translation', *Studies in Church History*, vol. 30 (1993), pp. 127–39.

3. Richard Eales, 'The Political Setting of the Becket Translation', *Studies in Church History*, vol. 30 (1993), pp. 127–39, at p. 136.

4. It was widely believed that Becket was born, baptised, exiled and also martyred on a Tuesday. He fled Northampton and returned from exile on a Tuesday too. Nicholas Vincent, 'Stephen Langton, Archbishop of Canterbury', in *Étienne Langton: prédicateur, bibliste, théologien*, ed. Louis-Jacques Bataillon, Nicole Bériou, Gilbert Dahan and Riccardo Quinto, Turnhout: Brepols, 2010, pp. 51–123, esp. p. 100.

5. Leviticus 25:10, King James Version.

6. Raymonde Foreville, *Le jubilé de saint Thomas Becket du 13e au 15e siècle, 1220–1470: étude et documents*, Paris: SEVPEN, 1958, pp. 1–11, 21–45.

7. Jonathan Phillips, *The Fourth Crusade and the Sack of Constantinople*, London: Vintage, 2011, pp. 321–2; Elizabeth J. Mylod, Guy Perry, Thomas W. Smith and Jan Vandeburie, eds, *The Fifth Crusade in Context: The Crusading Movement in the Early Thirteenth Century*, London: Routledge, 2017, p. 1.

8. Stephen Church, *King John: England, Magna Carta and the Making of a Tyrant*, London: Pan Macmillan, 2016.

9. Charles Duggan, 'Richard [Richard of Dover] (d. 1184), Archbishop of Canterbury', *Oxford Dictionary of National Biography*, 23 September 2004, www.oxforddnb.com/view/10.1093/ref:odnb/9780198614128.001.0001/odnb-9780198614128-e-23514 (accessed 7 August 2020).

10. James Barnaby discusses how the Canterbury monks used a gift of relics as a means of gaining support at a later date: see 'Becket Vault: The Appropriation of St Thomas Becket's Image during the Canterbury Dispute 1184–1200', in *Anglo-Norman Studies XL: Proceedings of the Battle Conference*, ed. Elisabeth van Houts, Woodbridge: The Boydell Press, 2018, pp. 65–76, at p. 71. Rachel Koopmans, 'Gifts of Thomas Becket's Clothin: Made by the Monks of Canterbury Cathedral', *Journal of the British Archaeological Association*, vol. 173 (2020), pp. 39–60, esp. pp. 49–59.

11. Claudia Quattrocchi, *Un martire inglese alla curia di Roma: l'oratorio di San Thomas Becket di Canterbury nella cattedrale di Anagni*, Rome: Campisano Editore, 2017.

12. Costanza Cipollaro and Veronika Decker, 'Shaping a Saint's Identity: The Imagery of Thomas Becket in Medieval Italy', in *Medieval Art, Architecture and Archaeology at Canterbury*, ed. Alixe Bovey, Leeds: Maney Publishing, 2013, pp. 116–38, at pp. 124–6.

13. Ibid.

14. Richard Gameson, 'The Early Imagery of Thomas Becket', in *Pilgrimage: The English Experience from Becket to Bunyan*, ed. Colin Morris and Peter Roberts, Cambridge: Cambridge University Press, 2002, pp. 46–89, at pp. 48–9; Caroline Vogt, 'Episcopal Self-Fashioning: The Thomas Becket Mitres', in *Iconography of Liturgical Textiles in the Middle Ages*, ed. Evelin Wetter, Riggisberg: Abegg-Stiftung, 2010, pp. 117–28.

15. Colette Bowie, *The Daughters of Henry II and Eleanor of Aquitaine*, Turnhout: Brepols, 2014, p. 89.

16. Margaret Harris, 'Alan of Tewkesbury and St Thomas of Canterbury', *Reading Medieval Studies*, vol. 16 (1990), pp. 39–53, at p. 47. Barnaby, 'Becket Vault: The Appropriation of St Thomas Becket's Image', p. 66.

17. Christopher Cheney, *Pope Innocent III and England*, Stuttgart: Hiersemann, 1976, pp. 209–20; Jane Sayers, 'Peter's Throne and Augustine's Chair: Rome and Canterbury from Baldwin (1184–90) to Robert Winchelsey (1297–1313)', *Journal of Ecclesiastical History*, vol. 51 (2000), pp. 249–66; Marie-Pierre Gelin, 'Gervase of Canterbury, Christ Church and the Archbishops', *Journal of Ecclesiastical History*, vol. 60 (2009), pp. 449–63.

18. Cheney, *Pope Innocent III*, pp. 209–20. See also Hugh M. Thomas, *The Secular Clergy in England, 1066–1216*, Oxford: Oxford University Press, 2014, pp. 350–1.

19. These were: Bath, Canterbury, Carlisle, Coventry, Durham, Ely, Norwich, Winchester and Worcester.

20. David Knowles, *The Monastic Order in England: A History of its Development from the Times of St Dunstan to the Fourth Lateran Council: 940–1216*, 2nd edn, Cambridge: Cambridge University Press, 1966, pp. 318–22; Sheila Sweetinburgh, 'Caught in the Cross-Fire: Patronage and Institutional Politics in

Late Twelfth-Century Canterbury', in *Cathedrals, Community and Conflict in the Anglo-Norman World*, ed. Paul Dalton, Charles Insley and Louise J. Wilkinson, Woodbridge: The Boydell Press, 2011, pp. 187–202.

21. Cheney, *Pope Innocent III*, p. 210; Knowles, *The Monastic Order*, pp. 322–30; Peter R. Coss, 'Bishops, Chroniclers and Historians: The Case of Twelfth-Century Coventry', in *Episcopal Power and Local Society in Medieval Europe, 900–1400*, ed. Peter Coss, Chris Dennis, Melissa Julian-Jones and Angelo Silvestri, Turnhout: Brepols, 2017, pp. 21–40.

22. Michael Staunton, 'Thomas Becket in the Chronicles', in *The Cult of St Thomas Becket in the Plantagenet World, c.1170–c.1220*, ed. Paul Webster and Marie-Pierre Gelin, Woodbridge: The Boydell Press, 2016, pp. 95–112, at p. 107; Barnaby, 'Becket Vult: The Appropriation of St Thomas Becket's Image', for the visions see pp. 69–70.

23. Thomas, *The Secular Clergy in England*, p. 351.

24. Barnaby, 'Becket Vult: The Appropriation of St Thomas Becket's Image', p. 68.

25. Christopher Holdsworth, 'Baldwin [Baldwin of Forde] (c. 1125–1190), Archbishop of Canterbury', *Oxford Dictionary of National Biography*, 23 September 2004, www.oxforddnb.com/view/10.1093/ref:odnb/9780198614128.001.0001/odnb-9780198614128-e-1164 (accessed 18 September 2020).

26. Eales, 'The Political Setting of the Becket Translation', p. 133; Alan J. Forey, 'The Military Order of St Thomas of Acre', *English Historical Review*, vol. 92 (1977), pp. 481–503. The foundation went through two phases: first it was a hospital whose purpose was to care for crusading knights, and then in the thirteenth century the order took on a military role. See also John Jenkins, 'St Thomas Becket and Medieval London', *History*, vol. 105 (2020), pp. 652–72, at pp. 659–62.

27. Derek J. Keene and Vanessa Harding, 'St. Mary Colechurch 105/18', in *Historical Gazetteer of London before the Great Fire Cheapside; Parishes of All Hallows Honey Lane, St Martin Pomary, St Mary Le Bow, St Mary Colechurch and St Pancras Soper Lane*, London: British History Online, 1987, pp. 490–517, available at www.british-history.ac.uk/no-series/london-gazetteer-pre-fire/pp490-517 (accessed 9 August 2020). Jenkins, 'St Thomas Becket and Medieval London', p. 659.

28. For a biography of Hubert Walter, see Christopher Cheney, *Hubert Walter*, London: Nelson, 1967.

29. Neil Stratford, Pamela Tudor-Craig and Anna Maria Muthesius, 'Archbishop Hubert Walter's Tomb and its Furnishings', in *Medieval Art and Architecture at Canterbury before 1220*, ed. Nicola Coldstream and Peter Draper, British Archaeological Association Conference Transactions 5, Leeds: British Archaeological Association and Kent Archaeological Society, 1982, pp. 71–93, at pp. 87–93; Paul Binski, *Becket's Crown: Art and Imagination in Gothic England, 1170–1300*, New Haven and London: Yale University Press, 2004, pp. 36–40.

30. Kay Slocum, '*Martir quod stillat primatis ab ore sigillat*: Sealed with the Blood of Becket', *Journal of the British Archaeological Association*, vol. 165 (2012), pp. 61–88.

31. The inscription reads 'Martir quod stillat, primatis ab ore sigillat', translated in Margaret Gibson, 'Normans and Angevins, 1070–1220', in *A History of Canterbury Cathedral*, ed. Patrick Collinson, Nigel Ramsay and Margaret Sparks, Oxford: Oxford University Press, 1995, pp. 38–68, at p. 67, n. 184.

32. For a summary of seals with Becket's martyrdom, see Slocum, 'Sealed with the Blood of Becket'.

33. At the end of his life Walter took up a project, later abandoned after he died, to refound a secular college at Wolverhampton as a Cistercian monastery. See Paul Webster, *King John and Religion*, Woodbridge: The Boydell Press, 2015, pp. 35–6.

34. See Matthew M. Reeve, 'A Seat of Authority: The Archbishop's Throne at Canterbury Cathedral', *Gesta*, vol. 42 (2003), pp. 131–42; Binski, *Becket's Crown*, pp. 37–8.

35. Christopher Wilson, 'The Medieval Monuments', in *A History of Canterbury Cathedral*, ed. Patrick Collinson, Nigel Ramsay and Margaret Sparks, Oxford: Oxford University Press, 1995, pp. 451–511, at pp. 454–8.

36. Ibid., p. 454.

37. Translation taken from David Carpenter, *Magna Carta*, London: Penguin Books, 2015, p. 39. Another translation can be found online at 'Treasures in Full: Magna Carta: Translation', British Library website, www.bl.uk/treasuresmagnacarta/translation/mc_trans.html (accessed 3 August 2020).

38. The most recent overview of the situation is Paul Webster, 'Crown versus Church after Becket: King John, St Thomas and the Interdict', in Webster and Gelin, eds, *The Cult of St Thomas Becket in the Plantagenet World*, pp. 147–69. See also Webster, *King John and Religion*, chapters 6 and 7, pp. 131–72.

39. Webster, 'Crown versus Church', p. 148. See also Paul Webster, 'Crown, Cathedral and Conflict: King John and Canterbury', in *Cathedrals, Community and Conflict in the Anglo-Norman World*, ed. Paul Dalton, Charles Insley and Louise J. Wilkinson, Woodbridge: The Boydell Press, 2011, pp. 203–19.

40. Cheney, *Hubert Walter*, p. 87: see n. 5, which references Matthew Paris, *Matthaei Parisiensis, monachi Sancti Albani, Historia Anglorum: sive, ut vulgo dicitur, Historia minor*, vol. II, ed. Frederic Madden, London: Longman & Co., 1866, p. 104.

41. David Knowles, 'The Canterbury Election of 1205–6', *English Historical Review*, vol. 53 (1938), pp. 211–20. Cheney, *Pope Innocent III*, pp. 147–54.

42. Vincent, 'Stephen Langton, Archbishop of Canterbury'. He had been in York too: Christopher Holdsworth, 'Langton, Stephen (c. 1150–1228), Archbishop of Canterbury', *Oxford Dictionary of National Biography*, 23 September 2004, www.oxforddnb.com/view/10.1093/ref:odnb/9780198614128.001.0001/odnb-9780198614128-e-16044 (accessed 8 August 2020).

43. The classic study of Langton is Frederick M. Powicke, *Stephen Langton*, Oxford: Oxford University Press, 1928, but this has been updated by work by Nicholas Vincent and others. Knowles, 'The Canterbury Election of 1205–6'.

44. Brenda Bolton, 'Pastor Bonus: Matthew Paris's Life of Stephen Langton, Archbishop of Canterbury (1207–28)', *Dutch Review of Church History*, vol. 84 (2004), pp. 57–70.

45. Powicke, *Stephen Langton*, p. 75.

46. They first went to St Bertin for a year (the group included the prior and sixteen monks) but then Langton arranged for them to be dispersed to other abbeys around France: see Powicke, *Stephen Langton*, p. 76. See also Webster, 'Crown versus Church', p. 154.

47. Innocent III, *Selected Letters of Pope Innocent III*, ed. Christopher Cheney and William H. Semple, London: Nelson, 1953, pp. 89–90.

48. Christopher Cheney, *From Becket to Langton: English Church Government 1170–1213*, Manchester: Manchester University Press, 1956, p. 1.

49. Powicke, *Stephen Langton*, p. 12. Anne Duggan has also noted that Langton compared himself to Becket and King John to Henry II, see Anne Duggan, 'The Cult of Thomas Becket in the Thirteenth Century', in *Thomas Becket: Friends, Networks, Texts and Cult*, Aldershot: Ashgate, 2007, pp. 21–44, at p. 37.

50. Thomas Wright, *The Political Songs of England: From the Reign of King John to that of Edward II*, London: J. B. Nichols and Son, 1839, pp. 6–7.

51. 'Mors expressa foris tibi vita sit intus amoris'. The translation is in Anne Duggan, 'Becket's Cap and the Broken Sword', *Journal of the British Archaeological Association*, vol. 173 (2020), p. 14. See also Duggan, 'The Cult of Thomas Becket', p. 37, n. 93.

52. Webster, 'Crown versus Church', p. 161.

53. Michael Staunton, *The Historians of Angevin England*, Oxford: Oxford University Press, 2017, p. 102.

54. Gerald of Wales, *De principis instructione*, trans. Robert Bartlett, Oxford: Oxford University Press, 2018, pp. 35–7.

55. Christopher Cheney, 'King John and the Papal Interdict', *Bulletin of the John Rylands Library*, vol. 31 (1948), pp. 295–317; Christopher R. Cheney, 'King John's Reaction to the Interdict on England', *Transactions of the Royal Historical Society*, 4th series, vol. 31 (1949), pp. 129–50; Christopher R. Cheney, 'A Recent View of the General Interdict on England, 1208–1214', *Studies in Church History*, vol. 3 (1966), pp. 159–68.

56. Paul Webster, 'Religion, Politics, and Reputation: The Interdict and King John's Excommunication', in *King John and Religion*, pp. 131–52; esp. pp. 138–44.

57. David Carpenter, *The Struggle for Mastery: Britain 1066–1284*, London: Penguin Books, 2004, p. 276.

58. Webster, *King John and Religion*, chapter 7; Cheney discusses the settlement between Innocent and John in *Pope Innocent III*, pp. 326–56.

59. Carpenter, *The Struggle for Mastery*, p. 286.

60. For the most recent overview, see Carpenter, *Magna Carta*; Carpenter, *The Struggle for Mastery*, p. 287.

61. Nicholas Vincent, 'The Seal(s) of Robert Fitzwalter', in *Seals and Status: The Power of Objects*, ed. John Cherry, Jessica Berenbeim and Lloyd de Beer, London: British Museum Press, 2018, pp. 84–94.

62. Christopher Holdsworth, 'Langton, Stephen (*c.* 1150–1228), Archbishop of Canterbury', *Oxford Dictionary of National Biography*, 23 September 2004, www.oxforddnb.com/view/10.1093/ref:odnb/9780198614128.001.0001/odnb-9780198614128-e-16044 (accessed 13 August 2020); John W. Baldwin, 'Master Stephen Langton, Future Archbishop of Canterbury: The Paris Schools and Magna Carta', *English Historical Review*, vol. 123 (2008), pp. 811–46; David A. Carpenter, 'Archbishop Langton and Magna Carta: His Contribution, his Doubts and his Hypocrisy', *English Historical Review*, vol. 126 (2011), pp. 1041–65.

63. This copy is now BL, Cotton MS Augustus II.106.

64. Carpenter, 'Archbishop Langton and Magna Carta', p. 1050. See also Carpenter, *Magna Carta*, pp. 332–5, 347–52. David d'Avray, 'Magna Carta: Its Background in Stephen Langton's Academic Biblical Exegesis and its Episcopal Reception', *Studi Medievali*, vol. 38 (1997), pp. 423–38.

65. Carpenter, *Magna Carta*, pp. 395–403.

66. Matthew Paris, quoted in Mason, *What Became of the Bones of St Thomas?*, p. 80.

67. Carpenter, *Magna Carta*, pp. 406–16.

68. See David A. Carpenter, *The Minority of Henry III*, Berkeley: University of California Press, 1990, pp. 187–221.

69. Christopher Wilson, 'Calling the Tune? The Involvement of King Henry III in the Design of the Abbey Church at Westminster', *Journal of the British Archaeological Association*, vol. 161 (2008), pp. 59–93; Paul Binski, *Westminster Abbey and the Plantagenets: Kingship and the Representation of Power, 1200–1400*, New Haven and London: Yale University Press, 1995, pp. 10–51.

70. The Waverley annalist notes that Langton had sent out an edict about the translation two years before, in 1218. See Mason, *What Became of the Bones of St Thomas?*, pp. 80–1.

71. Foreville, *Le jubilé de saint Thomas Becket*, pp. 165–6. The term Honorius used was 'renovatio'.

72. For the painted vaults, see Madeleine Caviness, 'A Lost Cycle of Canterbury Paintings of 1220', *Antiquaries Journal*, vol. 54 (1974), pp. 66–74.

73. Mason, *What Became of the Bones of St Thomas?*, p. 75; 'Appendix ad Quodrilogum', *MTB*, vol. IV, 1879, p. 426.

74. See also Laura Slater, *Art and Political Thought in Medieval England, c.1150–1350*, Woodbridge: The Boydell Press, 2018, pp. 95–101.

75. Kay Slocum, *Liturgies in Honour of Thomas Becket*, Toronto: University of Toronto Press, 2003, p. 242.

76. Quoted in Sherry L. Reames, 'Reconstructing and Interpreting a Thirteenth-Century Office for the Translation of Thomas Becket', *Speculum*, vol. 80 (2005), pp. 118–70, at p. 119.

77. Ibid., p. 124; Foreville, *Le jubilé de saint Thomas Becket*, pp. 165–6.

78. C. Eveleigh Woodruff, 'The Financial Aspect of the Cult of St Thomas of Canterbury', *Archaeologia Cantina*, vol. 44 (1932), pp. 13–32, at p. 19. Ben Nilson, *Cathedral Shrines of Medieval England*, Woodbridge: The Boydell Press, 1998, pp. 147–154, 168–90, 211–15.

79. Phyllis Roberts, *Thomas Becket in the Medieval Latin Preaching Tradition*, The Hague: Martinus Nijhoff International, 1992, no. 124, p. 178; 'Appendix ad Quodrilogum', *MTB*, vol. IV, 1879, p. 427; Walter of Coventry, *Memoriale fratris Walteri de Coventria: The Historical Collections of Walter of Coventry*, vol. II, ed. William Stubbs, London: Longman & Co., 1873, p. 246.

80. English translation from 'Magna Carta, 1225', TNA, www.nationalarchives.gov.uk/education/resources/magna-carta/magna-carta-1225-westminster (accessed 9 August 2020). For the most recent translation of the 1215 document and for context, see Carpenter, *Magna Carta*, pp. 36–69, 395–429. See also Nicholas Vincent, *Magna Carta: Origins and Legacy*, Oxford: Bodleian Library, 2015, pp. 224–31.

81. David Carpenter, 'Archbishop Langton and Magna Carta', p. 1056.

82. J. M. Theilmann, 'Political Canonisation and Political Symbolism in medieval England', *Journal of British Studies*, vol. 29 (1970), pp. 242–66. A. M. Kleinberg, 'Proving Sanctity: Selection and Authentication of Saints in the Later Middle Ages', *Viator*, vol. 20 (1989), pp. 183–205. Binski, *Becket's Crown*, pp. 81–4. Ian Bass, 'England's Two Thomases: Episcopal Models of Sanctity Embodied in Thomas Becket and Thomas de Cantilupe', in *Episcopal Power and Personality in Medieval Europe, 900–1480*, ed. Peter Coss et al., Turnhout: Brepols, 2020, pp. 159–79. John Jenkins, 'Replication or Rivalry? The "Becketization" of Pilgrimage in English Cathedrals', *Religion*, vol. 49, (2019), pp. 24–47.

83. Binski, *Becket's Crown*, pp. 53–77. This poem is by Henry d'Avranches and titled *De translatione veteris ecclesie Saresberiensis et constructione nove*. He composed it between 1220 and 1225, and it can be found in a manuscript in Cambridge University Library, MS Dd.11.78, f. 92v.

Chapter 6

1. Transcription of the original in Richard Leighton Green, ed., *The Early English Carols*, Oxford: Clarendon Press, 1925, pp. 72–3, no. 114. Translation from Eleanor Parker's blog: https://aclerkofoxford.blogspot.com/2011/12/song-for-st-thomas-becket.html (accessed 5 November 2020).

2. See Michael Staunton, *Thomas Becket and his Biographers*, Woodbridge: The Boydell Press, 2006.

See also Paul Alonzo Brown, 'The Development of the Legend of Thomas Becket', PhD thesis, Philadelphia: University of Pennsylvania, 1930, pp. 14–27.

3. Anne Duggan, 'Master Herbert: Becket's Eruditus, Envoy, Adviser and Ghost Writer?', in *Herbert of Bosham: A Medieval Polymath*, ed. Michael Staunton, Woodbridge: The Boydell Press, 2019, pp. 29–54.

4. See Ian Short, 'An Early Draft of Guernes' "Vie de Saint Thomas Becket"', *Medium Ævum*, vol. 46 (1977), pp. 20–34; Beneit of St Albans, *La vie de Thomas Becket par Beneit: poème anglo-normand du XIIe siècle*, ed. Börje Schlyter, Lund: C. W. K. Gleerup, 1941. For Scandinavia see Haki Antonsson, 'The Lives of Thomas Becket and Early Scandinavian Literature', *Studi e materiali di storia delle religioni*, vol. 81 (2015), pp. 392–413.

5. Rachel Koopmans, *Wonderful to Relate: Miracle Stories and Miracle Collecting in High Medieval Europe*, Philadelphia: University of Pennsylvania Press, 2011, p. 130.

6. A number of versions of Grandison's life survive, for instance at Exeter Cathedral, Venerable English College, Parker Library. For Grandison and the Pope, see Margaret Walvoord Steele, 'A Study of the Books Owned or Used by John Grandisson, Bishop of Exeter (1327–1369)', PhD thesis, University of Oxford, 1994, p. 215, see also pp. 213–67.

7. British Museum registration numbers 1861,0416.1 and 1926,0712.1.

8. Islwyn Thomas, 'The Cult of Saints' Relics in Medieval England', PhD thesis, Queen Mary University, London, 1977, pp. 98–9.

9. Ibid., p. 98.

10. Steele, 'A Study of the Books', p. 214.

11. Ibid., p. 215.

12. Phyllis Roberts, *Thomas Becket in the Medieval Latin Preaching Tradition: An Inventory of Sermons about St Thomas Becket c.1170–c.1400*, Turnhout: Brepols, 1992.

13. Brown, 'The Development of the Legend of Thomas Becket', pp. 28–153.

14. Ibid., pp. 92–5.

15. Katherine Emery, 'Music, Politics and Sanctity: The Cult of Thomas Becket, 1170–1580', PhD thesis, King's College London. Our sincere thanks to Katherine Emery for discussing her research with us and for sharing her PhD before it was submitted. See also Anne Duggan, 'Becket is Dead! Long Live St Thomas', in *The Cult of St Thomas Becket in the Plantagenet World, c.1170–c.1220*, ed. Paul Webster and Marie-Pierre Gelin, Woodbridge: The Boydell Press, 2016, pp. 25–52, esp. pp. 28–36.

16. Rossell Hope Robbins, 'Middle English Carols as Processional Hymns', *Studies in Philology*, vol. 56 (1959), pp. 559–82. Thanks to Katherine Emery for supplying this reference.

17. Richard Leighton Greene, ed., *A Selection of English Carols*, Oxford: Clarendon Press, 1962, p. 80. 'Saint Thomas honour we,/ Through whose blood Holy

Church is made free./ All Holy Church was but a thrall,/ Through king and temporal lords all,/ Till he was slain in Christ's hall/ And set all things in unity:/ His death has such auctorite [power]'. Translation from Eleanor Parker's blog, https://aclerkofoxford.blogspot.com/2012/07/translation-of-st-thomas-becket.html (accessed 11 November 2020).

18. For images, see Tancred Borenius, *St Thomas Becket in Art*, London: Methuen & Co., 1932.

19. Francis Cheetham, *Alabaster Images of Medieval England*, Woodbridge: The Boydell Press, 2003. For images of Becket see pp. 65–6.

20. Robert Morris, *Medieval Feast Menus: 1380–1450*, Bristol: Stuart Press, 2001, pp. 20–1.

21. For the period between Henry II's reign to that of Edward I see Antonia Gransden, *Historical Writing in England c.550 to c.1307*, Ithaca: Cornell University Press, 1974, pp. 219–486.

22. See also Arthur James Mason, *What Became of the Bones of St Thomas? A Contribution to his Fiftieth Jubilee*, Cambridge: The University Press, 1920. For Paris, see Richard Vaughan, *Matthew Paris*, New York: Cambridge University Press, 2008; Suzanne Lewis, *The Art of Matthew Paris in the Chronica majora*, Berkeley: University of California Press, 1987.

23. Lewis, *Matthew Paris*, p. 87.

24. Ibid., pp. 88–9.

25. Paris knew of Langton's seal as he records a letter between Langton and Robert Grosseteste in the *Chronica majora*, see ibid., p. 89, n. 79. Vaughan, *Matthew Paris*, p. 160; Frederick M. Powicke, *Stephen Langton*, Oxford: Oxford University Press, 1928, pp. 102–3.

26. Michael A. Michael, *St Albans Cathedral Wall Paintings*, London: Scala, 2019, pp. 42–3, 70–1.

27. Janet Backhouse and Christopher de Hamel, *The Becket Leaves*, London: British Library, 1988, p. 14. M. R. James, *La estoire de seint Aedward le rei; The Life of St. Edward the Confessor, Reproduced in Facsimile from the Unique Manuscript (Cambridge University Library Ee.3.59) Together with Some Pages of the Manuscript of the Life of St. Alban at Trinity College, Dublin*, Oxford: Oxford University Press, 1920, p. 21. For a discussion of Arundel, see Paul Binski, *Becket's Crown: Art and Imagination in Gothic England, 1170–1300*, New Haven and London: Yale University Press, 2004, p. 123.

28. Paul Meyer, ed., *Fragments d'une vie de Saint Thomas de Cantorbéry en vers accouplés*, Paris: Firmin Didot, 1885; Vaughan, *Matthew Paris*, pp. 159–81; Sotheby's sale, London, 24 June 1986, lot 40; Nigel Morgan, *Early Gothic Manuscripts*, vol. 1: *1190–1250*, 2 vols, London: Harvey Miller, 1982–8, pp. 107–8; Nigel Morgan, 'Matthew Paris, St Albans, London, and the Leaves of the "Life of St Thomas Becket"', *Burlington Magazine*, vol. 13 (special issue on English Gothic art) (1988), pp. 85–96; Backhouse and de Hamel, *The Becket Leaves*, pp. 11, 13–19; Binski, *Becket's Crown*, pp. 122–8; Katherine Rachel Handel, 'French Writing in the Cloister: Four Texts from St Albans Abbey Featuring Thomas Becket and Alexander the

Great, c.1184–c.1275', PhD thesis, University of York, 2015, pp. 108–72.

29. Backhouse and de Hamel hypothesise that it might have originally been a gathering of eight leaves, which means there were probably around thirty-four images, see Backhouse and de Hamel, *The Becket Leaves*, p. 13. Dating of the leaves has ranged from 1230 to 1240, for a summary see Morgan, 'Matthew Paris'.

30. For a summary of the events on each folio, see Backhouse and de Hamel, *The Becket Leaves*, pp. 31–2.

31. Ibid., p. 31; Laura Slater, *Art and Political Thought in Medieval England, c.1150–1350*, Woodbridge: The Boydell Press, 2018, p. 100.

32. Backhouse and de Hamel, *The Becket Leaves*, p. 6.

33. Henry R. Luard, ed., *Matthaei Parisiensis, monachi Sancti Albani Chronica majora*, 7 vols, London: Longman, 1872–83, vol. IV, pp. 93–4; Lewis, *Matthew Paris*, pp. 310–20; John Jenkins, 'St Thomas Becket and Medieval London', *History*, vol. 105 (2020), pp. 652–72, at pp. 662–3.

34. See also Lewis, *Matthew Paris*, pp. 319–20. Jenkins provides a slightly different translation from Lewis, see Jenkins, 'St Thomas Becket and Medieval London', pp. 662–3.

35. For the manuscripts in which this story can be found and the most detailed discussion of the origin of the legend, see Brown, 'The Development of the Legend of Thomas Becket', pp. 28–74, pp. 274–7. See also Robert Mills, 'Invisible Translation, Language Difference and the Scandal of Becket's Mother', in *Rethinking Medieval Translation: Ethics, Politics, Theory*, ed. Robert Mills and Emma Campbell, Woodbridge: The Boydell Press, 2012, pp. 125–46; Jenkins, 'St Thomas Becket and Medieval London', pp. 668–70.

36. See Brown, 'The Development of the Legend of Thomas Becket', pp. 51–74. It has been kept alive through the English folk ballad tradition, see Mills, 'Invisible Translation'.

37. Brown, 'The Development of the Legend of Thomas Becket', p. 35. The naming of Matilda as Alisaundre is in the *South English Legendary*, see Charlotte D'Evelyn and Anna J. Mill, eds, *The South English Legendary: Edited from Corpus Christi College Cambridge Ms. 145 and British Museum Ms. Harley 2277 with Variants from Bodley Ms Ahsmole 43 and British Museum Ms. Cotton Julius D.IX, vol. II*, Oxford: Oxford University Press, 1959, p. 41.

38. See appendices A to C in Brown, 'The Development of the Legend of Thomas Becket', pp. 262–73. Jacobus de Voragine, *The Golden Legend or Lives of the Saints, as Englished by William Caxton*, ed. F. S. Ellis, London: Dent, 1900, vol. II, pp. 182–4.

39. Anne Rudloff Stanton, 'The Queen Mary Psalter: A Study of Affect and Audience', *Transactions of the American Philosophical Society*, new series, vol. 91 (2001), pp. 53, 142, 146, 186, 195.

40. Rachel Koopmans, 'Early Sixteenth-Century Stained Glass at St Michael-Le-Belfrey and the

Commemoration of Thomas Becket in Late Medieval York', *Speculum*, vol. 89 (2014), pp. 1040–1100.

41. Ibid., pp. 1055–9.

42. Ibid., pp. 1047–50.

43. Brown provides a full translation of the Latin version in Brown, 'The Development of the Legend of Thomas Becket', pp. 29–32.

44. In another version, in a fifteenth-century manuscript in the Bodleian Library, Oxford, MS Rawlinson poet. 225 (SC 14716), it is 'Iewes' who imprison Gilbert and his companion. See ibid., p. 34.

45. Ibid., p. 30.

46. Ibid., p. 31.

47. Clifford Davidson, *Festivals and Plays in Late Medieval Britain*, Aldershot: Ashgate, 2007, p. 40. Clifford Davidson, 'The Middle English Saint Play and its Iconography', in *The Saint Play in Medieval Europe*, ed. Davidson, Kalamazoo: Medieval Institute Publications, 1986, pp. 52–60.

48. Mary Blackstone, 'A Survey and Annotated Bibliography of Records Research and Performance History Relating to Early British Drama and Minstrelsy for 1984–8 (Continued)', *Records of Early English Drama*, vol. 15 (1990), pp. 1–104, at p. 85. See also Meg Twycross, 'Two Maid Marians and a Jewess', *Medieval English Theatre*, vol. 9 (1987), pp. 6–7.

49. Jenkins, 'St Thomas Becket and Medieval London', p. 654.

50. Ibid.

51. Brown, 'The Development of the Legend of Thomas Becket', p. 21.

52. *The Travels of Leo of Rozmital*, ed. and trans. Malcolm Letts, Cambridge: The University Press, 1957, p. 51.

53. Derek Keene, 'London Bridge and the Identity of the Medieval City', *Transactions of the London and Middlesex Archaeological Society*, vol. 51 (2000), pp. 143–56, at pp. 146–53; Bruce Watson, Trevor Brigham and Tony Dyson, *London Bridge: 2000 Years of a River Crossing*, London: Museum of London, 2001, pp. 83–155. Christopher Wilson, 'The Architect as Civic Benefactor: Henry Yevele and the Chapel of London Bridge', *Revue de l'Art*, vol. 166 (2009), pp. 43–51.

54. Elizabeth New, 'The Common Seal and Communal Identity in Medieval London', in *Medieval Coins and Seals: Constructing Identity, Signifying Power*, ed. Susan Solway, Turnhout: Brepols, 2015, pp. 297–318; Jenkins, 'St Thomas Becket and Medieval London', pp. 656–7.

55. Caroline Barron, 'The Political Culture of Medieval London', in *Political Culture in Late Medieval Britain*, ed. Linda Clark and Christine Carpenter, Woodbridge: The Boydell Press, 2004, pp. 111–34, at pp. 113–14. See also Jenkins, 'St Thomas Becket and Medieval London', p. 657.

56. John R. Maddicott, 'Follower, Leader, Pilgrim, Saint: Robert de Vere, Earl of Oxford, at the Shrine of Simon de Montfort, 1273', *English Historical Review*, vol. 109 (1994), pp. 641–53; Claire Valente, 'Simon

de Montfort, Earl of Leicester, and the Utility of Sanctity in Thirteenth-Century England', *Journal of Medieval History*, vol. 21 (1995), pp. 27–49; Simon Walker, 'Political Saints in Later Medieval England', in *The McFarlane Legacy: Studies in Late Medieval Politics and Society*, ed. Richard J. Britnell and Anthony J. Pollard, New York: St Martin's Press, 1995, pp. 77–106, at p. 82.

57. Thomas Wright, *The Political Songs of England: From the Reign of King John to that of Edward II*, London: J. B. Nichols and Son, 1839, pp. 125–6.

58. Walker, 'Political Saints in Later Medieval England', pp. 82, 96. For a discussion of his miracles, see John Edward St Lawrence, 'The *Liber miraculorum* of Simon de Montfort: Contested Sanctity and Contesting Authority in Late Thirteenth-century England', PhD thesis, University of Texas, 2005.

59. John R. Maddicott, *Thomas of Lancaster, 1307–1322: A Study in the Reign of Edward II*, Oxford: Oxford University Press, 1970; Arthur R. Echerd, Jr, 'Canonization and Politics in Late Medieval England: The Cult of Thomas of Lancaster', PhD thesis, University of North Carolina at Chapel Hill, 1983; John Edwards, 'The Cult of "St" Thomas of Lancaster and its Iconography', *Yorkshire Archaeological Journal*, vol. 64 (1992), pp. 103–22; John T. McQuillen, 'Who Was St Thomas of Lancaster? New Manuscript Evidence', in *Fourteenth Century England*, vol. IV, ed. J. S. Hamilton, Woodbridge: The Boydell Press, 2006, pp. 1–25; Danna Piroyansky, 'Bloody Miracles of a Political Martyr: The Case of Thomas Earl of Lancaster', in *Signs, Wonders, Miracles: Representations of Divine Power in the Life of the Church*, ed. Kate Cooper and Jeremy Gregory [Studies in Church History 41], Woodbridge: The Boydell Press, 2005, pp. 228–38. For context, see Walker, 'Political Saints in Later Medieval England'.

60. Walker, 'Political Saints in Later Medieval England', pp. 83, 92–3.

61. Piroyansky, 'Bloody Miracles of a Political Martyr', p. 230.

62. Ibid.

63. Ibid., pp. 230–1.

64. For a full list of the manuscripts, see McQuillen, 'Who Was St Thomas of Lancaster?', p. 1.

65. Piroyansky, 'Bloody Miracles of a Political Martyr', pp. 234–6.

66. Hugh Tait, 'Pilgrim-Signs and Thomas, Earl of Lancaster', *British Museum Quarterly*, vol. 20 (1955–6), pp. 39–47.

67. Ibid. Only two of these plaques have been found. One in London, now in the British Museum, 1954,0502.1. The other also in London between 2006 and 2009, now in the Museum of London. See Anthony Mackinder, *Roman and Medieval Revetments on the Thames Waterfront: Excavations at Riverbank House, City of London, 2006–9*, London: Museum of London Archaeology, 2015, pp. 94–6.

68. Tait, 'Pilgrim-Signs and Thomas, Earl of Lancaster', p. 46.

69. Lord Houghton, 'Observations on the History of Thomas Earl of Lancaster', *Journal of the British Archaeological Association*, vol. 20 (1864), pp. 16–17.

70. Walker, 'Political Saints in Later Medieval England', p. 83.

71. Diana Webb, *Pilgrims and Pilgrimage in the Medieval West*, London: I. B. Tauris, 1999, p. 137.

72. Simon Walker, 'Political Saints in Later Medieval England', p. 94.

73. Thomas Walsingham, *The Chronica maiora*, trans. David Preest, Woodbridge: The Boydell Press, 2005, pp. 125–8.

74. This idea has been suggested by Colin Torode and he is preparing a publication on the subject. Recently another Sudbury badge was discovered in London. See Walker, 'Political Saints in Later Medieval England', pp. 81–2.

75. Andrew Galloway, 'Gower in his Most Learned Role and the Peasants' Revolt of 1381', *Mediaevalia*, vol. 16 (1990), pp. 329–47, at pp. 335–6.

76. Sudbury's head was buried at St Gregory's, Sudbury.

77. John Jenkins, 'Replication or Rivalry? The "Becketization" of Pilgrimage in English Cathedrals', *Religion*, vol. 49 (2019), p. 37.

Chapter 7

1. Geoffrey Chaucer, 'General Prologue', *The Canterbury Tales*, in *The Riverside Chaucer*, ed. F. N. Robinson and Larry D. Benson, Oxford: Oxford University Press, 2008, ll. 12–18. Benson dates the work to *c.*1388–1400 and the Prologue to *c.*1388–92.

2. Anne Duggan, 'Becket is Dead! Long Live St Thomas', in *The Cult of St Thomas Becket in the Plantagenet World, c.1170–c.1220*, ed. Paul Webster and Marie-Pierre Gelin, Woodbridge: The Boydell Press, 2016, pp. 25–52, at pp. 44–7; Anne Duggan, 'The Cult of St Thomas Becket in the Thirteenth Century' in *St Thomas Cantilupe, Bishop of Hereford: Essays in his Honour*, ed. Meryl Jancey, Hereford: Friends of Hereford Cathedral, 1982, pp. 21–44, at pp. 24–9.

3. Tancred Borenius, *St Thomas Becket in Art*, London: Methuen & Co., 1932, pp. 19, 58–63; Jennifer Lee, 'The Merchants' Saint: Thomas Becket among the Merchants of Hamburg', *Journal of the British Archaeological Association*, vol. 173 (2020), pp. 174–82.

4. Anne F. Sutton and Livia Visser-Fuchs, *The Book of Privileges of the Merchant Adventurers of England, 1296–1483*, Oxford: Oxford University Press, 2011, p. 40.

5. Chaucer, 'General Prologue', ll. 769–70. Our thanks to Marion Turner for kindly providing modern translations.

6. Diana Webb, *Pilgrims and Pilgrimage in the Medieval West*, London: I. B. Tauris, 1999, p. 199.

7. Alnwick Castle, Northumberland 455. Thank you to Marion Turner for alerting us to the manuscript.

8. 'The Canterbury Interlude', in *The Canterbury Tales: Fifteenth-Century Continuations and Additions*, ed. John M. Bowers, Kalamazoo: Medieval Institute Publications, 1992, p. 64.

9. Webb, *Pilgrims and Pilgrimage*, pp. 11–47; Robert Bartlett, *Why Can the Dead Do Such Great Things? Saints and Worshippers from the Martyrs to the Reformation*, Princeton: Princeton University Press, 2015, pp. 410–43.

10. For two recent broad surveys of relic culture in Europe see: Cynthia J. Hahn, *Strange Beauty: Issues in the Making and Meaning of Reliquaries, 400–circa 1204*, University Park: Pennsylvania State University Press, 2015; Martina Bagnoli et al., eds, *Treasures of Heaven: Saints, Relics and Devotion in Medieval Europe*, London: British Museum Press, 2011.

11. Rachel Koopmans, 'Gifts of Thomas Becket's Clothing Made by the Monks of Canterbury Cathedral', *Journal of the British Archaeological Association*, vol. 173 (2020), pp. 39–60; Avinoam Shalem, ed., *The Chasuble of Thomas Becket: A Biography*, Munich: Hirmer, 2016.

12. Martina Bagnoli, 'The Stuff of Heaven: Materials and Craftsmanship in Medieval Reliquaries', in Bagnoli et al., *Treasures of Heaven*, pp. 136–47.

13. Webb, *Pilgrims and Pilgrimage*, pp. 51–63, 83–123, 133–47.

14. Ibid., p. 142.

15. Conrad Rudolph, 'The Tour Guide in the Middle Ages: Guide Culture and the Mediation of Public Art', *Art Bulletin*, vol. 100 (2018), pp. 36–67, at p. 27.

16. Webb, *Pilgrims and Pilgrimage*, pp. 83–123.

17. John Jenkins, 'St Thomas Becket and Medieval London', *History*, vol. 105 (2020), pp. 652–72, at p. 666.

18. Webb, *Pilgrims and Pilgrimage*, p. 203.

19. Chaucer, 'General Prologue', l. 618.

20. Ibid., l. 558.

21. Webb, *Pilgrims and Pilgrimage*, p. 202.

22. Ibid., p. 215. Ben Nilson, *Cathedral Shrines of Medieval England*, Woodbridge: The Boydell Press, 1998, pp. 92–121.

23. Eirikr Magnússon, 'Icelandic Pilgrims to the Tomb of Becket', *Archaeologia Cantiana*, vol. 13, 1880, p. 407.

24. Ibid., pp. 405–7.

25. See chapter 6 on royal pilgrimage in Diana Webb, *Pilgrimage in Medieval England*, London: Hambledon Continuum, 2007, pp. 111–40.

26. R. Barrie Dobson, 'The Monks of Canterbury in the Later Middle Ages, 1220–1540', in *A History of Canterbury Cathedral*, ed. Patrick Collinson, Nigel Ramsay and Margaret Sparks, Oxford: Oxford University Press, 1995, pp. 69–153, at pp. 142–3; Mark Ormrod, 'The Personal Religion of Edward III', *Speculum*, vol. 64 (1989), pp. 849–77, at pp. 857–8.

27. Dobson, 'The Monks of Canterbury in the Later Middle Ages', p. 141. Nilson, *Cathedral Shrines of Medieval England*, pp. 117–21.

28. Bartlett, *Why Can the Dead Do Such Great Things?*, pp. 417–20. For a medieval burial in pilgrimage garb, see Helen Lubin, *The Worcester Pilgrim*, Worcester: West Mercian Archaeological Consultants, 1990.

29. Chaucer, 'General Prologue', l. 685.

30. Medieval wills document numerous instructions for pilgrimages to Becket's shrine from knights, sailors, butchers, merchants and ladies. For a selection, see Webb, *Pilgrims and Pilgrimage*, pp. 146–7.

31. Margery Kempe, *The Book of Margery Kempe*, ed. Anthony Bale, Oxford: Oxford University Press, 2015.

32. For English pilgrims abroad, see Webb, *Pilgrims and Pilgrimage*, pp. 163–97.

33. Chaucer, 'General Prologue', ll. 465–6. For English pilgrims' travel accounts, see Robert Lutton, 'Pilgrimage and Travel Writing in Early Sixteenth-Century England: The Pilgrimage Accounts of Thomas Larke and Robert Langton', *Viator*, vol. 48 (2017), pp. 333–57. See also M. B. Parkes and Richard Beadle, eds, *The Poetical Works of Geoffrey Chaucer: A Facsimile of Cambridge University Library MS GG.4.27*, 3 vols, Norman: Pilgrim Books, 1979; Megan L. Cook, 'Joseph Holland and the Idea of the Chaucerian Book', *Manuscript Studies: A Journal of the Schoenberg Institute for Manuscript Studies*, vol. 1 (2016), pp. 165–88.

34. Marion Turner, *Chaucer: A European Life*, Princeton: Princeton University Press, 2019, pp. 70–119, 145–65.

35. Chaucer, 'General Prologue', ll. 51, 75–6.

36. Ibid., l. 278.

37. Ibid., ll. 407–9.

38. Ibid., ll. 401–4.

39. Ibid., ll. 159–62.

40. Helen Cooper, *Oxford Guides to Chaucer: The Canterbury Tales*, Oxford: Oxford University Press, 2010, p. 29. The Portable Antiquities Scheme database records over twenty-one medieval objects with the motto. The Prioress was based on a character from the *Roman de la Rose*, see Geoffrey Chaucer, *The Canterbury Tales: A Selection*, ed. Colin Wilcockson, London: Penguin Classics, 2008, pp. xvi–xvii.

41. Chaucer, 'General Prologue', l. 115.

42. 'The Canterbury Interlude', in *The Canterbury Tales: Fifteenth-Century Continuations and Additions*, ed. Bowers, p. 63.

43. Sarah Blick, 'Votives, Images, Interaction and Pilgrimage to the Tomb and Shrine of St Thomas Becket', in *Push Me, Pull You: Imaginative, Emotional, Physical, and Spatial Interaction in Late Medieval and Renaissance Art*, vol. II, ed. Sarah Blick and Laura Deborah Gelfand, Leiden: Brill, 2011, pp. 21–58, at pp. 37–53.

44. Ibid., pp. 45–53.

45. John Jenkins, 'Modelling the Cult of Thomas Becket at Canterbury Cathedral', *Journal of the British Archaeological Association*, vol. 173 (2020), pp. 100–23.

46. Ibid., pp. 102–4. See also John Jenkins, 'Replication or Rivalry? The "Becketization" of Pilgrimage in English Cathedrals', *Religion*, vol. 49 (2019), pp. 24–47, at pp. 34–8.

47. BL, Add. MS 59616. John Jenkins is currently preparing a full translation of the Customary. Our sincere gratitude to him for sharing his translation and for discussing his research with us prior to publication. What follows is drawn from his translation, see John Jenkins, *The Customary of the Shrine of Thomas Becket at Canterbury Cathedral: Latin Text and Translation*, York: Arc Humanities Press, forthcoming. See also D. H. Turner, 'The Customary of the Shrine of St Thomas Becket', *Canterbury Cathedral Chronicle*, vol. 70 (1976), pp. 16–22.

48. Rudolph, 'The Tour Guide in the Middle Ages', p. 41.

49. John Dart, *The History and Antiquities of the Cathedral Church of Canterbury*, London: J. Cole, 1726, p. 13.

50. Jenkins, 'Replication or Rivalry?', p. 33.

51. Eugenio Sidoli, Margherita Palumbo and Stephen Parkin, 'A Florentine Merchant's Visit to Canterbury Cathedral in 1444', *Journal of Medieval History*, vol. 46 (2020), pp. 572–95, at p. 594.

52. See Chapter 5, p. 149.

53. 'The Canterbury Interlude', in *The Canterbury Tales: Fifteenth-Century Continuations and Additions*, ed. Bowers, p. 64. Jenkins, 'Replication or Rivalry?', pp. 35–6.

54. Jenkins, 'Replication or Rivalry?', p. 37. For Becket relics in general see Luxford, 'The Relics of Thomas Becket in England'.

55. *The Travels of Leo of Rozmital*, ed. and trans. Malcolm Letts, Cambridge: The University Press, 1957, pp. 43–4.

56. Canon Scott Robertson, 'Relics of Decorative Painting Now or Formerly in Canterbury Cathedral', *Archaeologia Cantiana*, vol. 22 (1897), pp. 34–44, at pp. 42–4.

57. *The Travels of Leo of Rozmital*, pp. 43–4. The Florentine merchant mentioned on p. 195 of this book also had a guide: Sidoli et al., 'A Florentine Merchant's Visit'.

58. Desiderius Erasmus, *Pilgrimages to Saint Mary of Walsingham and Saint Thomas of Canterbury*, trans. John Gough Nichols, London: John Murray, 1875, p. 42.

59. Ibid.

60. John Wickham Legg and William H. St John Hope, *Inventories of Christ Church, Canterbury*, Westminster: Constable, 1902, p. 135.

61. Ibid.

62. Christopher de Hamel, *The Book in the Cathedral: The Last Relic of Thomas Becket*, London: Allen Lane, 2020.

63. C. Eveleigh Woodruff, 'The Financial Aspect of the Cult of St Thomas of Canterbury', *Archaeologia Cantiana*, vol. 44 (1932), pp. 13–32. Nilson, *Cathedral Shrines of Medieval England*, pp. 147–54, 168–90, 211–15.

64. Nilson, *Cathedral Shrines of Medieval England*, pp. 211–15. It is difficult to equate these amounts to a modern value.

65. Woodruff, 'The Financial Aspect', p. 18.

66. Ibid.

67. Dobson, 'The Monks of Canterbury in the Later Middle Ages', p. 140.

68. Woodruff, 'The Financial Aspect', p. 23; Dobson, 'The Monks of Canterbury in the Later Middle Ages', p. 140.

69. Dobson, 'The Monks of Canterbury in the Later Middle Ages', pp. 135–53; Nilson, *Cathedral Shrines of Medieval England*, pp. 150–2. Meriel Connor, 'Brotherhood and Confraternity at Canterbury Cathedral Priory in the 15th Century: The Evidence of John Stone's Chronicle', *Archaeologia Cantiana*, vol. 128 (2008), pp. 143–64.

70. See Simon Walker, 'Political Saints in Later Medieval England', in *The McFarlane Legacy: Studies in Late Medieval Politics and Society*, ed. Richard J. Britnell and Anthony J. Pollard, New York: St Martin's Press, 1995, pp. 77–106, at p. 79. Eamon Duffy, 'The Dynamics of Pilgrimage in Late Medieval England', in *Pilgrimage: The English Experience from Becket to Bunyan*, ed. Colin Morris and Peter Roberts, Cambridge: Cambridge University Press, 2002, pp. 164–77.

71. Woodruff, 'The Financial Aspect', p. 29; Sarah Blick, 'Reconstructing the Shrine of St Thomas Becket', in *Art and Architecture of Late Medieval Pilgrimage in Northern Europe and the British Isles*, vol. II, ed. Sarah Blick and Rita Tekippe, Leiden: Brill, 2005, pp. 405–44, at p. 426.

72. *The Travels of Leo of Rozmital*, pp. 43–4.

73. Richard Kelleher, '"Pilgrims, Pennies and the Ploughzone": Folded Coins in Medieval Britain', in *Divina Moneta: Coins in Religion and Ritual*, ed. Nanouschka Myrberg Burström and Gitte Tarnow Ingvardson, London: Routledge, 2017, pp. 68–86.

74. Webb, *Pilgrims and Pilgrimage*, p. 146. In 1522 a knight ordered in his will that a pilgrim should go to Canterbury and offer a gold coin to St Thomas, see ibid., p. 147.

75. Dobson, 'The Monks of Canterbury in the Later Middle Ages', p. 137.

76. Woodruff, 'The Financial Aspect', p. 29. See also Blick, 'Reconstructing the Shrine', p. 426.

77. For context for this donation, see Chris Given-Wilson, *Henry IV*, New Haven and London: Yale University Press, 2016, p. 521.

78. Dobson, 'The Monks of Canterbury in the Later Middle Ages', p. 137; Peter Marshall, 'Thomas Becket, William Warham and the Crisis of the Early Tudor Church', *Journal of Ecclesiastical History*, vol. 71 (2020), pp. 293–315, at p. 298.

79. Erasmus, *Pilgrimages*, p. 49.

80. For details of this visit, see Nichols's discussion in ibid., pp. lxxxv–lxxxvi.

81. *The Travels of Leo of Rozmital*, pp. 43–4.

82. Jenkins, 'Modelling the Cult', pp. 105–6.

83. Jenkins, 'Replication or Rivalry?', pp. 27–38. Rudolph, 'The Tour Guide in the Middle Ages', pp. 41–6. Markus Späth, 'Architectural Representation and Monastic Identity: The Medieval Seal Images of Christchurch Canterbury', in *Image, Memory,*

Devotion: Liber Amicorum, ed. Zoë Opačić and Achim Timmerman, Turnhout: Brepols, 2011, pp. 255–63.

84. Jeanne Krochalis, 'Magna Tabula: The Glastonbury Tablets', in *Glastonbury Abbey and the Arthurian Tradition*, ed. James P. Carley, Cambridge and New York: D. S. Brewer, 2001, pp. 435–567; Rudolph, 'The Tour Guide in the Middle Ages', p. 45.

85. Blick, 'Votives, Images, Interaction and Pilgrimage', pp. 32–6.

86. Tom Nickson, 'Light, Canterbury and the Cult of St Thomas', *Journal of the British Archaeological Association*, vol. 173 (2020), pp. 78–99, where he references Nicholas Vincent, ed., *The Letters and Charters of Henry II, King of England 1154–1189*, 6 vols, Oxford: Oxford University Press, forthcoming, vol. 1, no. 462.

87. Nickson, 'Light, Canterbury and the Cult of St Thomas', pp. 88–91; Jenkins, *The Customary of the Shrine of Thomas Becket*, forthcoming.

88. Jenkins, *The Customary of the Shrine of Thomas Becket*, forthcoming; Nickson, 'Light, Canterbury and the Cult of St Thomas', pp. 88–9.

89. Nickson, 'Light, Canterbury and the Cult of St Thomas', p. 81.

90. Blick, 'Votives, Images, Interaction and Pilgrimage', pp. 26–32. For ex-votos more generally, see Ittai Weinryb, *Agents of Faith: Votive Objects in Time and Place*, New York: Bard Graduate Center, 2018.

91. Nilson, *Cathedral Shrines of Medieval England*, p. 101.

92. U. M. Radford, 'The Wax Images Found in Exeter Cathedral', *Antiquaries Journal*, vol. 29 (1949), pp. 164–8; Blick, 'Votives, Images, Interaction and Pilgrimage', p. 26.

93. Dobson, 'The Monks of Canterbury in the Later Middle Ages', p. 137.

94. For the most complete survey of the medieval tombs in Canterbury Cathedral, see Christopher Wilson, 'The Medieval Monuments', in *A History of Canterbury Cathedral*, ed. Patrick Collinson, Nigel Ramsay and Margaret Sparks, Oxford: Oxford University Press, 1995, pp. 451–510.

95. For the most up-to-date assessment of the takings at Becket's shrine and how these changed over time, see Nilson, *Cathedral Shrines of Medieval England*, pp. 147–54, 168–90.

96. Paul Binski, *Westminster Abbey and the Plantagenets: Kingship and the Representation of Power, 1200–1400*, New Haven and London: Yale University Press, 1995, pp. 90–120.

97. Wilson, 'The Medieval Monuments', p. 495.

98. Christopher Wilson, 'The Tomb of Henry IV and the Holy Oil of St Thomas of Canterbury', in *Medieval Architecture and its Intellectual Context*, ed. Eric Fernie and Paul Crossley, London: The Hambledon Press, 1990, pp. 181–90. Edward II was also connected to a story about Thomas Becket and holy oil, see J. W. McKenna, 'The Coronation Oil of the Yorkist Kings', *English Historical Review*, vol. 82 (1967), pp. 102–4. Wilson, 'The Medieval Monuments', pp. 498–504.

99. Thomas of Walsingham, *The Chronica maiora*, trans. David Preest, Woodbridge: The Boydell Press, 2005, p. 312.

100. Ibid.; Walter Ullmann, 'Thomas Becket's Miraculous Oil', *Journal of Theological Studies*, vol. 8 (1957), pp. 129–33; McKenna, 'The Coronation Oil of the Yorkist Kings', pp. 102–4.

101. Walsingham, p. 312.

102. Ibid.

103. In 1399, after his coronation, Henry IV had a new Great Seal made and placed the Black Prince's shield of peace, comprising three ostrich-feather badges, at the base under his feet.

104. 'The Canterbury Interlude', in *The Canterbury Tales: Fifteenth-Century Continuations and Additions*, ed. Bowers, chapter 5, ll. 171–3.

105. The Kunera database can be searched for find spots of Thomas Becket badges and ampullae across Europe: www.kunera.nl (accessed 15 January 2021).

106. Brian Spencer, *Pilgrim Souvenirs and Secular Badges*, Woodbridge: The Boydell Press, 2010; Sarah Blick, 'A Canterbury Keepsake: English Medieval Pilgrim Souvenirs and Popular Culture', PhD thesis, University of Kansas, 1994; Jennifer Lee, 'Signs of Affinity: Canterbury Pilgrims' Signs Contextualized, 1171–1538', PhD thesis, Emory University, Atlanta, 2003.

107. Spencer, *Pilgrim Souvenirs*, pp. 37–128; Amy Jeffs, 'Pilgrim Souvenir: Ampulla of Thomas Becket', *British Art Studies*, issue 6; Alyce A. Jordan, 'The "Water of Thomas Becket": Water as Medium, Metaphor, and Relic', in *The Nature and Function of Water, Baths, Bathing and Hygiene from Antiquity through the Renaissance*, ed. Cynthia Kosso and Anne Scott, Leiden: Brill, 2009, pp. 479–500.

108. 'The Canterbury Interlude', in *The Canterbury Tales: Fifteenth-Century Continuations and Additions*, ed. Bowers, p. 65.

109. Jennifer M. Lee, 'Searching for Signs: Pilgrims' Identity and Experience Made Visible in the *Miracula Sancti Thomae Cantuariensis*', in *Art and Architecture of Late Medieval Pilgrimage in Northern Europe and the British Isles*, vol. II, ed. Sarah Blick and Rita Tekippe, Leiden: Brill, 2005, pp. 473–91, at p. 479.

110. Gerald of Wales, *Geraldi Cambrensis Opera*, ed. John S. Brewer, James F. Dimock and George F. Warner, 8 vols, Rolls Series 21, London: Longman & Co., 1870, vol. I, p. 169.

111. Webb, *Pilgrims and Pilgrimage*, p. 125.

112. Ibid., pp. 124–32. See the case of the collection of the Lombard queen Theodelinda in Bagnoli et al., *Treasures of Heaven*, p. 11.

113. Bartlett, *Why Can the Dead Do Such Great Things?*, pp. 439–43.

114. Paul Alonzo Brown, 'The Development of the Legend of Thomas Becket', PhD thesis, Philadelphia: University of Pennsylvania, 1930, p. 190.

115. Webb, *Pilgrims and Pilgrimage*, p. 129.

116. Brown, 'The Development of the Legend of Thomas Becket', p. 163.

117. 'The Canterbury Interlude', in *The Canterbury Tales: Fifteenth-Century Continuations and Additions*, ed. Bowers, p. 65.

118. Erasmus, *Pilgrimages*, pp. 1–2.

119. Chaucer, 'General Prologue', ll. 701–4.

120. John F. Davis, 'Lollards, Reformers and St Thomas of Canterbury', *University of Birmingham Historical Journal*, vol. 9 (1963), pp. 1–15, at pp. 8–12. Other useful references are Margaret Aston, *Lollards and Reformers: Images and Literacy in Late Medieval Religion*, London: Hambledon Press, 1984, and Robert Lutton, *Lollardy and Orthodox Religion in Pre-Reformation England*, Woodbridge: The Boydell Press, 2006.

121. Robert E. Scully, 'The Unmaking of a Saint: Thomas Becket and the English Reformation', *Catholic Historical Review*, vol. 86 (October 2000), pp. 579–602, at p. 586.

122. Anne Hudson, ed., *Two Wycliffite Texts: The Sermon of William Taylor 1406, and the Testimony of William Thorpe 1407*, Early English Text Society Original Series 301, Oxford: Oxford University Press, 1993; J. Patrick Hornbeck et al., *A Companion to Lollardy*, Leiden: Brill, 2016, pp. 40–1, 167–9.

123. Alfred W. Pollard, ed., *Fifteenth Century Prose and Verse*, Westminster: Constable, 1903, p. 140.

Chapter 8

1. *Tudor Royal Proclamations: The Early Tudors (1485–1553)*, vol. I, ed. Paul L. Hughes and James F. Larkin, New Haven and London: Yale University Press, 1964, p. 275.

2. For a recent summary of Becket's cult during Henry VIII's reign and the Catholic opposition to its suppression see Kay Slocum, *The Cult of Thomas Becket: History and Historiography through Eight Centuries*, London: Routledge, 2019, pp. 143–92.

3. Diarmaid MacCulloch, *Thomas Cromwell: A Life*, London: Allen Lane, 2018, pp. 464–5.

4. George Bernard, 'The Piety of Henry VIII', in *The Education of a Christian Society: Humanism and Reformation in Britain and the Netherlands. Papers Delivered to the Thirteenth Anglo-Dutch Historical Conference, 1997*, ed. N. S. Amos, A. Pettegree and H. van Nierop, Aldershot: Ashgate, 1999, pp. 63–88.

5. Richard C. Marius, 'Henry VIII, Thomas More, and the Bishop of Rome', *Albion*, vol. 10 (1978), pp. 89–107. Alec Ryrie, *Protestants: The Faith that Made the Modern World*, New York, Penguin, 2017, p. 44.

6. This text is RCIN 1006836. Margaret Mitchell, 'Works of Art from Rome for Henry VIII: A Study of Anglo-Papal Relations as Reflected in Papal Gifts to the English King', *Journal of the Warburg and Courtauld Institutes*, vol. 34 (1971), pp. 178–203, at p. 183.

7.   See, for example, BL, Cotton MS Vitellius B IV/1.

8.   He is known to have visited in 1513, 1514, 1520, 1522 and 1537. Peter Marshall, 'Thomas Becket, William Warham and the Crisis of the Early Tudor Church', *Journal of Ecclesiastical History*, vol. 71 (2020), pp. 293–315. See also Richard Rex, 'The Religion of Henry VIII', *Historical Journal*, vol. 57 (2014), pp. 1–32, at pp. 11, 15. For more information about the 1520 jubilee see R. Barrie Dobson, 'Contrasting Cults: St Cuthbert of Durham and St Thomas of Canterbury in the Fifteenth Century', in *Christianity and Community in the West: Essays for John Bossy*, ed. Simon Ditchfield, London: Routledge, 2017, pp. 24–43. In 1533 he visited Canterbury but didn't enter Christ Chuch of St Augustine's Abbey: R. Barrie Dobson, 'The Monks of Canterbury in the Later Middle Ages, 1220–1540', in *A History of Canterbury Cathedral*, ed. Patrick Collinson, Nigel Ramsay and Margaret Sparks, Oxford: Oxford University Press, 1995, pp. 69–153, at p. 150.

9.   'Henry VIII: June 1520', in *Letters and Papers, Foreign and Domestic, of the Reign of Henry VIII*, vol. III/1: *1519–1521*, ed. J. S. Brewer, London: HMSO, 1867, pp. 299–319, available at www.british-history.ac.uk/letters-papers-hen8/vol3/pp299-319 (accessed 23 November 2020).

10. Glenn Richardson estimates that both Henry VIII and Francis I brought retinues of around 6,000 people with them to their meeting at the Field of the Cloth of Gold in June 1520. See Glenn Richardson, *The Field of the Cloth of Gold*, New Haven and London: Yale University Press, 2013, p. 10. See also Robert E. Scully, 'The Unmaking of a Saint: Thomas Becket and the English Reformation', *Catholic Historical Review*, vol. 86 (2000), pp. 579–602, at p. 586.

11. The instrument case is now owned by the Worshipful Company of Barber Surgeons. David Starkey, ed., *Henry VIII: A European Court in England*, London: Collins & Brown, 1991, no. XI.5, p. 144; Ann Wickham, 'The Barbers' Company's Instrument Case', in *Barbers' Historical Group Presentations: Folio 3*, London: Worshipful Company of Barbers, 2002, pp. 83–93; Timothy Schroder, *'A Marvel to Behold': Gold and Silver at the Court of Henry VIII*, Woodbridge: The Boydell Press, 2020, pp. 176–7.

12. Starkey, *Henry VIII: A European Court in England*, no. XI.5, p. 144.

13. Nicholas Harris Nicolas, *Testamenta vetusta: Being Illustrations from Wills, of Manners, Customs, &c. as well as of the Descents and Possessions of Many Distinguished Families. From the Reign of Henry II. to the Accession of Queen Elizabeth*, vol. II, London: Nichols & Son, 1826, p. 534.

14. Philippa Glanville, *Silver in Tudor and Early Stuart England*, London: Victoria and Albert Museum, 1990, no. 7, pp. 394–7; Schroder, *'A Marvel to Behold'*, pp. 175–6.

15. Julian Luxford, 'The Relics of Thomas Becket in England', *Journal of the British Archaeological Association*, vol. 173 (2020), pp. 124–142.

16. *Archaeologia: or Miscellaneous Tracts Relating to Antiquity*, vol. III, London: Society of Antiquaries of London, 1775, pp. 20–1; William H. Dean, 'Sir Thomas Boleyn, the Courtier Diplomat, 1477–1539', PhD thesis, West Virginia University, 1987.

17. Jonathan Woolfson, 'Introduction', in *Reassessing Tudor Humanism*, ed. J. Woolfson, London: Palgrave Macmillan, 2002, pp. 1–21. For fig. 8.4 see Joseph B. Trapp and Hubertus S. Herbrüggen, *'The King's Good Servant': Sir Thomas More, 1477/8–1535*, London: National Portrait Gallery, 1977, no. 88, p. 56.

18. Desiderius Erasmus, *The Colloquies of Erasmus*, trans. Craig R. Thompson, Chicago and London: University of Chicago Press, 1965, pp. 285–312.

19. Ibid., p. 308.

20. Ibid., p. 285.

21. 'Yᵉ Pylgremage of Pure Devotyon', *The Earliest English Translations of Erasmus's 'Colloquia' 1536–1566*, ed. Henry de Vocht, *Humanistica Lovaniensia*, vol. II, Louvain: Librairie Universitaire, 1928, pp. xxxvi–lxxxvi, p. xlix.

22. Sheila Sweetinburgh, 'Looking to the Past: The St Thomas Pageant in Early Tudor Canterbury', *Archaeologia Cantiana*, vol. 137 (2016), pp. 163–84; for the Skinners' pageant, see Chapter 6 of this book, p. 181.

23. See the St Michael le Belfrey windows in Chapter 6 of this book. Dobson, 'The Monks of Canterbury in the Later Middle Ages', p. 138.

24. Eamon Duffy, *The Stripping of the Altars: Traditional Religion in England, c.1400–c.1580*, 2nd edn, New Haven and London: Yale University Press, 2005, p. 160.

25. Eamon Duffy, 'Late Medieval Religion', in *Gothic: Art for England 1400–1547*, ed. Richard Marks and Paul Williamson, London: 2003, pp. 56–67.

26. Peter Marshall, 'Thomas Becket, William Warham and the Crisis of the Early Tudor Church'.

27. Quoted in Peter Roberts, 'Politics, Drama and the Cult of Thomas Becket in the Sixteenth Century', in *Pilgrimage: The English Experience from Becket to Bunyan*, ed. Colin Morris and Peter Roberts, Cambridge: Cambridge University Press, 2002, pp. 199–237, at p. 200.

28. *Expositions and Notes on Sundry Portions of the Holy Scriptures, Together with the Practice of Prelates by William Tyndale, Martyr*, ed. Henry Walter, Cambridge: The University Press, 1849, pp. 247–344.

29. Ibid., pp. 273–4, 292–3.

30. Ibid., p. 292.

31. Ibid.

32. Roberts, 'Politics, Drama and the Cult of Thomas Becket', p. 202, n. 8.

33. Margaret Aston, *Broken Idols of the English Reformation*, Cambridge: Cambridge University Press, 2015, pp. 388–9.

34. Ibid.

35. 'Houses of Benedictine Monks: The Cathedral Priory of the Holy Trinity of Christ Church, Canterbury', in *The Victoria History of the County of Kent*, vol. II, ed. William Page, London: St Catherine Press, 1926, pp. 113–21, available at www.british-history.ac.uk/vch/kent/vol2/pp113-121 (accessed 20 November 2020).

36. William Sheils, 'Polemic as Piety: Thomas Stapleton's Tres Thomae and Catholic Controversy in the 1580s', *Journal of Ecclesiastical History*, vol. 60 (2009), pp. 74–94, at p. 81; Scully, 'The Unmaking of a Saint', pp. 587–8.

37. Sheils, 'Polemic as Piety', p. 81.

38. Letter from Thomas More to Margaret Roper, 5 July 1535, in *The Correspondence of Sir Thomas More*, ed. Elizabeth Frances Rogers, Princeton: Princeton University Press, 1947, no. 218, pp. 563–5.

39. Letter from Pope Paul III to Francis I, 26 July 1535. Roberts, 'Politics, Drama and the Cult of Thomas Becket', p. 207.

40. Helen L. Parish, *Monks, Miracles and Magic: Reformation Representations of the Medieval Church*, London and New York: Routledge, 2005, p. 101; Candace Lines, '"Secret Violence": Becket, More, and the Scripting of Martyrdom', *Religion & Literature*, vol. 32 (2000), pp. 11–28.

41. Their likenesses are copied from portraits by Holbein executed in the 1520s. A copy of this print is in the Royal Collection, RCIN 654620.

42. This ring is recorded as having come from the Messiter family, who were descended from Fisher's family. Thomas E. Bridgett, *Life of Blessed John Fisher, Bishop of Rochester, Cardinal of the Holy Roman Church and Martyr under Henry VIII*, London: Burns & Oates, 1890, p. 506.

43. These four items were presented to the English College, Liège, by the last male descendant of Thomas More, also of the same name (1722–1795). *Proceedings of the Society of Antiquaries of London November 21, 1861 to June 16, 1864*, 2nd series, vol. 2 (1864), pp. 117–18; Trapp and Herbrüggen, *'The King's Good Servant'*, no. 277, pp. 118–19.

44. It is also known as the Barnborough Jewel after Barnborough Hall, the Yorkshire estate of the More family.

45. Peter Davidson et al., 'The Harkirk Graveyard and William Blundell "the Recusant" (1560–1638): A Reconsideration', *British Catholic History*, vol. 34 (2018), pp. 29–76, at pp. 63–70.

46. Holbein's preparatory drawing for the now lost family portrait of the More family shows Alice wearing a crucifix, now in the Kunstmuseum, Basel, as does a later sixteenth-century copy of the painting, now at Nostrell Priory, owned by the National Trust. The reliquary cross can be seen in a portrait attributed to the studio of Hans Holbein the Younger, now in the Weiss Gallery, London. See Jan van der Stock, *In Search of Utopia: Art and Science in the Era of Thomas More*,

47. Trapp and Herbrüggen, 'The King's Good Servant', p. 119.

48. Sheils, 'Polemic as Piety', pp. 74–94.

49. Victor Houliston, 'St Thomas Becket in the Propaganda of the English Counter-Reformation', Renaissance Studies, vol. 7 (1993), pp. 43–70, at pp. 50–51; Lines, '"Secret Violence": Becket, More, and the Scripting of Martyrdom'; Sheils, 'Polemic as Piety'.

50. Trapp and Herbrüggen, 'The King's Good Servant', p. 138, no. 282.

51. Roberts, 'Politics, Drama and the Cult of Thomas Becket', p. 212.

52. Aston, Broken Idols, pp. 366–7.

53. Scully, 'The Unmaking of a Saint', p. 592.

54. Chris Skidmore, Edward VI: The Lost King of England, London: Phoenix, 2007, p. 13.

55. Roberts, 'Politics, Drama and the Cult of Thomas Becket', p. 223; John Bale, The Plays of John Bale, vol. I, ed. Peter Happé, Cambridge: D. S. Brewer, 1985, pp. 8–9; Houliston, 'St Thomas Becket in the Propaganda of the English Counter-Reformation', p. 45.

56. MacCulloch, Thomas Cromwell: A Life, p. 417.

57. Thomas Cranmer, Miscellaneous Writings and Letters of Thomas Cranmer, ed. John Edmund Cox, Cambridge: Cambridge University Press, 1846, pp. 377–8.

58. Ibid., p. 378.

59. Diarmaid MacCulloch, Thomas Cranmer: A Life, New Haven and London: Yale University Press, 1996, p. 226; Sarah Blick, 'Reconstructing the Shrine of St Thomas Becket, Canterbury Cathedral', in Art and Architecture of Late Medieval Pilgrimage in Northern Europe and the British Isles, vol. II, ed. Sarah Blick and Rita Tekippe, Leiden: Brill, 2005, pp. 405–41, at p. 405.

60. 'Henry VIII: September 1538 1–5', in Letters and Papers, Foreign and Domestic, of the Reign of Henry VIII, vol. XIII/2: August–December 1538, ed. James Gairdner, London: HMSO, 1893, Letter 257, pp. 101–16, available at www.british-history.ac.uk/letters-papers-hen8/vol13/no2/pp101-116 (accessed 20 November 2020).

61. Roberts argues that the decision was only made in September 1538 while the court was at Canterbury, see Roberts, 'Politics, Drama and the Cult of Thomas Becket', pp. 217–19.

62. MacCulloch, Thomas Cromwell: A Life, p. 464.

63. Parish, Monks, Miracles and Magic, pp. 95–6.

64. Aston, Broken Idols, p. 366.

65. 'Henry VIII: September 1538 1–5', in Letters and Papers, Foreign and Domestic, of the Reign of Henry VIII, vol. XIII/2: August–December 1538, ed. James Gairdner, London: HMSO, 1893, Letter 303, pp. 116–26, available at www.british-history.ac.uk/letters-papers-hen8/vol13/no2/pp116-126 (accessed 20 November 2020). A comprehensive discussion of the events at Canterbury can be found in Roberts,

66. Roberts, 'Politics, Drama and the Cult of Thomas Becket', pp. 222–4. It has been suggested that this was Bale's Becket play, see MacCulloch, Thomas Cranmer: A Life, p. 227.

67. Roberts, 'Politics, Drama and the Cult of Thomas Becket', pp. 220–1; Blick, 'Reconstructing the Shrine', p. 411.

68. Roberts, 'Politics, Drama and the Cult of Thomas Becket', p. 221.

69. The quote is from The Travels of Leo of Rozmital, ed. and trans. Malcolm Letts, Cambridge: The University Press, 1957, pp. 50–1. On the Regale, Butler argues that Louis gave the gem in 1179. See John R. Butler, The Quest for Becket's Bones: The Mystery of the Relics of St Thomas Becket, New Haven and London: Yale University Press, 1995, p. 25. Jenkins counteracts this in John Jenkins, 'Modelling the Cult of Thomas Becket in Canterbury Cathedral', Journal of the British Archaeological Association, vol. 173 (2020), pp. 100–23, at pp. 105–6.

70. Blick, 'Reconstructing the Shrine', p. 412. She references a quote about Henry's ring published in William Dugdale, Monasticon Anglicanum: A History of the Abbies and Other Monasteries, Hospitals, Frieries, and Cathedral and Collegiate Churches, with their Dependencies, in England and Wales, London: J. Bohn, 1846, plate facing p. 85.

71. On the treatment of shrines during the English Reformation see John Crook, English Medieval Shrines, Woodbridge: The Boydell Press, 2011, pp. 289–308.

72. Thomas F. Mayer, 'Becket's Bones Burnt! Cardinal Pole and the Invention and Dissemination of an Atrocity', in Martyrs and Martyrdom in England, c.1400–1700, ed. Thomas S. Freeman and Thomas F. Mayer, Woodbridge: The Boydell Press, 2007, pp. 126–43, at p. 130.

73. Mayer, 'Becket's Bones Burnt!'.

74. 'Letters and Papers: February 1539, 26–28', in Letters and Papers, Foreign and Domestic, of the Reign of Henry VIII, vol. XIV/1: January–July 1539, ed. James Gairdner and R. H. Brodie, London: HMSO, 1894, no. 402, pp. 143–66, available at www.british-history.ac.uk/letters-papers-hen8/vol14/no1/pp143-166, (accessed 20 November 2020); MacCulloch discusses this pamphlet in MacCulloch, Thomas Cromwell: A Life, pp. 487–8.

75. See Butler, The Quest for Becket's Bones.

76. Tudor Royal Proclamations, vol. I, p. 275.

77. James Bentley, Restless Bones: The Story of Relics, London: Constable, 1985, p. 151; Butler, The Quest for Becket's Bones, p. 120.

78. Another of Cranmer's seals was adapted, with Becket replaced by Christ's flagellation. MacCulloch, Thomas Cranmer: A Life, pp. 228–30.

79. Kay Slocum, 'Martir quod stillat primatis ab ore sigillat: Sealed with the Blood of Becket', Journal of the British Archaeological Association, vol. 165 (2012), pp. 61–88.

80. Wade's text is now in the Parker Library, Corpus Christi College, Cambridge, MS 298.

81. Roberts, 'Politics, Drama and the Cult of Thomas Becket', p. 204.

82. Tancred Borenius, St Thomas Becket in Art, London: Methuen & Co., 1932, pp. 22–4; Houliston, 'St Thomas Becket in the Propaganda of the English Counter-Reformation', p. 47.

83. Edward Foss, The Reigns of Henry VII., Henry VIII., Edward VI., Mary, and Elizabeth. 1485–1603, vol. V, London: Longman, 1857, p. 122.

84. Ibid.

85. Kirstin Barnard, 'The Mercers' Company, London, and St Thomas Becket during the Reformation', London Journal, vol. 45 (2020), pp. 299–317; Aston, Broken Idols, p. 372.

86. Aston, Broken Idols, p. 371. John McEwan notes that in 1542 the London Bridge Trust changed its seal to remove an image of Becket. See J. A. McEwan, Seals in Medieval London 1050–1300, London: London Record Society, 2016, p. 35. Likewise, other churches across the country were rededicated to the Apostle: see Robert Whiting, The Blind Devotion of the People: Popular Religion and the English Reformation, Cambridge: Cambridge University Press, 1991, pp. 116–17; Nicholas Orme, English Church Dedications: With a Survey of Cornwall and Devon, Exeter: University of Exeter Press, 1996, pp. 41, 49–50.

87. Nicholas Doggett, 'Whiting, Richard (d. 1539), abbot of Glastonbury', Oxford Dictionary of National Biography, 23 September 2004, https://doi.org/10.1093/ref:odnb/29315 (accessed 20 November 2020); Roberts, 'Politics, Drama and the Cult of Thomas Becket', p. 228; MacCulloch, Thomas Cromwell: A Life, pp. 509–10.

88. Margaret Aston, England's Iconoclasts, vol. I: Laws Against Images, Oxford: Clarendon Press, 1988, p. 318.

89. Eamon Duffy, Marking the Hours: English People and their Prayers 1240–1570, New Haven and London: Yale University Press, 2006, p. 152, fig. 99.

90. These can be seen on f. 7r and f. 12v.

91. For a discussion of the varied approaches people took to religious objects during the Reformation see Sarah Tarlow, 'Reformation and Transformation: What Happened to Catholic Things in a Protestant World', in The Archaeology of Reformation 1480–1580, ed. David Gaimster and Roberta Gilchrist, Leeds: Maney Publishing, 2003, pp. 108–121.

92. Duffy, The Stripping of the Altars, p. 419; Aston, Broken Idols, pp. 370–1.

93. Ibid. For more general discussions on the reuse and adaptation of Catholic objects during and after the Reformation, see Art Re-Formed: Re-Assessing the Impact of the Reformation on the Visual Arts, ed. Tara Hamling and Richard L. Williams, Newcastle: Cambridge Scholars Publishing, 2007; Alexandra Walsham, 'Recycling the Sacred: Material Culture and Cultural Memory after the English Reformation', Church History vol. 86 (2017), pp. 1121–54.

Amsterdam: Amsterdam University Press, 2016, no. 4, pp. 90–3.

94. Margaret Aston, 'Public Worship and Iconoclasm' in *The Archaeology of Reformation 1480–1580*, ed. David Gaimster and Roberta Gilchrist, Leeds: Maney Publishing, 2003, pp. 9–28.

95. *Proceedings of the Society of Antiquaries of London*, 2nd series, vol. 21 (1906), pp. 208–211. Our thanks to John Wilkins, Church Warden of All Saints, Tilsworth, for showing us the sculptures in person.

96. J. J. G. Alexander and Paul Binski, eds, *The Age of Chivalry: Art in Plantagenet England 1200–1400*, London: Weidenfeld and Nicolson, 1987, no. 26, pp. 210–11; Lloyd de Beer, 'Reassessing English Alabaster Carving: Medieval Sculpture and its Contexts', PhD thesis, University of East Anglia, Norwich, 2018, p. 45.

97. Stephen Glover, *The History of the County of Derby: Drawn Up from Actual Observation, and from the Best Authorities*, vol. II, Derby: Stephen Glover, 1829, p. 95.

98. The sculpture could also have been preserved as an important record of the union of two families.

99. K. Williams-Jones, 'Thomas Becket and Wales', *Welsh Historical Review*, vol. 5 (1971), pp. 350–65, at pp. 364–5; Ronald Hutton, 'The Local Impact of the Tudor Reformations', in *The English Reformation Revised*, ed. Christopher Haigh, Cambridge: Cambridge University Press, 1987, pp. 114–38, at p. 119; Edward Owen, 'The Parish Church of New Radnor at the Reformation', *Archaeologia Cambrensis*, vol. 18 (1918), pp. 263–78, at pp. 266–71.

100. The print is based on a painting now in the National Museum of Wales, NMW A 564. S. See Susan Doran in *Henry VIII: Man and Monarch*, ed. Susan Doran, London: British Library, 2009, no. 274, p. 270.

101. This was the king's injunction of 1547.

102. It should also be noted that the suppressed abbey in Wymondham had been jointly dedicated to Becket and the Virgin Mary and contained a Becket chapel. Jennifer Loach, *Edward VI*, New Haven and London: Yale University Press, 1999, p. 78; Scully, 'The Unmaking of a Saint', p. 581.

103. David Loades, 'The Personal Religion of Mary I', in *The Church of Mary Tudor*, ed. Eamon Duffy and David Loades, Aldershot: Ashgate, 2006, pp. 1–29, at p. 21.

104. Ibid.

105. J. B. Sheppard, 'The Canterbury Marching Watch and its Pageant of St Thomas', *Archaeologia Cantiana*, vol. 12 (1878), pp. 27–46, at p. 39; Houliston, 'St Thomas Becket in the Propaganda of the English Counter-Reformation', p. 47.

106. C. Eveleigh Woodruff, 'The Financial Aspect of the Cult of St Thomas of Canterbury,' *Archaeologia Cantiana*, vol. 44 (1932), pp. 13–32, at p. 25.

107. Borenius, *St Thomas Becket in Art*, p. 111.

108. Ibid.; Barnard, 'The Mercers' Company, London, and St Thomas Becket during the Reformation', pp. 306–7.

109. Barnard, 'The Mercers' Company, London, and St Thomas Becket during the Reformation', pp. 306–7.

110. Ibid., p. 307.

111. MacCulloch, *Cranmer: A Life*, pp. 601–4.

112. Ibid., p. 603.

113. John Foxe, *The Acts and Monuments of John Foxe*, vol. VIII, ed. G. Townsend and S. R. Cattley, London: Seeley and Burnside, 1841, p. 90.

114. Mayer, 'Becket's Bones Burnt!'.

115. Ibid.; Thomas Mayer, ed., *The Correspondence of Reginal Pole*, vol. I: *A Calendar, 1518–1546: Beginnings to Legate of Viterbo*, London and New York: Routledge, 2002, pp. 209–13.

116. Walter de Gray Birch, *Catalogue of Seals in the Department of Manuscripts in the British Museum*, vol. I, London: British Museum, 1887, p. 175; Slocum 'Sealed with the Blood of Becket', pp. 81, 83.

117. Thomas Mayer, *Reginald Pole: Prince & Prophet*, Cambridge: Cambridge University Press, 2000, p. 345; Thomas Mayer, ed., *The Correspondence of Reginald Pole*, vol. III: *A Calendar, 1555–1558: Restoring the English Church*, London and New York: Routledge, 2004, no. 2286, pp. 558–71.

118. On the treatment of images during Elizabeth's reign see Richard L. Williams, 'Religious Pictures and Sculpture in Elizabethan England: Censure, Appreciation and Devotion', PhD thesis, Courtauld Institute of Art, London, 2003; Richard L. Williams, 'Domestic Religious Painting in England, *c*.1530–*c*.1600', MA thesis, Courtauld Institute of Art, London, 1993.

119. Barnard, 'The Mercers' Company, London, and St Thomas Becket during the Reformation', pp. 299, 304.

120. Anthony Bale and Sebastian Sobecki, *Medieval English Travel*, Oxford: Oxford University Press, 2019, pp. 401–8. See also Peter Newton, *The English Hospice in Rome: The Venerable Sexcentenary Issue*, Rome: Catholic Records Press, 1962.

121. Carol M. Richardson, 'St Thomas at the English College in Rome', *Journal of the British Archaeological Association*, vol. 173 (2020), pp. 183–203, at p. 189.

122. Lines, '"Secret Violence": Becket, More, and the Scripting of Martyrdom', pp. 17–18.

123. Carol M. Richardson, 'Durante Alberti, the Martyrs' Picture and the Venerable English College, Rome', *Papers of the British School at Rome*, vol. 73 (2005), pp. 223–63; Richardson, 'St Thomas at the English College in Rome', pp. 190–2.

124. Richardson, 'Durante Alberti, the Martyrs' Picture and the Venerable English College, Rome', pp. 252–3.

125. Ibid., p. 239.

126. For the use of such relics see Alexandra Walsham, 'Miracles and the Counter-Reformation Mission to England', *Historical Journal*, vol. 46 (2003), pp. 779–815.

127. Victor Houliston, 'Breuis dialogismus', *English Literary Renaissance*, vol. 23 (1993), pp. 382–427; Houliston, 'St. Thomas Becket in the Propaganda of the English Counter-Reformation', pp. 41, 54–60;

Martin Wiggins and Catherine Teresa Richardson, *British Drama, 1533–1642*, vol. IV: *1598–1602*, Oxford: Oxford University Press, 2012, pp. 179–81. The script of the play is now at Hatfield House, Cecil Papers, 139/116.

Legacy

1. Janet Graffius, 'Relics and Cultures of Commemoration in the English Jesuit College of St. Omers in the Spanish Netherlands', in *Jesuit Intellectual and Physical Exchange between England and Mainland Europe, c.1580–1789*, ed. James Kelly and Hannah Thomas, Leiden: Brill, 2018, pp. 113–32, at p. 124.

2. Victor Houliston, 'St Thomas Becket in the Propaganda of the English Counter-Reformation', *Renaissance Studies*, vol. 7 (1993), pp. 43–70, at p. 54.

3. Kay Slocum, *The Cult of Thomas Becket: History and Historiography through Eight Centuries*, London: Routledge, 2019, pp. 279–301.

4. T. S. Eliot, *Murder in the Cathedral*, London: Faber and Faber, 1979, p. 52.

5. Michael Staunton, ed. and trans., *The Lives of Thomas Becket*, Manchester: Manchester University Press, 2001, pp. 41–2.

Select bibliography

Primary sources

Chaucer, Geoffrey, *The Canterbury Tales*, ed. Jill Mann, London: Penguin Classics, 2005

Duggan, Anne, ed. and trans., *The Correspondence of Thomas Becket, Archbishop of Canterbury, 1162–1170*, 2 vols, Oxford: Clarendon Press, 2000

Erasmus, Desiderius, *Peregrinatio religionis ergo* [London, 1631], trans. John Gough Nichols, in *Pilgrimages to Saint Mary of Walsingham and Saint Thomas of Canterbury*, London: John Murray, 1875

Garnier de Pont-Sainte-Maxence, *Garnier's Becket*, ed. and trans. Janet Shirley, London: Phillimore, 1975

———, *A Life of Thomas Becket in Verse*, ed. and trans. Ian Short, Turnhout: Brepols, 2014

John of Salisbury, *Policraticus: Of the Frivolities of Courtiers and the Footprints of Philosophers*, ed. and trans. Cary J. Nederman, Cambridge: Cambridge University Press, 1990

———, *Anselm & Becket: Two Canterbury Saints' Lives*, trans. Ronald E. Pepin, Toronto: Pontifical Institute of Mediaeval Studies, 2009

Magnússon, Eiríkr, ed., *Thómas Saga erkibyskups: A Life of Archbishop Thomas Becket, in Icelandic, with English Translation, Notes and Glossary*, 2 vols, London: Longman & Co., 1875–83

Robertson, James Craigie, and J. Brigstocke Sheppard, eds, *Materials for the History of Thomas Becket*, 7 vols, London: Longman & Co., 1875–85

Ryan, William Granger, trans., *Jacobus de Voragine, The Golden Legend: Readings on the Saints*, 2 vols, Princeton: Princeton University Press, 2012

Staunton, Michael, ed. and trans., *The Lives of Thomas Becket*, Manchester: Manchester University Press, 2001

Secondary sources

Aston, Margaret, *Broken Idols of the English Reformation*, Cambridge: Cambridge University Press, 2015

Barlow, Frank, *Thomas Becket*, Berkeley: University of California Press, 1986

Barnaby, James, 'Becket Vult: The Appropriation of St Thomas Becket's Image during the Canterbury Dispute 1184–1200', in *Anglo-Norman Studies XL: Proceedings of the Battle Conference 2017*, ed. Elisabeth van Houts, Woodbridge: The Boydell Press, 2018, pp. 63–76

Bartlett, Robert, *England Under the Norman and Angevin Kings, 1075–1225*, Oxford: Clarendon Press, 2000

Binski, Paul, *Becket's Crown: Art and Imagination in Gothic England, 1170–1300*, New Haven and London: Yale University Press, 2004

Blick, Sarah, 'Reconstructing the Shrine of St Thomas Becket, Canterbury Cathedral', in *Art and Architecture of Late Medieval Pilgrimage in Northern Europe and the British Isles*, vol. II, ed. Sarah Blick and Rita Tekippe, 2 vols, Leiden: Brill, 2005, pp. 405–41

Borenius, Tancred, *St Thomas Becket in Art*, London: Methuen & Co., 1932

Brown, Paul Alonzo, 'The Development of the Legend of Thomas Becket', PhD thesis, Philadelphia: University of Pennsylvania, 1930

Butler, John R., *The Quest for Becket's Bones: The Mystery of the Relics of St Thomas Becket*, New Haven and London: Yale University Press, 1995

Carpenter, David, *The Struggle for Mastery: Britain 1066–1284*, London: Penguin Books, 2004

———, *Magna Carta*, London: Penguin Books, 2015

Caviness, Madeline Harrison, *The Early Stained Glass of Canterbury Cathedral, circa 1175–1220*, Princeton: Princeton University Press, 1977

———, *The Windows of Christ Church Cathedral, Canterbury*, Corpus Vitrearum Medii Aevi, Great Britain 2, London: British Academy, 1981

Cheney, Christopher, *From Becket to Langton: English Church Government 1170–1213*, Manchester: Manchester University Press, 1956

Coldstream, Nicola, and Peter Draper, eds, *Medieval Art and Architecture at Canterbury before 1220*, British Archaeological Association Conference Transactions 5, Leeds: British Archaeological Association and Kent Archaeological Society, 1982

Collinson, Patrick, Nigel Ramsay and Margaret Sparks, eds, *A History of Canterbury Cathedral*, Oxford: Oxford University Press, 1995

Crook, John, *English Medieval Shrines*, Woodbridge: The Boydell Press, 2011

Draper, Peter, 'William of Sens and the Original Design of the Choir Termination of Canterbury Cathedral 1175–1179', *Journal of the Society of Architectural Historians*, vol. 42 (1983), pp. 238–48

———, *The Formation of English Gothic: Architecture and Identity, 1150–1250*, New Haven and London: Yale University Press, 2006

Duffy, Eamon, *The Stripping of the Altars: Traditional Religion in England 1400–1580*, New Haven and London: Yale University Press, 2005

Duggan, Anne, *Thomas Becket*, London: Arnold, 2004

———, 'The Coronation of the Young King in 1170', in *Thomas Becket: Friends, Networks, Texts and Cult*, Aldershot: Ashgate, 2007, pp. 165–78

———, 'The Cult of St Thomas Becket in the Thirteenth Century', in *Thomas Becket: Friends, Networks, Texts and Cult*, Aldershot: Ashgate, 2007, pp. 21–44

———, 'Diplomacy, Status and Conscience: Henry II's Penance for Murder', in *Thomas Becket: Friends, Networks, Texts and Cult*, Aldershot: Ashgate, 2007, pp. 265–90

———, 'Religious Networks in Action: The European Expansion of the Cult of St Thomas of Canterbury', in *International Religious Networks*, ed. Jeremy Gregory and Hugh McLeod, Woodbridge: Boydell and Brewer, 2012, pp. 20–43

Eales, Richard, 'The Political Setting of the Becket Translation', *Studies in Church History*, vol. 30 (1993), pp. 127–39

Fergusson, Peter, *Canterbury Cathedral Priory in the Age of Becket*, New Haven and London: Yale University Press, 2011

Foreville, Raymonde, *Le jubilé de saint Thomas Becket du 13e au 15e siècle, 1220–1470: étude et documents*, Paris: SEVPEN, 1958

———, ed., *Thomas Becket: Actes du Colloque International de Sédières, 19–24 août 1973*, Paris: Beauchesne, 1975

———, *Thomas Becket dans la tradition historique et hagiographique*, London: Variorum Reprints, 1981

Gameson, Richard, 'The Early Imagery of Thomas Becket', in *Pilgrimage: The English Experience from Becket to Bunyan*, ed. Colin Morris and Peter Roberts, Cambridge: Cambridge University Press, 2002, pp. 46–89

Gelin, Marie-Pierre, *'Lumen ad revelationem gentium': iconographie et liturgie à Christ Church, Canterbury, 1175–1220*, Turnhout: Brepols, 2006

Guy, John, *Thomas Becket: Warrior, Priest, Rebel, Victim*, London: Viking, 2012

Hamel, Christopher de, *The Book in the Cathedral: The Last Relic of Thomas Becket*, London: Allen Lane, 2020

Harper-Bill, Christopher, and Nicholas Vincent, eds, *Henry II: New Interpretations*, Woodbridge: The Boydell Press, 2007

Hearn, Millard F., 'Canterbury Cathedral and the Cult of Becket', *Art Bulletin*, vol. 76 (1994), pp. 19–52

Houliston, Victor, 'St Thomas Becket in the Propaganda of the English Counter-Reformation', *Renaissance Studies*, vol. 7 (1993), pp. 43–70

Keefe, Thomas K., 'Shrine Time: King Henry II's Visits to Thomas Becket's Tomb', *Haskins Society Journal*, vol. 11 (1998), pp. 115–22

Jenkins, John, 'Replication or Rivalry? The "Becketization" of Pilgrimage in English Cathedrals', *Religion*, vol. 49 (2019), pp. 24–47

———, 'St Thomas Becket and Medieval London', *History*, vol. 105 (2020), pp. 652–72

Jordan, Alyce, 'The "Water of Thomas Becket": Water as Medium, Metaphor, and Relic', in *The Nature and Function of Water, Baths, Bathing and Hygiene from Antiquity through the Renaissance*, ed. Cynthia Kosso and Anne Scott, Leiden: Brill, 2009, pp. 479–500

Kidson, Peter, 'Gervase, Becket and William of Sens', *Speculum*, vol. 68 (1993), pp. 969–91

Knowles, David, *The Monastic Order in England: A History of its Development from the Times of St Dunstan to the Fourth Lateran Council: 940–1216*, 2nd edn, Cambridge: Cambridge University Press, 1966

Koopmans, Rachel, *Wonderful to Relate: Miracle Stories and Miracle Collecting in High Medieval Europe*, Philadelphia: University of Pennsylvania Press, 2011

———, 'Early Sixteenth-Century Stained Glass at St Michael-Le-Belfrey and the Commemoration of Thomas Becket in Late Medieval York', *Speculum*, vol. 89, (2014), pp. 1040–1100

———, 'Visions, Reliquaries, and the Image of "Becket's Shrine" in the Miracle Windows of Canterbury Cathedral', *Gesta*, vol. 54 (2015), pp. 37–57

———, '"Water Mixed with the Blood of Thomas": Contact Relic Manufacture Pictured in Canterbury Cathedral's Stained Glass', *Journal of Medieval History*, vol. 42 (2016), pp. 535–58

———, 'Kentish Pilgrims in Canterbury Cathedral's Miracle Windows', *Journal of the Warburg and Courtauld Institutes*, vol. 80 (2017), pp. 1–27

Lee, Jennifer M., 'Searching for Signs: Pilgrims' Identity and Experience Made Visible in the *Miracula Sancti Thomae Cantuariensis*', in *Art and Architecture of Late Medieval Pilgrimage in Northern Europe and the British Isles*, vol. II, ed. Sarah Blick and Rita Tekippe, Leiden: Brill, 2005, pp. 473–91

Lines, Candace, '"Secret Violence": Becket, More, and the Scripting of Martyrdom', *Religion & Literature*, vol. 32 (2000), pp. 11–28

Luxford, Julian, 'The Relics of Thomas Becket in England', *Journal of the British Archaeological Association*, vol. 173 (2020), pp. 124–42

Marshall, Peter, 'Thomas Becket, William Warham and the Crisis of the Early Tudor Church', *Journal of Ecclesiastical History*, vol. 71 (2020), pp. 293–315

Mason, Arthur James, *What Became of the Bones of St Thomas? A Contribution to his Fiftieth Jubilee*, Cambridge: The University Press, 1920

Nilgen, Ursula, 'Intellectuality and Splendour: Thomas Becket as a Patron of the Arts', *Art and Patronage in the English Romanesque*, ed. Sarah Macready and F. H. Thompson, London: Society of Antiquaries of London, 1986, pp. 145–58

Nilson, Ben, *Cathedral Shrines of Medieval England*, Woodbridge: The Boydell Press, 1998

O'Reilly, Jennifer, 'The Double Martyrdom of Thomas Becket: Hagiography or History?', in *Studies in Medieval and Renaissance History*, vol. VII, ed. J. A. S. Evans and Richard Unger, New York: AMS Press, 1985, pp. 183–247

Roberts, Peter, 'Politics, Drama and the Cult of Thomas Becket in the Sixteenth Century', in *Pilgrimage: The English Experience from Becket to Bunyan*, ed. Colin Morris and Peter Roberts, Cambridge: Cambridge University Press, 2002, pp. 199–237

Scully, Robert E., 'The Unmaking of a Saint: Thomas Becket and the English Reformation', *Catholic Historical Review*, vol. 86 (2000), pp. 579–602

Slocum, Kay, *Liturgies in Honour of Thomas Becket*, Toronto: University of Toronto Press, 2003

———, *The Cult of Thomas Becket: History and Historiography through Eight Centuries*, London: Routledge, 2019

Smalley, Beryl, *The Becket Conflict and the Schools: A Study of Intellectuals in Politics*, Oxford: Blackwell, 1973

Southern, Richard W., *The Monks of Canterbury and the Murder of Archbishop Becket*, Canterbury: Friends of Canterbury Cathedral and the Trustees of the William Urry Memorial Fund, 1985

Staunton, Michael, *Thomas Becket and his Biographers*, Woodbridge: The Boydell Press, 2006

Strickland, Matthew, *Henry the Young King, 1155–1183*, New Haven and London: Yale University Press, 2016

Tatton-Brown, Tim, 'Canterbury and the Architecture of Pilgrimage Shrines in England', in *Pilgrimage: The English Experience from Becket to Bunyan*, ed. Colin Morris and Peter Roberts, Cambridge: Cambridge University Press, 2002, pp. 90–107

Turner, Ralph V., *Eleanor of Aquitaine: Queen of France, Queen of England*, New Haven and London: Yale University Press, 2011

Urry, William, *Canterbury Under the Angevin Kings*, London: Athlone Press, 1967

———, *Thomas Becket: His Last Days*, Stroud: Sutton, 2001

Vincent, Nicholas, 'The Murderers of Thomas Becket', in *Bischofsmord im Mittelalter*, ed. Natalie Fryde and Dirk Reitz, Göttingen: Vandenhoeck & Ruprecht, 2003, pp. 211–72

———, 'Stephen Langton, Archbishop of Canterbury', in *Étienne Langton: prédicateur, bibliste, théologien*, ed. Louis-Jacques Bataillon, Nicole Bériou, Gilbert Dahan and Riccardo Quinto, Turnhout: Brepols, 2010, pp. 51–123

———, *A Brief History of Britain 1066–1485*, London: Constable & Robinson, 2011

Ward, Benedicta, *Miracles and the Medieval Mind: Theory, Record and Event 1000–1215*, London: Scolar Press, 1982

Warren, Wilfred L., *Henry II*, New Haven and London: Yale University Press, 2000

Webster, Paul, and Marie-Pierre Gelin, eds, *The Cult of St Thomas Becket in the Plantagenet World, c.1170–c.1220*, Woodbridge: The Boydell Press, 2016

Willis, Robert, *The Architectural History of Canterbury Cathedral*, London: Longman & Co., 1845

Wilson, Christopher, *The Gothic Cathedral: The Architecture of the Great Church, 1130–1530*, London: Thames & Hudson, 1990

Woodman, Francis, *The Architectural History of Canterbury Cathedral*, London: Routledge, 1981

Woodruff, C. Eveleigh, 'The Financial Aspect of the Cult of St Thomas of Canterbury', *Archaeologia Cantiana*, vol. 44 (1932), pp. 13–32

Zarnecki, George, et al., *English Romanesque Art 1066–1200*, London: Arts Council of Great Britain, 1984

Acknowledgements

This book was almost entirely written, edited and proofed during a series of national lockdowns enforced due to the coronavirus pandemic. The British Museum, along with all other museums and libraries in the UK, was required by law to close its doors. As a result of these circumstances the exhibition was delayed to 2021, and we had precious little access to important reference material. We are therefore immensely grateful to those friends and colleagues who supplied scans of articles and book chapters when we needed them most. For the many relevant publications we have no doubt missed, we beg the reader's forgiveness. Likewise, image quality in a few instances could have been improved. Each chapter was read by an expert scholar and in each case they significantly enhanced the quality of the text. Our boundless thanks go to Peter Davidson, John Jenkins, Tom Nickson, Carol Richardson, Dora Thornton, Marion Turner, Nick Vincent and Paul Webster. All mistakes are, of course, our own. A very special note of thanks must go to Rachel Koopmans who contributed a section on the miracle windows, commented on large portions of the text, supplied new Latin translations, and shared her unpublished work and thoughts freely. We are in your debt.

We are enormously grateful to our supporters for their generosity: The Hintze Family Charitable Foundation, The Ruddock Foundation for the Arts and Jack Ryan and Zemen Paulos. We would also like to thank members of the Becket Curators' Circle for their support of the exhibition: Claudio Chittaro; Pamela Cross; Nicholas and Jane Ferguson; Nicholas and Judith Goodison; The Sandra Hindman Foundation; Steven Larcombe and Sonya Leydecker; Richard and Amicia Oldfield; and the Vogelgezang Foundation. Our thanks additionally go to Nicholas and Jane Ferguson for supporting the post of Curator of Medieval Europe and to the Paul Mellon Centre for Studies in British Art, who provided support for the post of Project Curator.

This exhibition would not have been possible without the support of over twenty lenders. These are named in the foreword, but we would like to express our sincere gratitude to all those colleagues who welcomed us so openly with a spirit of enthusiasm and generosity. Many other individuals helped in various ways, sharing their expert knowledge and advice, all of whom significantly contributed to the exhibition and book. To them we owe a debt of thanks: Martin Atherton, Anthony Bale, Don Paolo Barbisan, Isabelle Bardiès-Fronty, Kirstin Barnard, Caroline Barron, Ian Bass, Paul Binski, Barbara Drake Boehm, Karen Bollermann, Alixe Bovey, Craig Bowen, Claire Breay, Christine Brennen, Bernard Brousse, Sarah Brown, David Carpenter, Dan Clarke, Megan Cook, John Crook, Glyn Davies, Alex Devine, Emma Dillon, Keith Dowen, Kathleen Doyle, Paul Dryburgh, Anne Duggan, Dee Dyas and the team at the Centre for the Study of Christianity and Culture, York, Kjersti Marie Ellewsen, Katherine Emery, Sam Fogg, Michael Foljambe, Ralph Foljambe, Hazel Forsyth, James Freeman, Virginie Garret, Revd Dale Gingrich, Jan Graffius, Emily Guerry, Cynthia Hahn, Mark Hallett, Christopher de Hamel, Julian Harrison, Nicolas Hatot, Christian Heitzmann, Lynley Herbert, Sandy Heslop, Kate Higgins, Claudia Höhl, Matthew Holford, Mark Hosea, Philippa Hoskin, Fr Daniel Humphreys, Timothy Husband, Amelia Roché Hyde, Di Illsley, Mari James, Jitske Jasperse, Meriel Jeater, Amy Jeffs, Susan Jenkins, Christopher Kelly, Kirstin Kennedy, Isabelle Kent, Christopher Kerr-Smiley, Max Kramer, Pierre-Yves Le Pogam, Jan Leandro, Fra Luca, Gerhard Lutz, Julian Luxford, Ingeborg Magerøy, Bryan Maggs, C. Griffith Mann, Christina Martinsson, Anne McLaughlin, John McNeill, Alex McWhirter, Massimo Medica, Michael Michael, Robert Mills, Alma Monelli, Tessa Murdoch, Emily Naish, the Revd Dr Tim Naish, Cary Nederman, Heather Newton, Joshua O'Driscoll, Dan Olsson, Eleanor Parker, Erik Petersen, Paola Petrosino, Holly Pines, Richard Plant, Eyal Poleg, Nicolas Potier, Miriam Power, Elisabetta Raffo, Heikki Ranta, Joe Reed, Mitch Robertson, James Robinson, the Very Revd Dr Dean Sarah Rowland Jones, James Russell, Christine Sciacca, Leonie Seliger and her incredible team in the stained glass studio, Avinoam Shalem, Kay Brainerd Slocum, Kathryn A. Smith, Leslie Smith, Tim Tatton-Brown, Chiara Torresan, Barbara Tosti, Tony Trowles, Sarah Turner, Sarah Victoria Turner, Louise Wilkinson, Cressida Williams, the Very Revd Dr Robert Willis, Liv Barbro Veimodet and all the members of Hedalen parish council, Don Luca Vialetto, Matti Watton, Victoria West, Maurice Whitehead, Rodger Whitelocke, Mgr Philip Whitmore, Roger Wieck, John Wilkins, Fr Sławomir Witoń and Michaela Zöschg.

In particular, we would like to recognise the invaluable assistance of our colleagues at the British Museum. Thanks to everyone in the Department of Britain, Europe and Prehistory, but especially to Keeper Jill Cook for supporting and critically shaping this project, reading the entire book, and being a bastion of positivity during an extraordinary time. We'd also like to thank Hartwig Fischer, Jonathan Williams and Jill Maggs for believing in the exhibition and for championing the project. To the Becket project team and other colleagues across the museum we are grateful to you all, particularly: David Agar, Gaetano Ardito, Margot Black, Claudia Bloch, Maxwell Blowfield, Josh Cannon, Guy Carr, Hugo Chapman, Barrie Cook, Christopher Dobbs, Stephen Dodd, Joanna Fernandes, Stuart Frost, Paul Goodhead, Jess Hogg, Guy Howard-Evans, Elena Jones, Sarah Kavanagh, Beata Kibil, Deklan Kilfeather, Peter Kinsey, Kevin Lovelock, Peter Macdermid, Carolyn Marsden-Smith, Elizabeth Morrison, Saul Peckham, Rebecca Penrose, Jim Peters and his team, Michael Row, Callum Shaw, Kim Sloan, Chris Stewart, Bradley Timms, Sian Toogood, Vicci Ward, Rachel Weatherall, Morgan Whatford, Gareth Williams, John Williams, Keeley Wilson and Suzie Yarroll. Thank you to Adrian Hunt for his spectacular design and to our copyeditor Linda Schofield and proofreader Rosemary Roberts.

Above all, special thanks must go to project curator Sophie Kelly, project editor Lydia Cooper and project manager Holly Wright. Without you there would be no exhibition or book. We owe you our greatest debt of gratitude.

Finally, we'd like to thank our families and friends, particularly Esther and Matt, for their forbearance.

Picture credits

The publisher would like to thank the copyright holders for granting permission to reproduce the images illustrated. Every attempt has been made to trace accurate ownership of copyrighted images in this book. Any errors or omissions will be corrected in subsequent editions provided notification is sent to the publisher. Registration numbers for British Museum objects are included in the image captions.

Further information about the Museum and its collection can be found at britishmuseum.org. Unless otherwise stated below, copyright in photographs belongs to the institution mentioned in the caption. British Museum objects are © 2021 The Trustees of the British Museum, courtesy the Department of Photography and Imaging.

Fig. 0.1: © Victoria and Albert Museum, London; page 10: The Master and Fellows of Trinity College Cambridge; fig. 1.1: © The British Library Board (Royal MS 2 B VII); fig. 1.2: Paul Goodhead; fig. 1.3: © Museum of London; fig. 1.7: The Bodleian Libraries, University of Oxford 2021, MS Douce 5, f. 1v; fig. 1.9: © Victoria and Albert Museum, London; figs 1.10–1.11: The Chapter, Canterbury Cathedral; fig. 1.12: The National Archives; fig. 1.13: Canterbury Museums and Galleries; fig. 1.14: The Chapter, Canterbury Cathedral; figs 1.15–1.17: The Master and Fellows of Trinity College Cambridge; fig. 1.18: © The British Library Board (Royal MS 20 A II); fig. 1.19: Paul Goodhead; figs 1.20 and 1.22: By kind permission of the Provost and Scholars of King's College, Cambridge; fig. 1.24: Photo: Ellicrum/WikiCommons, Cathédrale Saint-Pierre de Poitiers; fig. 1.26: Canterbury City Council; fig. 1.28: By kind permission of the Administrator of Westminster Cathedral/© Victoria and Albert Museum, London; fig. 1.30: By permission of Dean and Chapter of Eglwys Gadeiriol Tyddewi/St Davids Cathedral; fig. 1.31: With the kind permission of Nicholas and Jane Ferguson/Photo: Lloyd de Beer; fig. 2.1: © The British Library Board (Royal MS 20 A II); fig. 2.2: © The British Library Board (Royal MS 2 B VII); fig. 2.3: The Wyvern Collection; fig. 2.4: Parker Library, Corpus Christi College, Cambridge; fig. 2.5: The Trustees of the Wormsley Fund; figs 2.6–2.7: © Dr Stuart Whatling; figs 2.8–2.10: The Trustees of the Wormsley Fund; fig. 2.11: © Dr Stuart Whatling; figs 2.12–2.13: © The British Library Board (Cotton MS Claudius B II); fig. 2.14: © The British Library Board (Harley MS 5102); fig. 2.15: © The British Library Board (Cotton MS Claudius B II); fig. 2.16: Photo: John Crook. Reproduced by kind permission of Salisbury Cathedral; fig. 2.17: The Metropolitan Museum of Art, Gift of J. Pierpont Morgan, 1917; fig. 2.20: By kind permission of Hedalen Stave Church; fig. 2.21: Mickelsson, Hilding/Hälsinglands Museum; fig. 3.1: Parker Library, Corpus Christi College, Cambridge; fig. 3.2: © The British Library Board (Royal MS 14 C VII); fig. 3.3: West Suffolk Heritage Services; fig. 3.4: The Bodleian Libraries, University of Oxford 2021, Selden End, Duke Humfrey Library/Photo: Lloyd de Beer; fig. 3.5: M.Brodie/Alamy Stock Photo; fig. 3.6: Image © National Museums Scotland; fig. 3.7: The Chapter, Canterbury Cathedral, fig. 3.8: Ian Dagnall/Alamy Stock Photo; fig. 3.9: Courtesy of St Nikolai, Wismar; fig. 3.10: Herzog August Bibliothek Wolfenbüttel: Cod. Guelf. 105 Noviss. 2°; fig. 3.11 (left): © Alfred Molon; fig. 3.11 (right): Photo courtesy of Professor Louise Wilkinson; fig. 3.12: The Picture Art Collection/Alamy Stock Photo; fig. 3.13: Album/Alamy Stock Photo; fig. 3.14: The Metropolitan Museum of Art. Purchase, Joseph Pulitzer Bequest, 1961; fig. 3.16: By kind permission of the Society of Antiquaries of London; fig. 3.17: © Dommuseum Hildesheim, Foto: Florian Monheim; fig. 3.18: Cleveland Museum of Art. Gift of the John Huntington Art and Polytechnic Trust; fig. 3.19: Dorling Kindersley ltd/Alamy Stock Photo; fig. 3.20: By kind permission of Lyngsjö Church; fig. 3.21: Su concessione del Direttore dell'Ufficio diocesano per l'arte sacra e I beni culturali don Paolo Barbisan; page 108: imageBROKER/Alamy Stock Photo; figs 4.1–4.2: Paul Goodhead; fig. 4.3: Bildarchiv Monheim GmbH/Alamy Stock Photo; fig. 4.4: imageBROKER/Alamy Stock Photo; figs 4.6–4.7: The Chapter, Canterbury Cathedral; fig. 4.8: © The Dean and Chapter of Westminster; fig. 4.9: Canterbury Museums and Galleries; fig. 4.10: © Museum of London; fig. 4.12: The Master and Fellows of Trinity College Cambridge; fig. 4.15: © Dr Stuart Whatling; fig. 4.16: Photo: © President and Fellows of Harvard College; figs 4.17–4.22: The Chapter, Canterbury Cathedral; fig. 4.23: The Chapter, Canterbury Cathedral; fig. 4.24: Photo © RMN-Grand Palais (musée de Cluny – musée national du Moyen Âge)/Jean-Gilles Berizzi; fig. 4.25: Charles Wild, *Twelve perspective views of the exterior and interior parts of the Metropolitical Church of Canterbury*, London: W. Bulmer, 1807/Photo: Rachel Koopmans; figs 4.26–4.27: The Chapter, Canterbury Cathedral; page 140: Paul Goodhead; pages 141–2: The Chapter, Canterbury Cathedral; pages 143–4: Paul Goodhead; pages 145–6: The Chapter, Canterbury Cathedral; page 147: Paul Goodhead; page 148: © The British Library Board (Stowe MS 12); figs 5.1–5.2: Su concessione del Capitolo della Cattedrale di Anagni; fig. 5.3: Courtesy of the Mercers' Company and Louis Sinclair Photography; figs 5.4–5.11: The Chapter, Canterbury Cathedral; fig. 5.12: Angelo Hornak/Alamy Stock Photo; fig. 5.13: © Aidan McRae Thomson; fig. 5.14: Property of the Queen's Most Excellent Majesty in Right of Her Duchy of Lancaster, reproduced by permission of the Chancellor and Council of the Duchy of Lancaster; fig. 5.16: Chronicle/Alamy Stock Photo; fig. 5.17: © The British Library Board (Stowe MS 12); fig. 5.18: Property of the Queen's Most Excellent Majesty in Right of Her Duchy of Lancaster, reproduced by permission of the Chancellor and Council of the Duchy of Lancaster; fig. 5.19: incamerastock/Alamy Stock Photo; figs 6.2–6.3: © Victoria and Albert Museum, London; fig. 6.6: Parker Library, Corpus Christi College, Cambridge; fig. 6.7: The Walters Art Museum, Acquired by Henry Walters; figs 6.8–6.15: The Trustees of the Wormsley Fund; fig. 6.16: © The British Library Board (Royal MS 2 B VII); fig. 6.17: Revd Gordon Plumb; fig. 6.18: Reproduced by kind permission of the Chapter of York; fig. 6.19: The National Archives/Photo: Lloyd de Beer; fig. 6.20: Reproduced by kind permission of St Peter ad Vincula, South Newington/Photo: Lloyd de Beer; fig. 7.1: bpk/Hamburger Kunsthalle; fig. 7.3: The Chapter, Canterbury Cathedral; fig. 7.4: Rijksmuseum, Amsterdam; fig. 7.5: Reproduced by kind permission of the Syndics of Cambridge University Library; fig. 7.10: © National Portrait Gallery, London; fig. 7.11–7.12: Parker Library, Corpus Christi College, Cambridge; fig. 7.13: By kind permission of the Society of Antiquaries of London; fig. 7.14: Reproduced by kind permission of the Chapter of York; fig. 7.15: Dean & Chapter of Exeter Cathedral; fig. 7.16: PA Images/Alamy Stock Photo; fig. 7.17: Granger Historical Picture Archive/Alamy Stock Photo; page 210: Angelo Hornak/Alamy Stock Photo; fig. 8.1: The Chapter, Canterbury Cathedral; fig. 8.2: The Worshipful Company of Barbers; fig. 8.3: © Victoria and Albert Museum, London; fig. 8.5: Angelo Hornak/Alamy Stock Photo; fig. 8.6: © National Portrait Gallery, London; fig. 8.8: By permission of the British Jesuit Province; fig. 8.9: By permission of the Governors of Stonyhurst College; fig. 8.11: © The British Library Board (Cotton MS Titus B I); fig. 8.12: Public domain: George Cornelius Gorham, *Gleanings of a Few Scattered Ears During the Period of the Reformation In England: Comprehending I. Engraving of Eleven Seals of Cranmer, Parkhurst, And Jewel : II. Letters &c. (for a Great Part Hitherto Unpublished) of Martyr, Bishop Parkhurst, Sandys, &c*, London: Bell and Daldy, 1857; fig. 8.13: Parker Library, Corpus Christi College, Cambridge; fig. 8.14: © The British Library Board (MS Harley 2985); fig. 8.15: By permission of the Governors of Stonyhurst College; fig. 8.16: Reproduced by kind permission of the Syndics of Cambridge University Library; fig. 8.17: Reproduced by kind permission of St Mary's in the Lace Market, Nottingham, www.stmarysnottingham.org/Photo: Naomi Speakman; fig. 8.18: Private Collection/Photo: Lloyd de Beer; fig. 8.22: Reproduced by kind permission of the Rector of the Venerable English College, Rome; figs 9.1–9.2: By permission of the British Jesuit Province; pages 244–5: The Chapter, Canterbury Cathedral.

Index